ACTIVITY & TEST PREP

SIDE by SIDE

THIRD EDITION

Steven J. Molinsky • Bill Bliss

with

Carolyn Graham • Peter S. Bliss

Contributing Authors

Dorothy Lynde • Elizabeth Handley

Illustrated by

Richard E. Hill

PEARSON Longman

To the Teacher

This enhanced edition of *Side by Side Activity Workbook 1* provides all-skills activities, lifeskills lessons, and achievement tests to reinforce, expand, and assess the learning objectives in the *Side by Side 1* and *Side by Side Plus 1* Student Books. It includes two audio CDs and an answer key, providing students with the resources they need to extend their language learning through self-study outside the classroom. The audio CDs contain all workbook listening activities and GrammarRaps and GrammarSongs that motivate learners and promote language mastery through entertaining practice with rhythm, stress, intonation, and music.

The achievement tests in the second section of the workbook (pages T1–T58) provide intensified coverage of lifeskill competencies, assess student progress, and prepare students for the types of standardized tests and performance assessments used by many instructional programs. The tests include: multiple-choice questions that assess vocabulary, grammar, reading, and listening skills; short-answer questions that cover lifeskill competencies and basic literacy tasks (such as reading medicine labels and filling out forms); writing assessments that can be evaluated using a standardized scoring rubric and collected in portfolios of students' work; and speaking performance assessments designed to stimulate face-to-face interactions between students, for evaluation by the teacher using a standardized scoring rubric, or for self-evaluation by students. Test pages are perforated so that completed tests can be handed in and can serve as a record of students' participation and progress in the instructional program.

Listening scripts and answer keys for the tests are provided in *Side by Side Plus* Teacher's Guide 1. Test preparation strategies, scoring rubrics, and resources for documenting students' progress are provided in *Side by Side Plus* Multilevel Activity & Achievement Test Book 1 and its accompanying CD-ROM.

Side by Side, 3rd edition
Activity & Test Prep Workbook 1

Pearson Education, 10 Bank Street, White Plains, NY 10606

Editorial director: *Pam Fishman*
Vice president, director of design and production: *Rhea Banker*
Director of electronic production: *Aliza Greenblatt*
Production manager: *Ray Keating*
Director of manufacturing: *Patrice Fraccio*
Associate digital layout manager: *Paula Williams*

Associate art director: *Elizabeth Carlson*
Interior design: *Elizabeth Carlson, Wendy Wolf*
Cover design: *Elizabeth Carlson, Warren Fischbach*

The authors gratefully acknowledge the contribution of Tina Carver in the development of the original *Side by Side* program.

ISBN 978-0-13-607059-7; 0-13-607059-0

Printed in the United States of America
6 7 8 9 10 – V011 – 12 11 10

Contents

*Listening scripts and answer keys for the achievement tests are provided in *Side by Side Plus* Teacher's Guide 1.

A WHAT ARE THEY SAYING?

what's	is	my	from	name	phone number
where	are	your	I'm	address	

1. What's your name?
My ________ is Janet Miller.

2. What's your ____________?
________ address ________ 456 Main Street.

3. What's ________ phone number?
My ________ ________ is 654-3960.

4. What's ________ name?
My ________ is Ken Green.

5. ________ your address?
My ____________ is 15 Park Street.

6. What's your ________ number?
______ phone ________ is 379-1029.

7. ________ ________ you from?
________ ________ Detroit.

B NAME/ADDRESS/PHONE NUMBER

STUDENT IDENTIFICATION CARD

Name: Maria (First Name) Gonzalez (Last Name)

Address: 235 Main Street

Bronx, New York

Phone Number: 741-8906

My name is Maria Gonzalez.
My address is 235 Main Street.
My phone number is 741-8906.

How about you? What's YOUR name, address, and phone number?

STUDENT IDENTIFICATION CARD

Name: __________ (First Name) __________ (Last Name)

Address: __________

____

Phone Number: __________

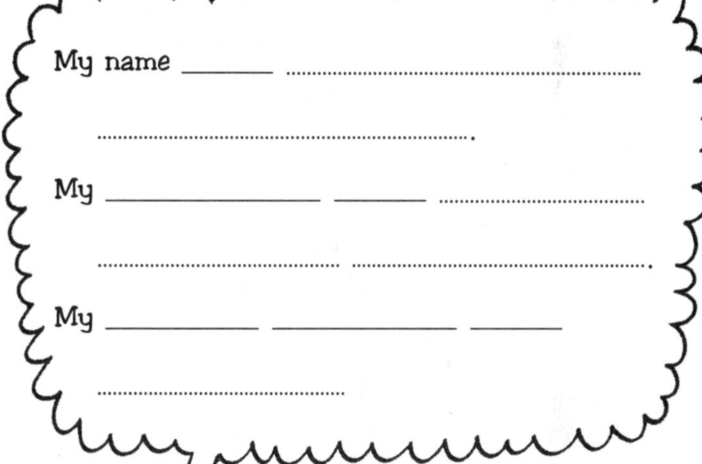
My name ____ ....
....
My ____ ____ ....
....
My ____ ____ ____
....

C LISTENING 

Listen and circle the number you hear.

1. (5) / 9
2. 3 / 7
3. 1 / 2
4. 6 / 3
5. 4 / 1
6. 3 / 6
7. 5 / 4
8. 8 / 2
9. 10 / 0
10. 5 / 9

D NUMBERS

zero	0
one	1
two	2
three	3
four	4
five	5
six	6
seven	7
eight	8
nine	9
ten	10

Write the number.

four	4
seven	______
one	______
eight	______
ten	______
two	______
nine	______
six	______
five	______
three	______

Write the word.

6	six
2	______
7	______
3	______
1	______
8	______
10	______
4	______
9	______
5	______

E LISTENING 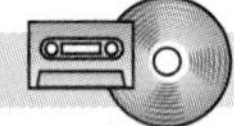

Listen and write the missing numbers.

1. What's your phone number?

My phone number is 389-793 2 .

2. 
What's your telephone number?
My telephone number is 837-29___3.

3. 
What's your apartment number?
My apartment number is ___-B.

4. 
What's your address?
My address is ___ Main Street.

5. 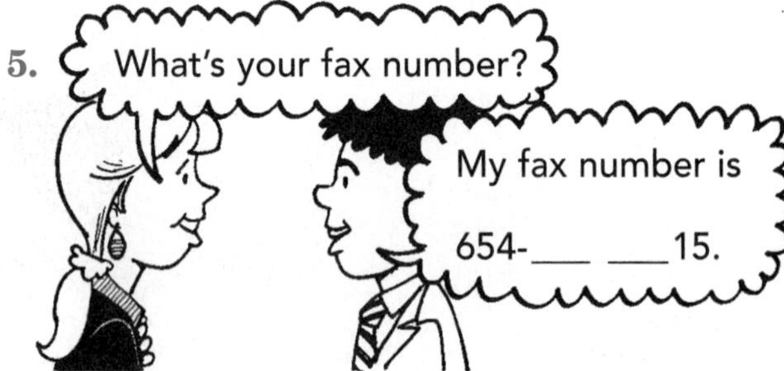
What's your fax number?
My fax number is 654-___ ___15.

6. 
What's your license number?
My license number is 26___3___9___.

F LISTENING

Listen and write the missing letters.

1. C-A-_R_-T-___-R
2. J-O-___-N-___-O-___
3. ___-E-R-___-L-___
4. A-N-D-E-___-S-___-N
5. ___-H-I-L-___-I-P
6. ___-A-R-___-I-N-E-___

G WHAT ARE THEY SAYING?

name	meet	you	Hi	Nice

A. Hello. My ___name___ [1] is Dan Harris.

B. ________ [2]. I'm Susan Wilson.

Nice to ________ [3] you.

A. ________ [4] to meet ________ [5], too.

is	you	Hello	I'm	My	to

A. Hi. ________ [6] name ________ [7] Alice Lane.

B. ________ [8]. ________ [9] Bob Chang.

A. Nice ________ [10] meet you.

B. Nice to meet ________ [11], too.

H GRAMMARRAP: *Hi! Hello!*

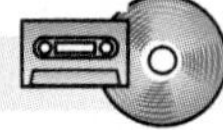

Listen. Then clap and practice.

A. Hi. I'm Jack.
B. Hello. I'm Jill.
C. Hi. I'm Mary.
D. Hello. I'm Bill.
All. Nice to meet you.
Nice to meet you, too.

A. Hi. I'm Bob.
B. Hello. I'm Tim.
C. Hi. I'm Susie.
D. Hello. I'm Jim.
All. Nice to meet you.
Nice to meet you, too.

A PUZZLE

Across

1.  
5.  
6.  
8. 
10. 
12. 

Down

1.  
2. 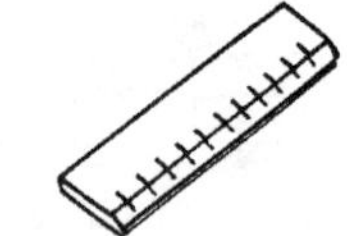 
3. 
4. 
7. 

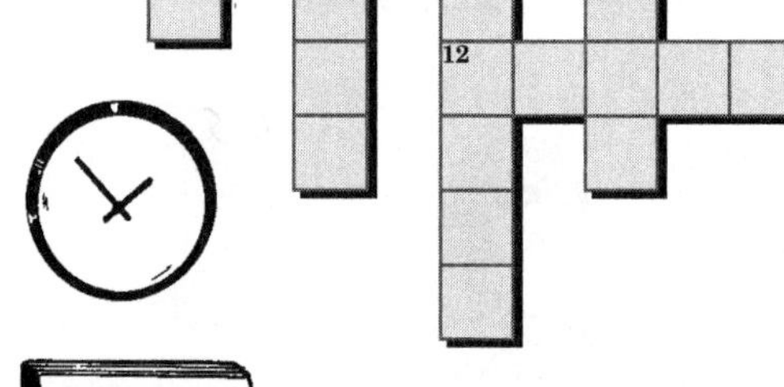

8. 
9. 
11. 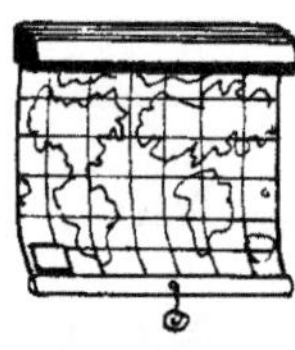

B LISTENING

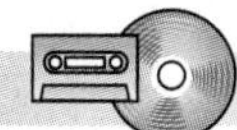

Listen and put a check (✓) under the correct picture.

1. ✔ ______ ______
2. ______ ______
3. ______ ______

  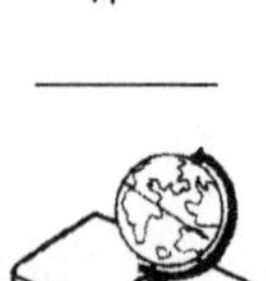    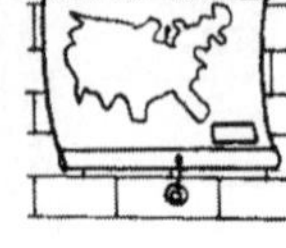

4. ______ ______
5. ______ ______
6. ______ ______

C WHAT ARE THEY SAYING?

I'm	are	basement	attic	living room
we're	where	dining room	yard	bedroom
they're	you	kitchen	bathroom	

1.
Where are you?
I'm in the ______.
2.
Where ______ Susan and Joe?
______ in the ______.
3.
Where ______ you and Julie?
______ in the ______.
4.
______ are you?
______ in the ______.
5.
______ ______ Ben and Maria?
______ in the ______.
6.
Where ______ you and Betty?
______ in the ______.
7.
______ ______ Pam and Peter?
______ in the ______.
8.
______ ______ you?
______ in the ______.

D WHAT ARE THEY SAYING?

where's	she's	classroom	garage	he's	living room	it's

1. Where's David?
He's in the ______.
2. ______ Millie?
______ in the ______.
3. ______ the computer?
______ in the ______.

E WHERE ARE THEY?

we	he she it	they

(Mr. and Mrs. Chen) 1. They are in the kitchen.

(Ms. Carter) 2. ______ is in the dining room.

(Mr. Grant) 3. ______ is in the bathroom.

(Harry and Mary) 4. ______ are in the basement.

(Ellen and I) 5. ______ are in the attic.

(The bookshelf) 6. ______ is in the living room.

(Mr. White) 7. ______ is in the garage.

(Mrs. Miller) 8. ______ is in the classroom.

(The telephone book) 9. ______ is in the bedroom.

F WHERE ARE THEY?

I'm	we're you're they're	he's she's it's	where's

(He is) 1. He's in the bedroom.

(They are) 2. ______ in the basement.

(We are) 3. ______ in the attic.

(I am) 4. ______ in the bathroom.

(It is) 5. ______ in the dining room.

(She is) 6. ______ in the living room.

(You are) 7. ______ in the garage.

(Where is) 8. ______ the cell phone?

G THE BAKER FAMILY

The Baker family is at home today. (1) Mrs. Baker is ___in___ ___the___ ___living___ ___room___. (2) Mr. Baker is ______ ______ ____________. (3) Peggy and Jim are ______ ______ ________. (4) Kevin is ______ ______ ____________. (5) Susie is ______ ______ ____________. (6) And the car is ______ ______ ____________.

H WHERE ARE THEY?

he's she's it's	they're

1. Where's Mrs. Baker? ___She's in the living room.___
2. Where's Mr. Baker? ________________________
3. Where are Peggy and Jim? ________________________
4. Where's Kevin? ________________________
5. Where's Susie? ________________________
6. Where's the car? ________________________

I WHAT'S THE SIGN?

Fill in the signs. Then complete the sentences.

1. Helen is ___in the park___.

2. Mr. and Mrs. Grant are ______________________.

3. Edward is ______________________.

4. Maria is ______________________.

5. Jim and Sarah are ______________________.

6. Billy is ______________________.

7. The monkey is ______________________.

8. Ms. Johnson is ______________________.

J LISTENING

Listen and write the number under the correct picture.

_____

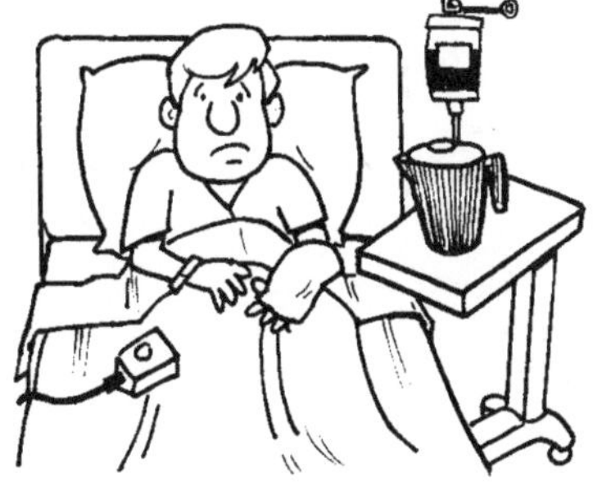

__1__

_____

_____

_____

_____

K LISTENING

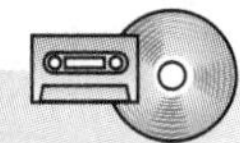

Listen and circle the word you hear.

1.	zoo	(you)	3.	We're	They're	5.	Where	Where's	7.	on	in
2.	Ms.	Mr.	4.	Where	How	6.	She's	He's	8.	Is	It's

L MATCHING

Match the nationality and the city.

__c__	1.	We're Mexican. We're from ______.	a.	Shanghai
_____	2.	She's Greek. She's from ______.	b.	San Juan
_____	3.	He's Chinese. He's from ______.	c.	Mexico City
_____	4.	I'm Italian. I'm from______.	d.	Seoul
_____	5.	They're Puerto Rican. They're from ______.	e.	Athens
_____	6.	We're Korean. We're from ______.	f.	Tokyo
_____	7.	She's Japanese. She's from ______.	g.	Rome

M GrammarRap: *Where's Jack?*

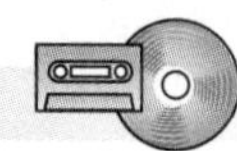

Listen. Then clap and practice.

A. Where's Jack?
B. He's in the kitchen.
A. Where's Jill?
B. She's in the dining room.
A. Where's Mom?
B. She's in the living room.
A. Where's Fred? Fred's in bed.
All. Fred's in bed.
Fred's in bed.
A. Jack's in the kitchen.
All. Fred's in bed.
A. Jack's in the kitchen.
B. Jill's in the dining room.
A. Mom's in the living room.
All. Fred's in bed.

N GrammarRap: *Where Are Fred and Mary?*

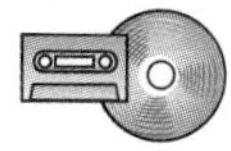

Listen. Then clap and practice.

Where are   Fred and Mary

A. Where's Jack?
B. Where's Jill?
C. Where are Fred and Mary?
D. Where's Bill?
A. Where's Ed?
B. Where's Sue?
C. Where are Bob and Betty?
D. Where are Tom and Lou?

A. Jack and Jill.
B. Betty and Bill.
C. Bob and Lou.
D. Mary and Sue.
A. Jack and Jill.
B. Betty and Bill.
C. Bob and Lou.
D. Mary and Sue.

A WHAT ARE THEY SAYING?

doing	watching	I'm	we're	you
reading	sleeping	he's	they're	what
playing	eating	she's	are	what's
studying	cooking			

1. ___What___ are you doing?
   I'm ________ English.

2. What's Carla ________?
   ________ ________.

3. ________ Walter doing?
   ________ ________.

4. ________ ________ Julie and David doing?
   ________ ________ the newspaper.

5. ________ ________ you and George doing?
   ________ ________ TV.

6. ________ ________ you ________?
   ________ ________ the piano.

7. ________ William doing?
   ________ ________ dinner.

B WHAT ARE THEY DOING?

cooking	eating	playing	singing	studying	watching
drinking	listening	reading	sleeping	teaching	

1. He's ____eating____ breakfast.

2. She's ________________ milk.

3. They're ________________ mathematics.

4. He's ________________ the newspaper.

5. They're ________________.

6. She's ________________.

7. He's ________________ to music.

8. They're ________________ TV.

9. She's ________________ dinner.

10. He's ________________.

11. They're ________________ baseball.

C LISTENING

Listen and put a check (✓) under the correct picture.

1. ✔ ______ ______
2. ______ ______
3. ______ ______
4. ______ ______
5. ______ ______
6. ______ ______
7. ______ ______
8. ______ ______
9. ______ ______
10. ______ ______

D GRAMMARRAP: *Frank?! At the Bank?!*

Listen. Then clap and practice.

A. Where's Frank?
B. He's working at the bank.
A. Frank?! At the bank?!
B. Yes, that's right.
He's working at the bank.
All. Frank?! At the bank?! Oh, no!

A. Where's Sue?
B. She's working at the zoo.
A. Sue?! At the zoo?!
B. Yes, that's right.
She's working at the zoo.
All. Sue?! At the zoo?! Oh, no!

A. Where's Paul?
B. He's working at the mall.
A. Paul?! At the mall?!
B. Yes, that's right.
He's working at the mall.
All. Paul?! At the mall?! Oh, no!

E WHAT'S THE QUESTION?

Where is	he / she / it	?	
What's	he / she / it	doing?	
Where are	you / they	?	
What are	you / they	doing?	

1. Where are you ?
I'm in the garage
2. What's he doing ?
He's cooking dinner.
3. ?
They're in the park.
4. ?
We're playing with the dog.
5. ?
He's in the attic.
6. ?
She's listening to the radio.
7. ?
She's in the yard.
8. ?
We're at the beach.
9. ?
He's sleeping.
10. ?
It's in the classroom.
11. ?
They're eating lunch.
12. ?
I'm in the hospital.

F GRAMMARRAP: *Eating Lunch* 

Listen. Then clap and practice.

What's he   Where are   What are

A.	Where's	Charlie?		
B.	He's in the	kitchen.		
A.	What's he	doing?		
B.	Eating	lunch.		
All.	Charlie's in the	kitchen	eating	lunch.
	Charlie's in the	kitchen	eating	lunch.
A.	Who's in the	kitchen?		
B.	Charlie's in the	kitchen.		
A.	What's he	doing?		
B.	Eating	lunch.		

A.	Where's	Betty?
B.	She's in the	bedroom.
A.	What's she	doing?
B.	Reading a	book.

All. Betty's in the bedroom reading a book.
Betty's in the bedroom reading a book.

A. Who's in the bedroom?

B. Betty's in the bedroom.

A. What's she doing?

B. Reading a book.

A. Where are Mom and Dad?

B. They're in the living room.

A. What are they doing?

B. Watching Channel Seven.

All. Betty's in the bedroom.
Mom's in the living room.
Dad's in the living room.
Charlie's in the kitchen.

A. Where's Charlie?

All. He's in the kitchen.

A. What's he doing?

All. Eating lunch.

✓ CHECK-UP TEST: Chapters 1-3

A. Answer the questions.

Ex. What's your telephone number?

My telephone number is 567-1032.

1. What's your name?

....

2. What's your address?

....

3. Where are you from?

....

B. Circle the correct answer.

Ex. The map is on the yard / (wall) / park .

1. We're eating milk / cards / lunch .

2. What / Where's / What's Ben doing?

3. Max is planting flowers / swimming / singing in the bathroom.

4. Ms. Park is teaching dinner / mathematics / the radio. .

5. Nice to hello / hi / meet you.

6. The pencil / attic / shower is in the classroom.

C. Fill in the blanks.

Ex. What's Bill doing?

1. Maria is ________ the hospital.
2. I'm ______________ the newspaper.
3. Where's Joe? ________ in the cafeteria.
4. They're ________________ TV.
5. What are you and Peter doing? __________ reading.
6. ____________ the car? It's in the garage.
7. What are you ____________? I'm studying.
8. Where's the cell phone? ________ in the basement.
9. ________ are Mr. and Mrs. Chen doing?
10. Carol ________ Bob are eating breakfast.

D. Listen and write the letter or number you hear.

Ex. M-A-R-K

1. C-A-R-___E-R
2. 354-9___12
3. 890-74___2
4. ___-U-L-I-E
5. 6___2-3059
6. 517___349

A WHAT ARE THEY DOING?

what	my	our	cleaning	apartment
what's	his	their	doing	children
are	her		fixing	homework
				sink

1. Hi! __What's__ Jason doing?
   He's ______________ ______________ room.

2. What's Peggy ______________?
   She's ______________ ______________ car.

3. ______________ are you doing?
   I'm cleaning ______________ ______________.

4. What are your ______________ doing?
   They're doing ______________ ______________.

5. What ______________ you doing?
   We're fixing ______________ ______________.

B WHAT'S THE WORD?

my	his	her	its	our	your	their

1. I'm feeding ___my___ cat.
2. We're washing __________ clothes.
3. They're painting __________ bedroom.
4. She's fixing __________ sink.
5. It's eating __________ dinner.
6. You're cleaning __________ yard.
7. He's reading __________ e-mail.

C LISTENING

Listen and circle the word you hear.

1.	your	(our)	3.	her	his	5.	your	our
2.	his	her	4.	our	their	6.	my	its

D PUZZLE

Across

1. I'm painting ______ apartment.
3. We're fixing ______ TV.
6. Bobby and Tim are cleaning ______ room.
7. Bill is doing ______ homework.

Down

2. You're doing ______ exercises.
4. The dog is eating ______ dinner.
5. Ruth is brushing ______ teeth.

E WHAT ARE THEY SAYING?

Yes, I am.	Yes, { he / she / it } is.	Yes, { we / you / they } are.

1. A. Is Harry feeding his cat?
   B. Yes, he is.

2. A. Are you and Tom cleaning your yard?
   B. ________ ________ ________

3. A. Is Mrs. Chen doing her exercises?
   B. ________ ________ ________

4. A. Are your children brushing their teeth?
   B. ________ ________ ________

5. A. Is George sleeping?
   B. ________ ________ ________

6. A. Is Irene planting flowers?
   B. ________ ________ ________

7. A. Are you washing your windows?
   B. ________ ________ ________

8. A. Am I in the hospital?
   B. ________ ________ ________

F GRAMMARRAP: *Busy! Busy! Busy!*

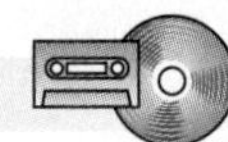

Listen. Then clap and practice.

What are	Is he	Yes, he	What's he

A. Are you busy?
B. Yes, I am.
A. What are you doing?
B. I'm talking to Sam.

A. Is he busy?
B. Yes, he is.
A. What's he doing?
B. He's talking to Liz.

A. Are they busy?
B. Yes, they are.
A. What are they doing?
B. They're washing their car.

All. I'm talking to Sam.
He's talking to Liz.
They're washing their car.
They're busy!

G LISTENING

Listen and circle the word you hear.

1.	(he's)	she's	3.	feeding	eating	5.	our	their
2.	his	her	4.	apartment	yard	6.	washing	watching

H WHAT ARE THEY DOING?

1. He's ___washing___ his hair.

2. They're __________ their yard.

3. We're __________ our exercises.

4. I'm __________ my e-mail.

5. She's __________ her living room.

6. You're __________ your cat.

I WHAT'S THE WORD?

Circle the correct words.

1. (They're) / Their washing they're / their windows.
2. Where / We're are Mr. and Mrs. Tanaka?
3. He's / His doing he's / his exercises.
4. Where are / Where's the cell phone?
5. We're brushing are / our teeth.
6. His / Is Richard busy?
7. What are / our you doing?
8. The cat is eating it's / its dinner.

J A BUSY DAY

laundromat	doing	playing	they're	what's	her	are
library	eating	reading	he's	where's	their	and
park	fixing	washing	she's	in	his	
restaurant	listening					

Everybody is busy today. Ms. Roberts is in the restaurant 1. She's ______ 2 dinner. Mr. and Mrs. Lopez are ______ 3 the health club. ______ 4 doing ______ 5 exercises. Patty and Danny Williams are in the ______ 6. She's ______ 7 the newspaper. He's ______ 8 to music. Mr. ______ 9 Mrs. Sharp are also in the park. What are they ______ 10? They're ______ 11 cards.

Jenny Chang is in the ______ 12. ______ 13 washing ______ 14 clothes. Charlie Harris and Julie Carter ______ 15 in the parking lot. He's ______ 16 ______ 17 car. She's ______ 18 her bicycle. ______ 19 Mr. Molina? He's in the ______ 20. ______ 21 he doing? ______ 22 reading a book.

A MATCHING OPPOSITES

d	1. large	a.	thin	____	8. tall	h.	heavy
____	2. heavy	b.	rich	____	9. difficult	i.	old
____	3. single	c.	beautiful	____	10. new	j.	ugly
____	4. ugly	d.	small	____	11. handsome	k.	big
____	5. cheap	e.	young	____	12. thin	l.	easy
____	6. poor	f.	expensive	____	13. little	m.	noisy
____	7. old	g.	married	____	14. quiet	n.	short

B WHAT ARE THEY SAYING?

Tell me about your new friend.
1. Is he short or ____tall____?
2. Is he heavy or ________?
3. Is he old or ________?
4. Is he single or ________?

Tell me about the apartment.
5. Is it large or ________?
6. Is it quiet or ________?
7. Is it cheap or ________?
8. Is it beautiful or ________?

C LISTENING

Listen and circle the word you hear.

1. small	(tall)	3. easy	noisy	5. ugly	young
2. ugly	heavy	4. thin	single	6. cheap	easy

D WHAT'S WRONG?

He She It	isn't	They aren't

1. It's new.

It isn't new.

It's old.

2. They're quiet.

____

____

3. It's large.

____

____

4. He's single.

____

____

5. She's young.

____

____

6. They're short.

____

____

E SCRAMBLED QUESTIONS

Unscramble the questions. Begin each question with a capital letter.

1. Are you busy?
busy you are

2. ______________________?
dog your large is

3. ______________________?
they are married

4. ______________________?
I beautiful am

5. ______________________?
difficult English is

6. ______________________?
new is car their

7. ______________________?
tall she is short or

8. ______________________?
noisy quiet he is or

F GRAMMARRAP: *Old! Cold! Tall! Small!*

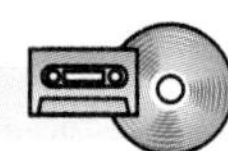

Listen. Then clap and practice.

All. Is he young? *(clap) (clap)*
Is he old? *(clap) (clap)*
Is it hot? *(clap) (clap)*
Is it cold? *(clap) (clap)*
Is she short? *(clap) (clap)*
Is she tall? *(clap) (clap)*
Is it large? *(clap) (clap)*
Is it small? *(clap) (clap)*
Young! Old!
Hot! Cold!
Young! Old!
Hot! Cold!

A. Is he young or old?
B. He's very old.
A. Is it hot or cold?
B. It's very cold.

A. Is she short or tall?
B. She's very tall.
A. Is it large or small?
B. It's extremely small.

All. Young! Old!
Hot! Cold!
Short! Tall!
Large! Small!

G WHOSE THINGS?

bicycle	book	car	cat	computer	dog	guitar	house	piano	TV

1. Albert's car

2. ______ ______

3. ______ ______

4. ______ ______

5. ______ ______

6. ______ ______

7. ______ ______

8. ______ ______

9. ______ ______

10. ______ ______

H WHAT'S THE WORD?

His	Her	Their	Its

1. Mary's brother isn't short. (His **Her**) brother is tall.
2. Mr. and Mrs. Miller's apartment isn't cheap. (His Their) apartment is expensive.
3. Robert's sister isn't single. (His Her) sister is married.
4. Ms. Clark's neighbors aren't quiet. (Their Her) neighbors are noisy.
5. Their dog's name isn't Rover. (Its Their) name is Fido.
6. Mrs. Hunter's car isn't large. (His Her) car is small.
7. Timmy's bicycle isn't new. (His Its) bicycle is old.
8. Mr. and Mrs. Lee's son isn't single. (Her Their) son is married.

I MR. AND MRS. GRANT

Read the story and answer the questions.

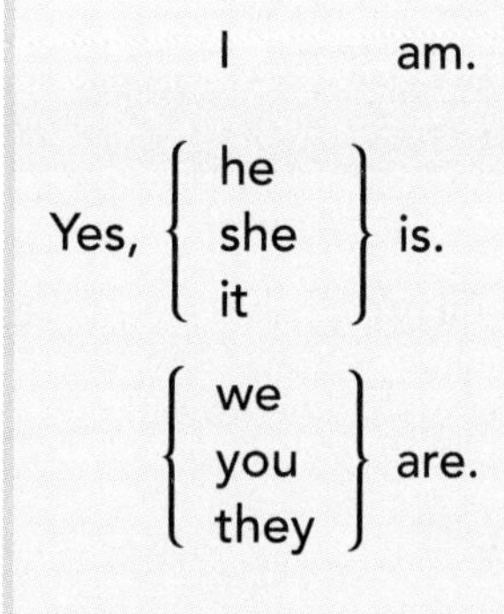

I am.

Yes, { he / she / it } is.

{ we / you / they } are.

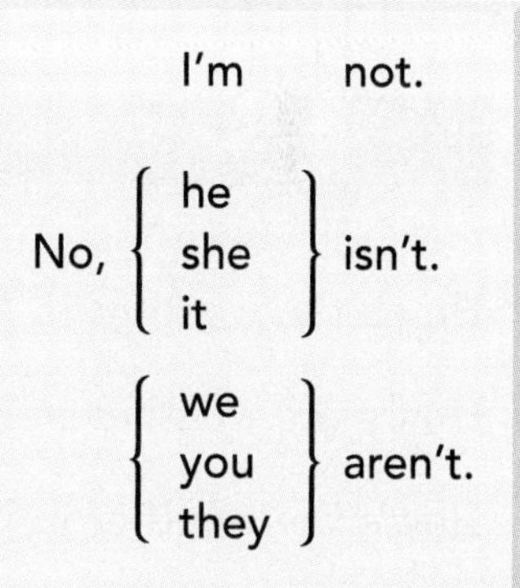

I'm not.

No, { he / she / it } isn't.

{ we / you / they } aren't.

Meet Mr. and Mrs. Grant. Mr. Grant is short and heavy. Mrs. Grant is tall and thin. Their house is small and old. Their car is new and expensive. Their neighbors are noisy. And their cat is ugly.

1. Is Mr. Grant short? Yes, he is.
2. Is he tall? ______
3. Is he thin? ______
4. Is he heavy? ______
5. Is Mrs. Grant tall? ______
6. Is she heavy? ______
7. Is she thin? ______
8. Is their house large? ______
9. Is it old? ______
10. Is their car new? ______
11. Is it cheap? ______
12. Are their neighbors quiet? ______
13. Are they noisy? ______
14. Is their cat pretty? ______

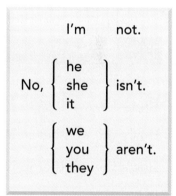

J HOW'S THE WEATHER?

it's sunny	it's raining	it's warm	it's hot
it's cloudy	it's snowing	it's cool	it's cold

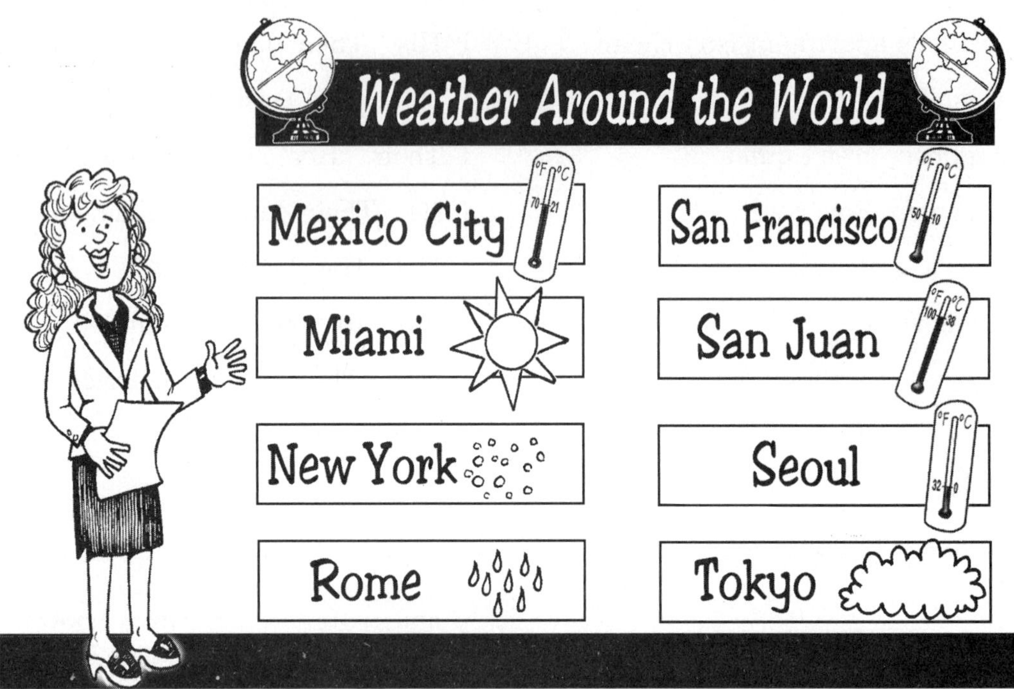

1. How's the weather in Mexico City? It's warm.
2. How's the weather in Miami? ______ ______________
3. How's the weather in New York? ______ ______________
4. How's the weather in Rome? ______ ______________
5. How's the weather in San Francisco? ______ ______________
6. How's the weather in San Juan? ______ ______________
7. How's the weather in Seoul? ______ ______________
8. How's the weather in Tokyo? ______ ______________
9. How's the weather in YOUR city? ______ ______________

K LISTENING 

Listen and circle the word you hear.

1. cold (cool)
2. snowing sunny
3. sunny snowing
4. cool hot
5. raining snowing
6. sunny cloudy

Numbers

0	zero	10	ten	20	twenty	30	thirty
1	one	11	eleven	21	twenty-one	40	forty
2	two	12	twelve	22	twenty-two	50	fifty
3	three	13	thirteen	23	twenty-three	60	sixty
4	four	14	fourteen	24	twenty-four	70	seventy
5	five	15	fifteen	25	twenty-five	80	eighty
6	six	16	sixteen	26	twenty-six	90	ninety
7	seven	17	seventeen	27	twenty-seven	100	one hundred
8	eight	18	eighteen	28	twenty-eight		
9	nine	19	nineteen	29	twenty-nine		

L WHAT'S THE NUMBER?

1. twenty-four ____24____
2. thirty-one ________
3. seventy-two ________
4. forty-six ________
5. ninety-seven ________

M WHAT'S THE WORD?

38 ____thirty-eight____

83 ________

55 ________

99 ________

64 ________

N NUMBER PUZZLE

Across

2. 46
5. 29
8. 8
9. 0
10. 11
11. 50

Down

1. 60
3. 15
4. 7
5. 20
6. 12
7. 90

O LISTENING

Listen to the temperature in Fahrenheit and Celsius. Write the numbers you hear.

1. Los Angeles ___86°___ F/ ___30°___ C
2. Seoul ________ F/ ________ C
3. San Juan ________ F/ ________ C
4. Hong Kong ________ F/ ________ C
5. Miami ________ F/ ________ C
6. London ________ F/ ________ C
7. Mexico City ________ F/ ________ C
8. Moscow ________ F/ ________ C

P GRAMMARRAP: *Terrible Weather! Beautiful Weather!*

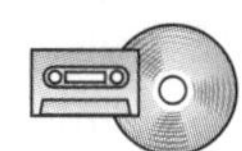

Listen. Then clap and practice.

It's raining in Alaska.
It's snowing in L.A.
It's cloudy in Caracas.
It's TERRIBLE today!
It's warm in Pennsylvania.
It's sunny in Bombay.
It's cool in Guatemala.
It's BEAUTIFUL today!

Q MATCHING

Match the questions and answers.

__e__ 1.	Is your brother tall?	a.	Yes, I am. I'm studying.
____ 2.	Is your computer new?	b.	No, she isn't. She's single.
____ 3.	Is it hot today?	c.	No, she isn't. She's old.
____ 4.	Hi! Are you busy?	d.	No, it isn't. It's cold.
____ 5.	Are your neighbors quiet?	e.	No, he isn't. He's short.
____ 6.	Is she young?	f.	No, he isn't. He's thin.
____ 7.	Is her husband heavy?	g.	No, they aren't. They're easy.
____ 8.	Is your sister married?	h.	No, it isn't. It's old.
____ 9.	Are these questions difficult?	i.	No, they aren't. They're noisy.

A FAMILY

6

Walter
Helen
Jane
Timmy
Sally

brother	sister
children	son
daughter	wife
husband	

father	grandmother
grandchildren	grandparents
granddaughter	grandson
grandfather	mother

Bill and Jane are married. Jane is Bill's ____wife____ 1. Bill is Jane's ____________ 2. Timmy and Sally are their ____________ 3. Timmy is their ____________ 4, and Sally is their ____________ 5. Timmy is Sally's ____________ 6, and Sally is Timmy's ____________ 7.

Walter and Helen are Jane's parents. Walter is Jane's ____________ 8, and Helen is Jane's ____________ 9. Walter and Helen are Timmy and Sally's ____________ 10. Walter is their ____________ 11, and Helen is their ____________ 12. Timmy and Sally are Walter and Helen's ____________ 13. Timmy is their ____________ 14, and Sally is their ____________ 15.

aunt	nephew	uncle
cousin	niece	

John is Jane's brother. Judy is John's wife. Danny is their son. John is Timmy and Sally's ____________ 16, and Judy is their ____________ 17. Timmy is John and Judy's ____________ 18, and Sally is their ____________ 19. Danny is Timmy and Sally's ____________ 20.

B LISTENING

Listen and put a check (✓) under the correct picture.

C THE WRONG WORD!

Put a circle around the wrong word.

1.	large	small	(cheap)	little	6.	rugs	parents	cousins	children
2.	kitchen	bathroom	bedroom	park	7.	pencil	book	pen	bank
3.	guitar	baseball	drums	piano	8.	Miss	Mr.	Ms.	Mrs.
4.	handsome	beautiful	tall	pretty	9.	quiet	noisy	poor	loud
5.	hot	dinner	warm	cool	10.	son	sister	nephew	brother

D GrammarSong: *Pictures on the Wall*

Listen and fill in the words to the song. Then listen again and sing along.

crying	dancing	hanging	having	living	looking	smiling	working

I'm looking at the photographs.

They're hanging in the hall.

I'm ___smiling___ 1 at the memories,

looking at the pictures on the wall.

My son Robert's married now.

I'm ______________ 2 *in L.A. (Hi, Dad!)*

My daughter's ______________ 3 in Detroit.

I'm very far away. (I love you, Dad!)

I'm ______________ 4 at the photographs.

They're ______________ 5 in the hall.

I'm smiling at the memories,

looking at the pictures on the wall.

My mom and dad are ______________ 6.

It's a very special day.

(*We're* ______________ 7 *a good time!*)

My little sister's ______________ 8.

It's my brother's wedding day.
(I'm so happy!)

I'm ______________ 9 at the photographs.

They're ______________ 10 in the hall.

I'm ______________ 11 at the memories,

______________ 12 at the pictures on the wall.

I'm smiling at the memories,

looking at the pictures on the wall.

E AN E-MAIL FROM LOS ANGELES

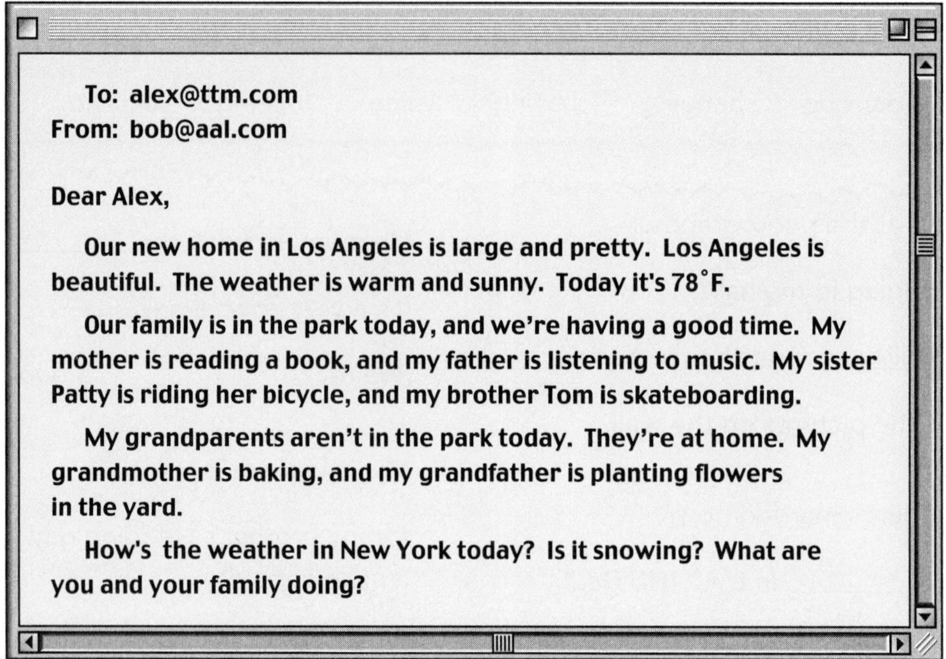
To: alex@ttm.com
From: bob@aal.com

Dear Alex,

Our new home in Los Angeles is large and pretty. Los Angeles is beautiful. The weather is warm and sunny. Today it's 78°F.

Our family is in the park today, and we're having a good time. My mother is reading a book, and my father is listening to music. My sister Patty is riding her bicycle, and my brother Tom is skateboarding.

My grandparents aren't in the park today. They're at home. My grandmother is baking, and my grandfather is planting flowers in the yard.

How's the weather in New York today? Is it snowing? What are you and your family doing?

Answer these questions in complete sentences.

1. Where is Bob's new home? It's in Los Angeles.
2. How's the weather in Los Angeles? __________
3. What's the temperature? __________
4. Where are Bob and his family today? __________
5. What's Bob's mother doing? __________
6. What's his father doing? __________
7. Who is Patty? __________
8. What's she doing? __________
9. Who is Tom? __________
10. What's he doing? __________
11. Are Bob's grandparents in the park? __________
12. Where are they? __________
13. What's his grandmother doing? __________
14. What's his grandfather doing? __________
15. Is Alex in Los Angeles? __________
16. Where is he? __________

F GrammarRap: *No. She's in Spain.*

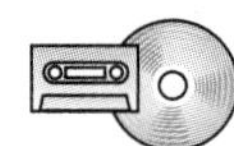

Listen. Then clap and practice.

A. What's Jack doing?
B. He's working in Rome.
A. What's BOB doing?
B. He's working at HOME.

A. Is Jack at home?
B. No. HE'S in ROME.
A. Is BOB in Rome?
B. No. HE'S at HOME.

All. Jack's in Rome.
Jack's in Rome.
What's BOB doing?
He's working at HOME.

A. What's Jane doing?
B. She's working in Spain.
A. What's MARY doing?
B. She's working in MAINE.

A. Is Jane in Maine?
B. No. SHE'S in SPAIN.
A. Is Mary in Spain?
B. No. SHE'S in MAINE.

All. Jane's in Spain.
Jane's in Spain.
What's MARY doing?
She's working in MAINE.

✓ CHECK-UP TEST: Chapters 4-6

A. Circle the correct answers.

Ex. Jack is sitting on his (computer / TV / **(bicycle)**).

1. He's my (nephew / wife / sister).
2. We're standing (on / at / in) front of our house.
3. They're swimming at the (yard / kitchen / beach).
4. He's feeding the dog (its / it's / he) dinner.
5. He's sleeping (at / on / in) the sofa.
6. Mrs. Kent is (raining / feeding / reading) in the park.
7. We're (fixing / snowing / riding) our car.
8. They're (painting / eating / brushing) their teeth.

B. Fill in the blanks.

Ex. ___What's___ his name?

1. __________ are they? They're in Tahiti.
2. My mother's mother is my ______________.
3. My sister's daughter is my ____________.
4. __________ is he? He's my cousin.
5. Mr. Jones is playing a game on __________ computer.
6. My children are doing ____________ homework.
7. Ms. Kim is busy. She's fixing __________ sink.

C. Write a sentence with the opposite adjective.

Ex. Their car isn't cheap. ___It's expensive.___

1. My brother isn't heavy. ____________________
2. They aren't short. ____________________
3. My computer isn't old. ____________________

D. Write the question.

Ex. ___Is it ugly?___ No, it isn't. It's beautiful.

1. _____________ No, I'm not. I'm single.
2. _____________ No, she isn't. She's old.
3. _____________ No, they aren't. They're noisy.

E. Listen and choose the correct response.

Ex. No, he isn't. **(a.)** He's young. b. He's thin.

1. No, it isn't. a. It's difficult. b. It's small.
2. No, she isn't. a. She's rich. b. She's short.
3. No, it isn't. a. It's easy. b. It's cloudy.
4. No, he isn't. a. He's tall. b. He's loud.

A WHERE IS IT?

7

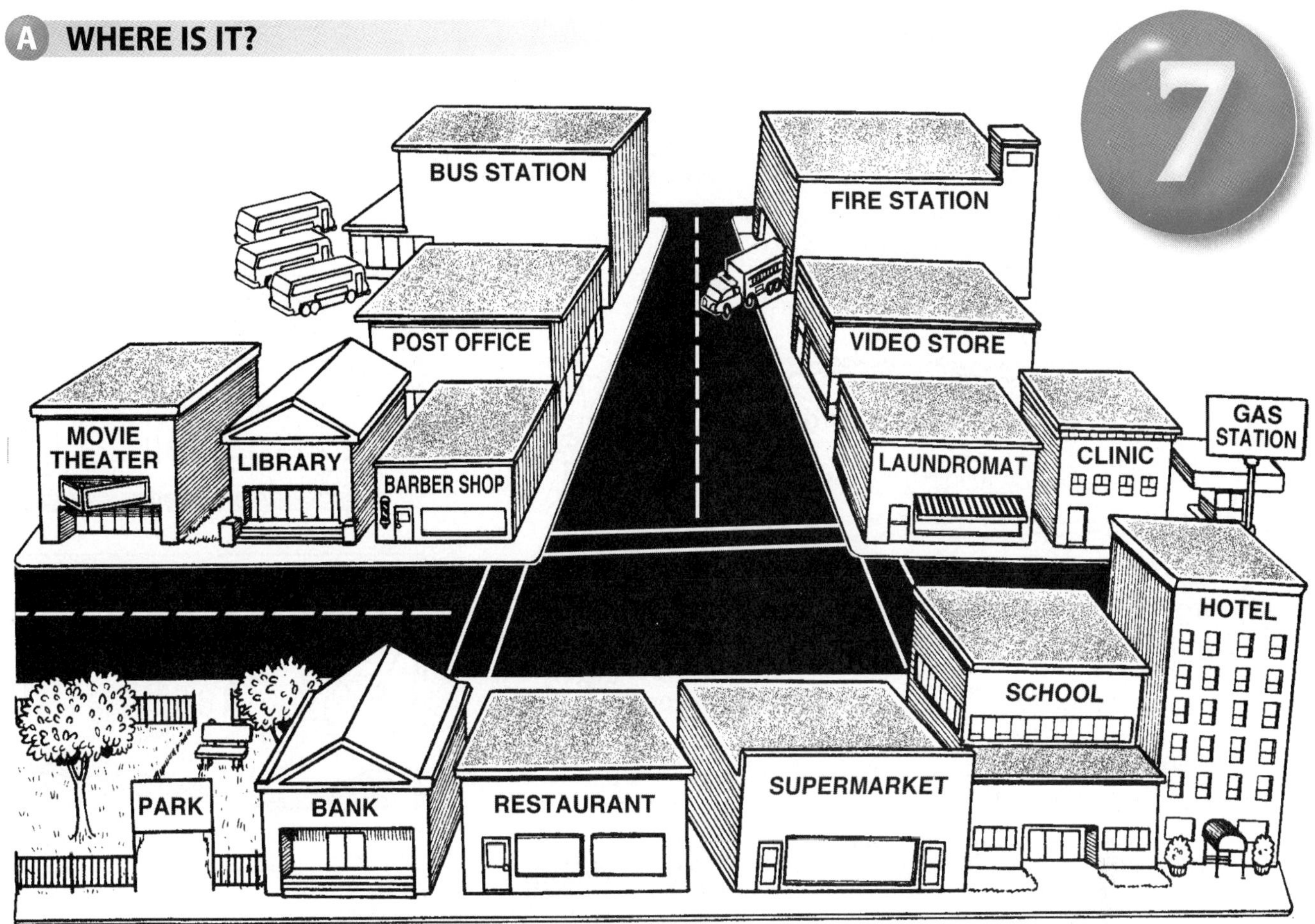

across from	around the corner from	next to	between

1. The bank is ___*next to*___ the restaurant.
2. The bus station is ______________ the fire station.
3. The library is ______________ the movie theater and the barber shop.
4. The laundromat is ______________________ the video store.
5. The laundromat is ______________ the clinic.
6. The clinic is ______________ the laundromat and the gas station.
7. The clinic and the gas station are ______________ the hotel.
8. The barber shop is ______________________ the post office.
9. The restaurant is ______________ the supermarket.
10. The school is ______________ the supermarket and the hotel.
11. The school is ______________ the laundromat.

B WHAT ARE THEY SAYING?

Is there	There's	across from	around the corner from
there		between	next to

1. Excuse me. Is there a bank in this neighborhood?

   Yes, there is. ___There's___ a bank on Park Street, ___next to___ the school.

   PARK STREET
   SCHOOL
   BANK

2. Excuse me. ______________ a video store in this neighborhood?

   Yes, there is. ______________ a video store on Main Street, ______________________________ the clinic.

   CLINIC
   MAIN STREET
   VIDEO STORE

3. Excuse me. Is there a supermarket in this neighborhood?

   Yes, ________ is. ____________ a supermarket on School Street, ____________________ the post office.

   SCHOOL STREET
   SUPERMARKET
   POST OFFICE

4. Excuse me. ______________ a park in this neighborhood?

   Yes, there is. ______________ a park on State Street, ____________________ the drug store and the library.

   STATE STREET
   DRUG STORE
   PARK
   LIBRARY

5. Excuse me. ______________ a gas station in this neighborhood?

   Yes, ________ is. ____________ a gas station on ______________ Avenue, ______________ the fire station.

   CENTRAL AVENUE
   GAS STATION
   FIRE STATION

C LISTENING

Listen to the sentences about the buildings on the map. After each sentence, write the name on the correct building.

1. bakery	4. library	7. hair salon	10. park
2. school	5. hospital	8. supermarket	11. health club
3. department store	6. police station	9. video store	12. train station

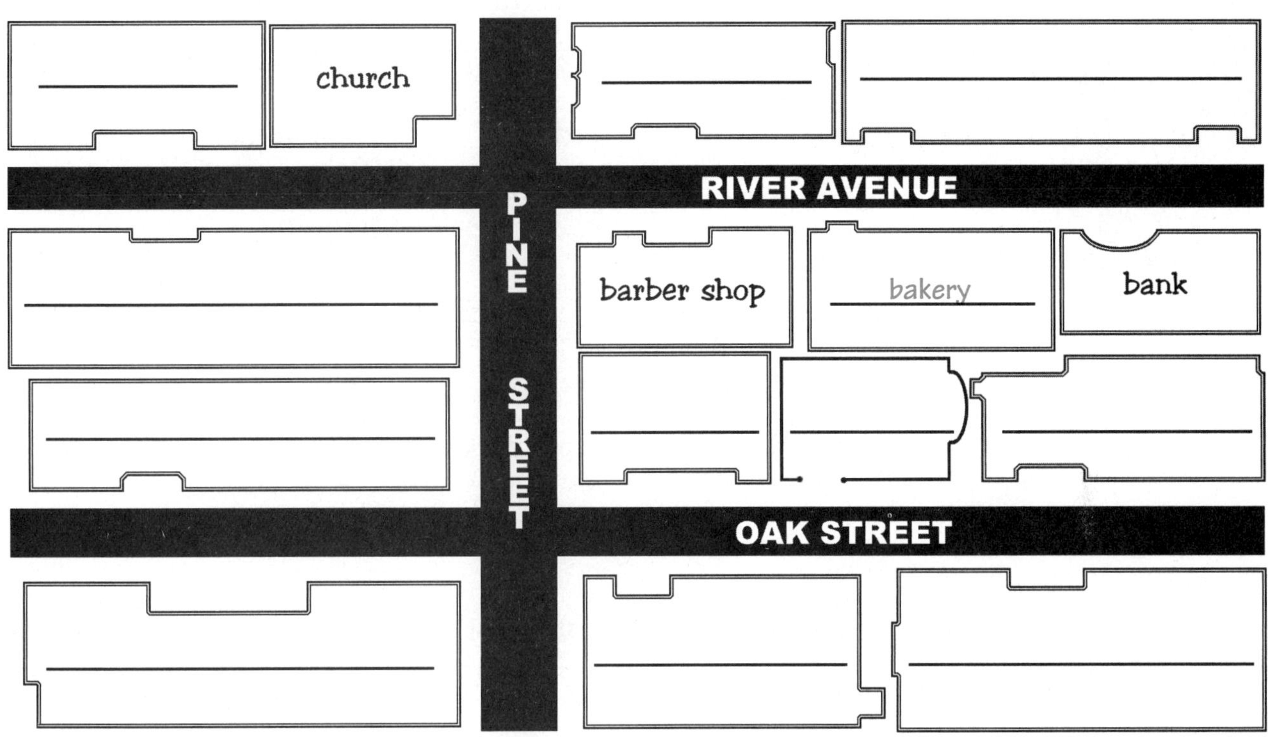

D YES OR NO?

Look at the map and answer the questions.

1. Is there a fire station on Oak Street? Yes, there is. (No, there isn't.)
2. Is there a hair salon across from the barber shop? Yes, there is. No, there isn't.
3. Is there a supermarket around the corner from the bank? Yes, there is. No, there isn't.
4. Is there a police station next to the hospital? Yes, there is. No, there isn't.
5. Is there a department store across from the school? Yes, there is. No, there isn't.
6. Is there a drug store on Oak Street? Yes, there is. No, there isn't.
7. Is there a laundromat next to the park? Yes, there is. No, there isn't.
8. Is there a church on River Avenue? Yes, there is. No, there isn't.
9. Is there a bank between the barber shop and the bakery? Yes, there is. No, there isn't.

E GRAMMARRAP: *Just Around the Corner*

Listen. Then clap and practice.

All. There's a nice big supermarket just around the corner.
There's a good cheap restaurant just around the corner.
There's a nice clean laundromat just around the corner.
There's a quiet little park just around the corner.
Just around the corner? Thanks very much.

A. Is there a nice big supermarket anywhere around here?
B. Yes, there is. Yes, there is.
There's a nice big supermarket just around the corner.
A. Just around the corner? Thanks very much.

A. Is there a good cheap restaurant anywhere around here?
B. Yes, there is. Yes, there is.
There's a good cheap restaurant just around the corner.
A. Just around the corner? Thanks very much.

A. Is there a nice clean laundromat anywhere around here?
B. Yes, there is. Yes, there is.
There's a nice clean laundromat just around the corner.
A. Just around the corner? Thanks very much.

A. Is there a quiet little park anywhere around here?
B. Yes, there is. Yes, there is.
There's a quiet little park just around the corner.
A. Just around the corner? Thanks very much.

F WHAT ARE THEY SAYING?

is there	there is	there isn't	there are
are there	there's		there aren't

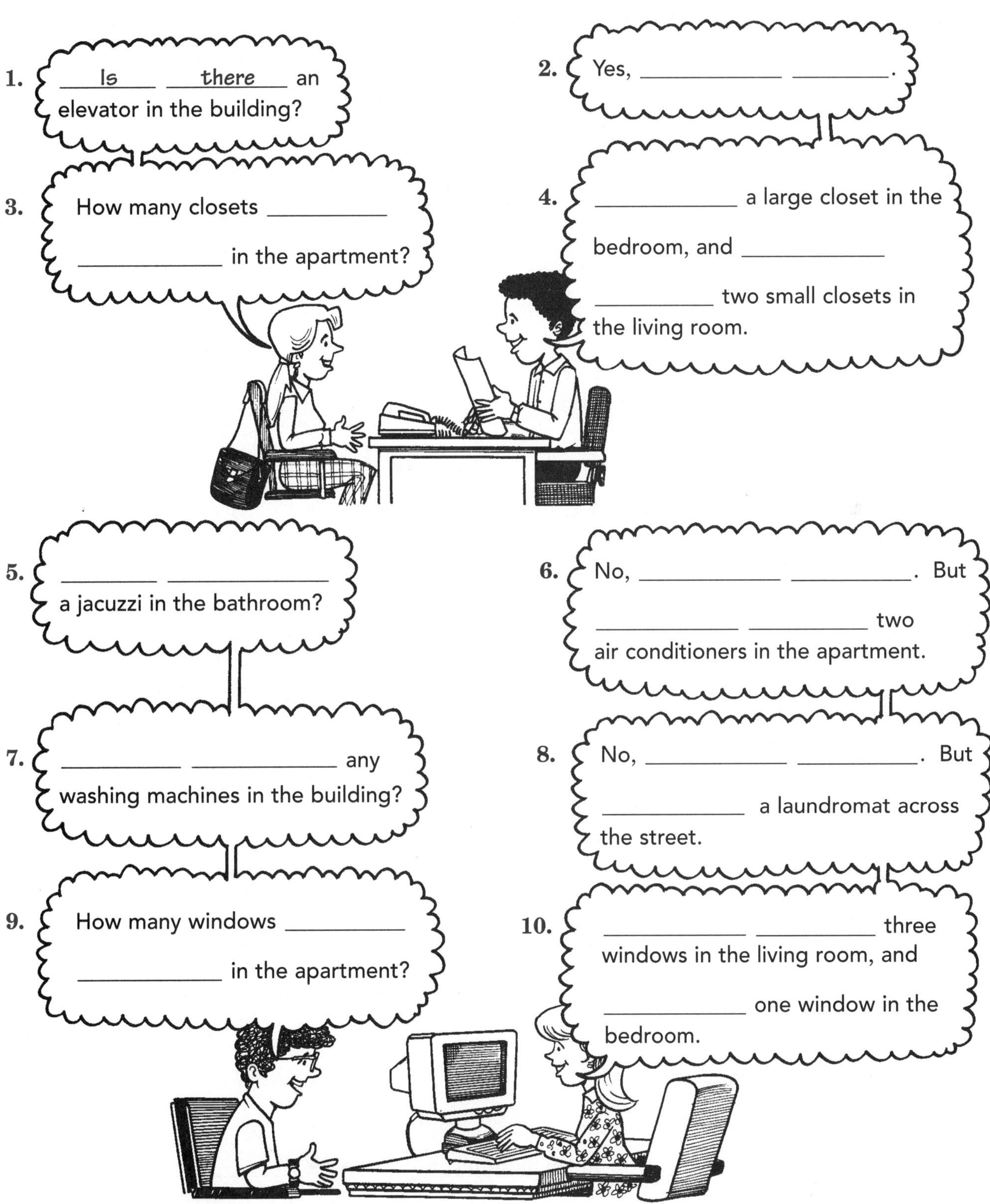

1. __Is__ __there__ an elevator in the building?
2. Yes, __________ __________.
3. How many closets __________ __________ in the apartment?
4. __________ a large closet in the bedroom, and __________ __________ two small closets in the living room.
5. __________ __________ a jacuzzi in the bathroom?
6. No, __________ __________. But __________ __________ two air conditioners in the apartment.
7. __________ __________ any washing machines in the building?
8. No, __________ __________. But __________ a laundromat across the street.
9. How many windows __________ __________ in the apartment?
10. __________ __________ three windows in the living room, and __________ one window in the bedroom.

G OUR APARTMENT BUILDING

broken	closets	escape	machines	satellite dish	mice
cats	dogs	hole	mailbox	refrigerator	stop

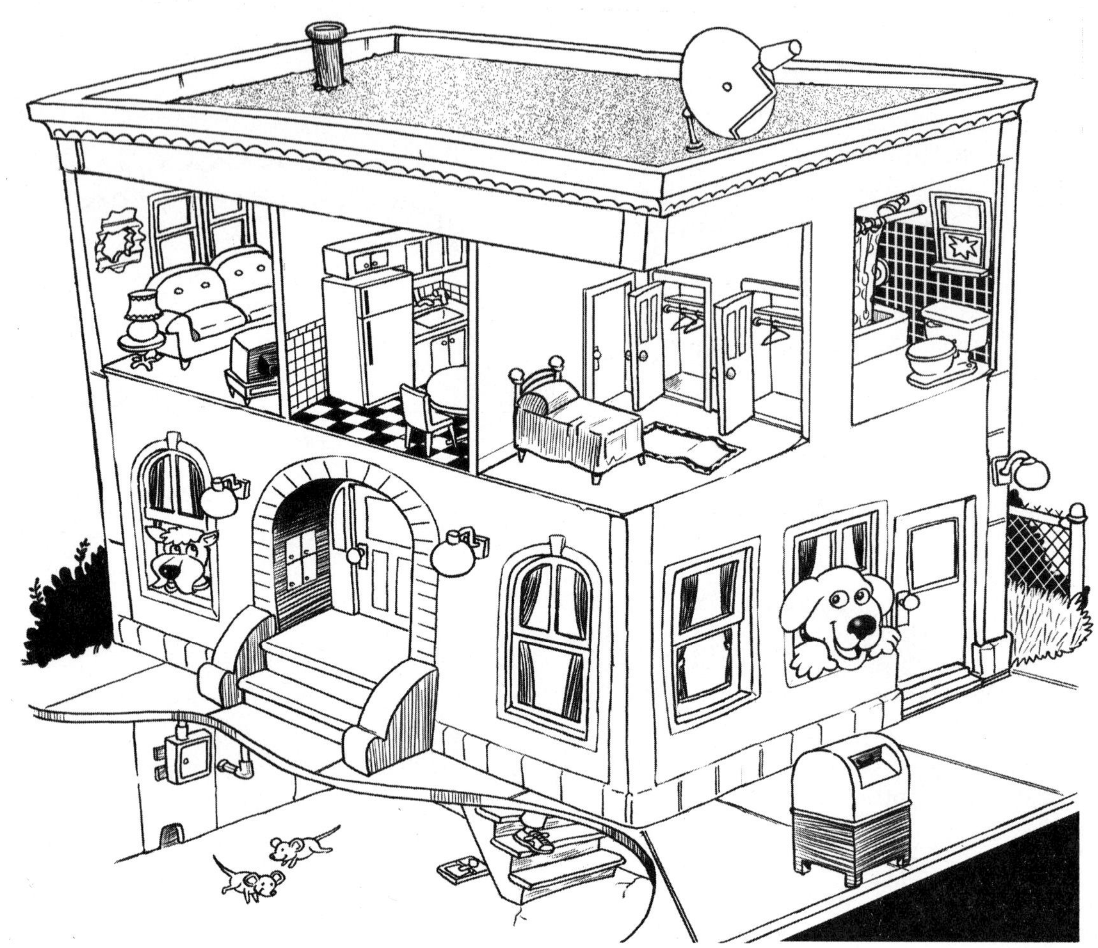

1. There aren't any washing ___machines___ in the basement.
2. There's a ______________ window in the bathroom.
3. There are ______________ in the basement.
4. There isn't a fire ______________.
5. There's a ______________ in the wall in the living room.
6. There's a ______________________ on the roof.
7. There's a ______________________ in the kitchen.
8. There are two __________________ in the bedroom.
9. There aren't any ______________ in the building, but there are ______________.
10. There isn't a bus ______________ outside the building, but there's a ______________.

H JANE'S LIVING ROOM

Yes, there is.   No, there isn't.   Yes, there are.   No, there aren't.

1. Is there a computer in Jane's living room?

   Yes, there is.

2. Is there a desk in the living room?

   ____

3. Are there any flowers in the living room?

   ____

4. Is there a newspaper on the table?

   ____

5. Are there any photographs on the table?

   ____

6. Are there any clothes in the closet?

   ____

7. Are there any windows in the living room?

   ____

8. Is there a cat in the living room?

   ____

9. Are there any chairs in front of the windows?

   ____

10. Is there a bookshelf in the living room?

    ____

11. Is there a cell phone next to the computer?

    ____

12. Is there a television next to the bookshelf?

    ____

13. Are there any books on the sofa?

    ____

14. Is there a guitar on the chair?

    ____

I LOOKING FOR AN APARTMENT

a/c. = air conditioner	beaut. = beautiful	frpl(s). = fireplace(s)	nr. = near
apt. = apartment	bldg. = building	kit. = kitchen	rm(s). = room(s)
bath(s). = bathroom(s)	dinrm. = dining room	lge. = large	schl. = school
bdrm(s). = bedroom(s)	elev. = elevator	livrm. = living room	

www.UShomes.com **CHICAGO**

Quiet, sunny apt., kit., livrm., bdrm., bath., 2 frpls., no children, $900. 800-874-5555.

1. The apartment is in ___Chicago___.
2. It's quiet and ______________.
3. There's a kitchen, a living room, a ______________, and a ______________.
4. There are two ______________ in the apartment.
5. There aren't any ______________ in the building.

www.UShomes.com **MIAMI**

Beaut. new apt., kit., livrm., 3 bdrms., 2 baths., elev. in building., $1200. 800-874-5555.

6. The apartment is in ______________.
7. It's ______________ and new.
8. There are three ______________ in the apartment.
9. There are __________ bathrooms.
10. There's an ______________ in the building.

www.UShomes.com **NEW YORK**

Sunny, lge. apt., kit., livrm., bdrm., bath., 2 a/c., nr. schl. $1800. 800-874-5555.

11. The apartment is in ______________.
12. It's sunny and ______________.
13. There's a kitchen, a ______________, a bedroom, and a bathroom.
14. There are two ______________.
15. The apartment is near a ______________.

www.UShomes.com **DALLAS**

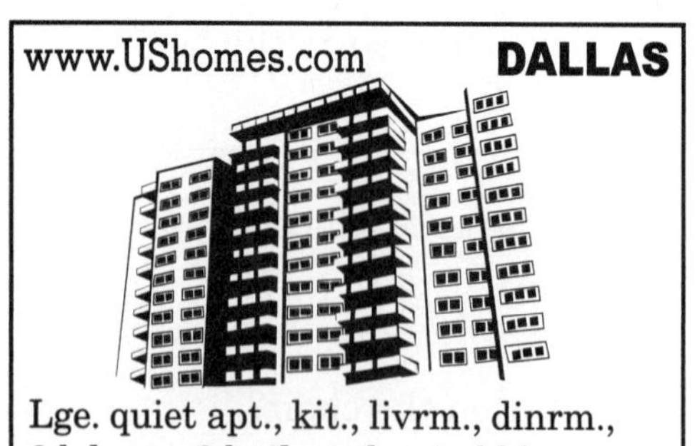

Lge. quiet apt., kit., livrm., dinrm., 2 bdrms., 2 baths., elev. in bldg., nr. bus. $850. 800-874-5555.

16. The apartment is in ______________.
17. It's large and ______________.
18. There's a ______________, a kitchen, and a living room.
19. There's an elevator in the ______________.
20. The apartment is ______________ a bus stop.

J GRAMMARRAP: *Tell Me About the Apartment*

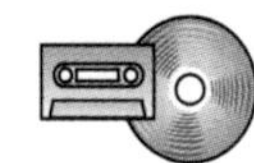

Listen. Then clap and practice.

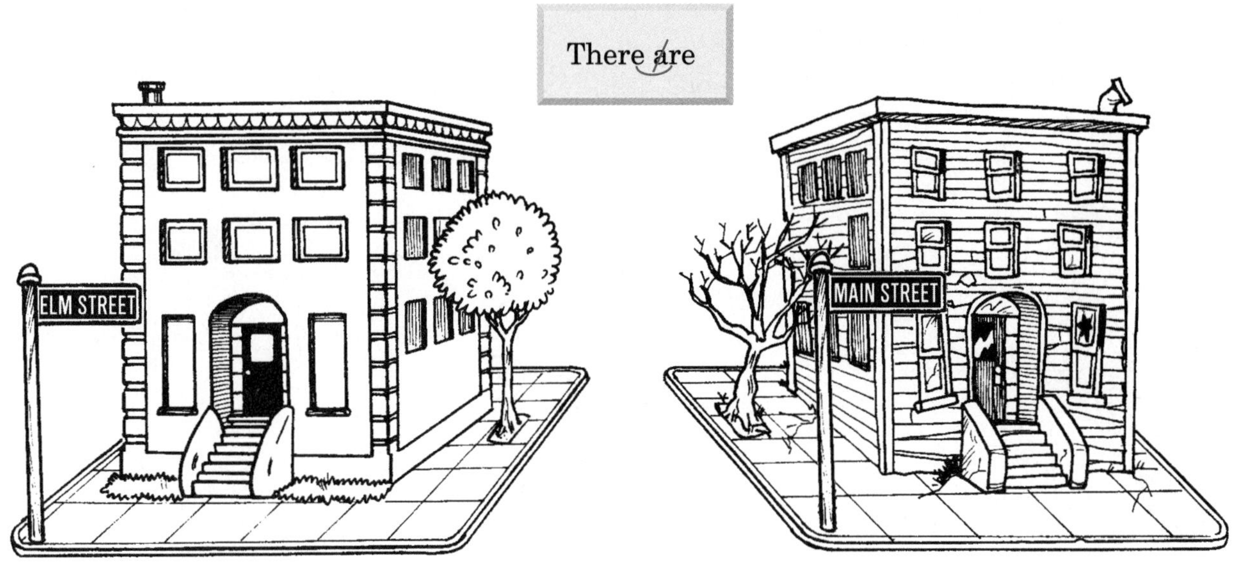

A.	Tell me about the apartment on		Elm Street.	•
B.	It's nice, but it	isn't very	cheap.	•
	There's a brand new	stove in the	kitchen.	•
	There's a beautiful	carpet on the	floor.	•
	There are three large	windows in the	living room.	•
	And the bedroom has a	sliding glass	door.	•
All.	The bedroom has a	sliding glass	door?!	•
B.	Yes, the bedroom has a	sliding glass	door.	•
A.	Tell me about the apartment on		Main Street.	•
B.	It's cheap, but it	isn't very	nice.	•
	There isn't a	tub in the	bathroom.	•
	There aren't any	lights in the	hall.	•
	There's a broken	window in the	dining room.	•
	And there are ten big	holes in the	wall!	•
All.	There are ten big	holes in the	wall?!	•
B.	Yes, there are ten big	holes in the	wall.	•

A WHAT'S THE WORD?

belt	briefcase	glasses	jeans	purse	sock	tie
blouse	coat	glove	mitten	shirt	stocking	umbrella
boots	dress	hat	necklace	shoe	suit	watch
bracelet	earring	jacket	pants	skirt	sweater	

1. tie
2. ______
3. ______
4. ______
5. ______
6. ______
7. ______
8. ______
9. ______
10. ______
11. ______
12. ______
13. ______
14. ______
15. ______

16. ______
17. ______
18. ______
19. ______
20. ______
21. ______
22. ______
23. ______
24. ______
25. ______
26. ______
27. ______

B A OR AN?

1.	a bus station	7.	______ hospital	13.	______ exercise	19.	______ uncle
2.	an umbrella	8.	______ antenna	14.	______ house	20.	______ attic
3.	______ school	9.	______ e-mail	15.	______ bank	21.	______ flower
4.	______ office	10.	______ yard	16.	______ woman	22.	______ aunt
5.	______ radio	11.	______ library	17.	______ apartment	23.	______ fax
6.	______ earring	12.	______ cell phone	18.	______ laundromat	24.	______ hotel

C SINGULAR/PLURAL

1.	a hat	hats	10.	______	rooms
2.	______	basements	11.	an earring	______
3.	a dress	______	12.	______	purses
4.	a boss	______	13.	a niece	______
5.	an exercise	______	14.	a woman	______
6.	______	watches	15.	______	children
7.	______	gloves	16.	a mouse	______
8.	a sock	______	17.	______	teeth
9.	a drum	______	18.	______	people

D LISTENING 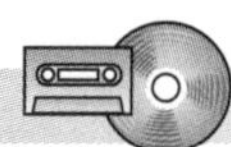

Listen and circle the word you hear.

1.	umbrella	(umbrellas)	9.	necklace	necklaces
2.	blouse	blouses	10.	earring	earrings
3.	coat	coats	11.	belt	belts
4.	computer	computers	12.	watch	watches
5.	shoe	shoes	13.	niece	nieces
6.	exercise	exercises	14.	nephew	nephews
7.	dress	dresses	15.	shirt	shirts
8.	restaurant	restaurants	16.	tie	ties

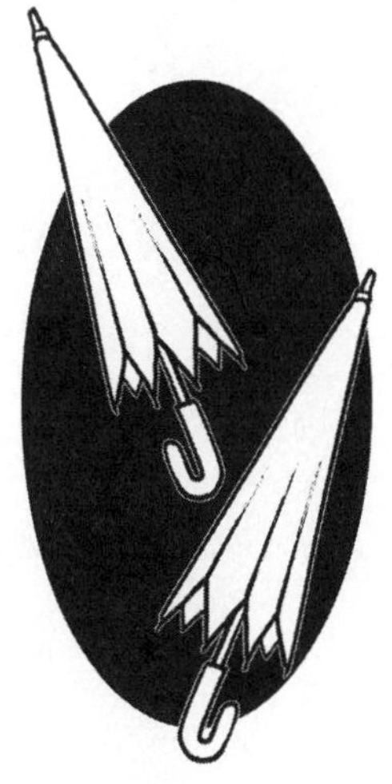

E LISTENING

Listen and circle the color you hear.

1.	(blue)	black	3.	gray	gold	5.	purple	yellow
2.	red	green	4.	pink	silver	6.	orange	brown

F COLORS

Write sentences about yourself, using colors.

black	gray	pink	silver
blue	green	purple	white
brown	orange	red	yellow
gold			

1. My house/apartment is. . . . .
2. My bedroom is . . . .
3. My kitchen is . . . .
4. My bathroom is . . . .
5. My living room is . . . .
6. My classroom is . . . .
7. My English book is . . . .
8. My pencils are . . . .
9. My notebook is . . . .
10. My desk is . . . .
11. My shirt/blouse is. . . . .
12. My watch is . . . .
13. My socks/stockings are . . . .
14. My coat is . . . .
15. My hat is . . . .
16. My jeans are . . . .
17. My shoes are . . . .
18. My . . . . (is/are) . . . .
19. My . . . . (is/are) . . . .
20. My . . . . (is/are) . . . .
21. My . . . . (is/are) . . . .
22. My . . . . (is/are) . . . .
23. My . . . . (is/are) . . . .
24. My . . . . (is/are) . . . .

G WHAT ARE THEY LOOKING FOR?

1. Yes, please. I'm looking for a pair of pants.

2. Yes, please. I'm looking for ______________________.

3. Yes, please. I'm looking for ______________________.

4. Yes, please. I'm looking for ______________________.

5. Yes, please. I'm looking for ______________________.

6. Yes, please. I'm looking for ______________________.

7. Yes, please. I'm looking for ______________________.

8. Yes, please. I'm looking for ______________________.

9. Yes, please. I'm looking for ______________________.

H LISTENING

Listen and put a check (✓) under the correct picture.

1. ______ ✓ ______ 2. ______ ______

3. ______ ______ 4. ______ ______

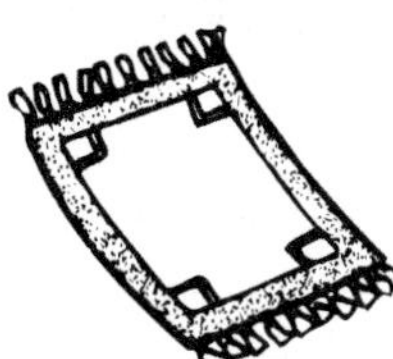 

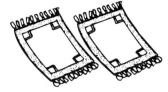

5. ______ ______ 6. ______ ______

7. ______ ______ 8. ______ ______

I LISTENING

Listen and circle the correct word to complete the sentence.

1. (is) / are red.
2. is / are easy.
3. is / are large.
4. is / are gold.
5. is / are beautiful.
6. is / are new.
7. is / are expensive.
8. is / are small.
9. is / are big.

J THIS/THAT/THESE/THOSE

this
these

that
those

orange

yellow

1. This hat is orange.

2. That hat is yellow.

brown

black

3. ______________________

4. ______________________

expensive

cheap

5. ______________________

6. ______________________

small

large

7. ______________________

8. ______________________

pretty

ugly

9. ______________________

10. ______________________

gold

silver

11. ______________________

12. ______________________

K SINGULAR → PLURAL

Write the sentence in the plural.

1. That coat is blue. _Those coats are blue._
2. This bracelet is new. ______
3. That watch is beautiful. ______
4. This is Tom's jacket. ______
5. This isn't your shoe. ______
6. Is that your earring? ______
7. That isn't your notebook. ______
8. This person isn't rich. ______

L PLURAL → SINGULAR

Write the sentence in the singular.

1. These sweaters are pretty. _This sweater is pretty._
2. Those purses are expensive. ______
3. Are these your neighbors? ______
4. Are those your dresses? ______
5. Those are Bill's shirts. ______
6. These women are my friends. ______
7. These aren't my gloves. ______
8. Those are her cats. ______

M SCRAMBLED SENTENCES

Unscramble the sentences. Begin each sentence with a capital letter.

1. _I think that's my jacket._
   jacket I that's think my
2. ______
   my these gloves new are
3. ______
   boots aren't those black your
4. ______
   year blue very this suits popular are
5. ______
   of here's nice sunglasses pair a
6. ______
   old that's car brother's my

N GrammarRap: *Clothes In My Closet*

Listen. Then clap and practice.

This shirt is	red.	Old	red	shirt!
That skirt is	blue.	New	blue	skirt!
This shirt is	old.	Old	red	shirt!
That skirt is	new.	New	blue	skirt!

These suits are	silver.	New	silver	suits!
Those boots are	gold.	Old	gold	boots!
These suits are	new.	New	silver	suits!
Those boots are	old.	Old	gold	boots!

O GrammarRap: *Black Leather Jacket*

Listen. Then clap and practice.

Blue jeans, gray pants,
Black leather jacket!
Blue jeans, gray pants,
Black leather jacket!

White shirt, silver boots,
Black leather jacket!
White shirt, silver boots,
Black leather jacket!

Cool blue jeans!
Nice gray pants!
White shirt, silver boots,
Black leather jacket!

P THIS/ THAT/ THESE/ THOSE

this these	that those

1. ___This___ is my favorite pair of jeans.
   ________ are my new sweaters, and
   ________ is my new coat.

2. ___That___'s a pretty coat.
   Are ________ your new boots?

3. ________ is my classroom.
   ________ is the bulletin board, and
   ________ are the computers.

4. Are ________ your books, and
   is ________ your pencil?

5. ________ is my favorite photograph.
   ________ is my mother, and
   ________ are my sisters and brothers.

6. Are ________ your cousins?
   Who's ________ handsome man?

Q GrammarSong: *At the Laundromat*

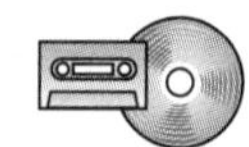

Listen and fill in the words to the song. Then listen again and sing along.

hat	those	shirt	suits	that	are	skirt	that's	boots	these	this

Is ___this___ 1 your sweater?

Is ________ 2 your ________ 3?

________ 4 my blue jacket.

That's my pink ________ 5.

I think ________ 6 is my new ________ 7.

We're looking for ________ 8 and ________ 9.

We're washing all our clothes at the laundromat.

________ 10 and that. At the laundromat.

This and ________ 11. At the laundromat.

________ 12 and ________ 13. At the laundromat.

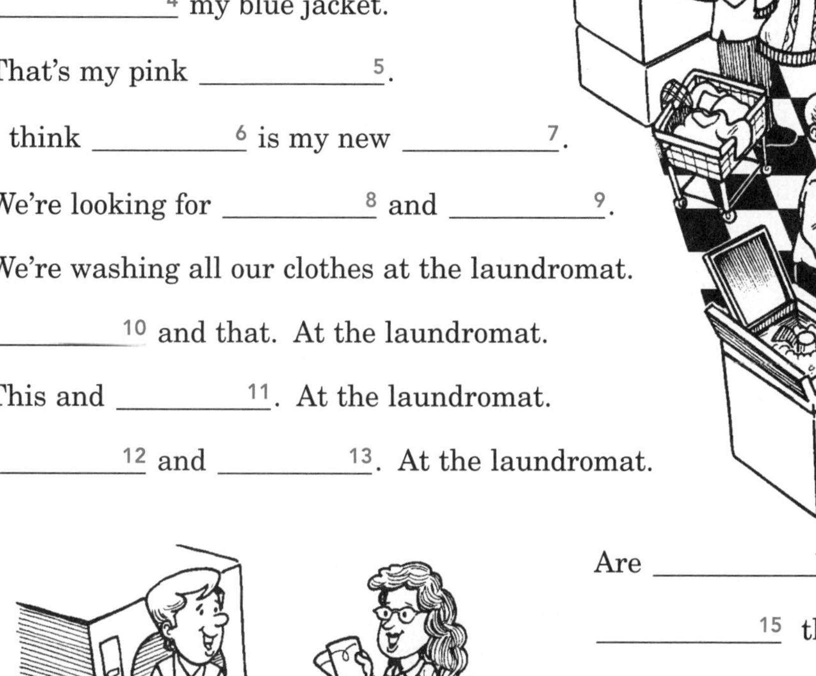

Are ________ 14 your mittens?

________ 15 these your ________ 16?

________ 17 are my socks.

Those are my bathing ________ 18.

Where ________ 19 my pantyhose?

We're looking for ________ 20 and ________ 21.

We're washing all our clothes at the laundromat.

________ 22 and ________ 23.

Washing all our clothes.

________ 24 and ________ 25.

At the laundromat. At the laundromat.

(Hey! Give me ________ 26!)

At the laundromat!

✓ CHECK-UP TEST: Chapters 7-8

A. Circle the correct answers.

Ex. My favorite color is [broken / **(blue)** / big].

1. Are [these / this / that] your children?

2. Here's a nice pair [to / on / of] stockings.

3. [Are there / Is there / There] a jacuzzi in the apartment?

4. There's an [earring / sweater / umbrellas] on the table.

5. [Who / What / How] many windows are there in the living room?

6. There aren't any [man / people / hole] in the room.

7. Dresses are over [there / their / they're].

8. Is there a stove in the kitchen?

   No, there aren't.
   No, they isn't.
   No, there isn't.

B. Answer the questions.

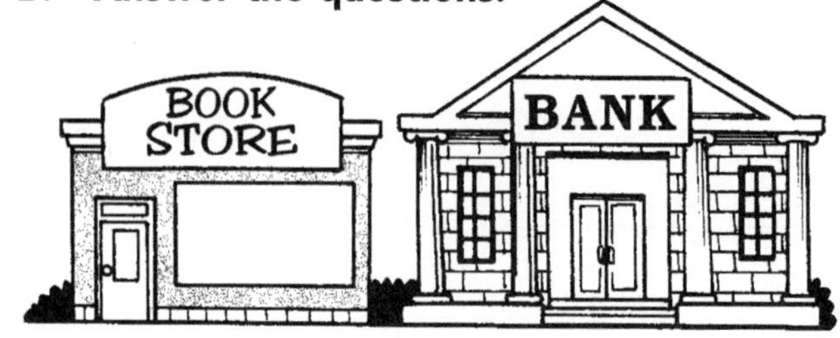

Ex. Where's the book store?

It's next to the bank.

1. Where's the bakery?

____

2. Where's the hospital?

____

3. Where's the video store?

____

C. Circle the word that doesn't belong.

Ex.	cotton	wool	vinyl	(cheap)
1.	this	those	their	these
2.	orange	striped	gray	pink
3.	closet	bakery	hotel	school
4.	boots	necklace	shoes	socks

D. Write sentences with *this, that, these,* and *those.*

old

Ex. This car is old.

large

1. ______________________

broken

2. ______________________

black

3. ______________________

E. Write these sentences in the plural.

Ex. That house is large.

Those houses are large.

1. This room is small.

____

2. That isn't my pencil.

____

3. Is this your boot?

____

F. Listen and circle the correct word to complete the sentence.

Ex. is / (are) green.

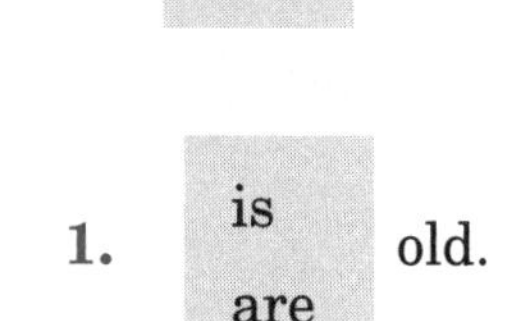

1. is / are old.

2. is / are nice.

3. is / are beautiful.

4. is / are expensive.

A INTERVIEWS AROUND THE WORLD

what	language	we	our	is	eat	read
what's	name	you	your	are	live	watch
where	names	they	their	do	sing	speak

A. What's (1) your name?

B. My ______ (2) ______ (3) Sung Hee.

A. Where ______ (4) ______ (5) live?

B. I ______ (6) in Seoul.

A. ______ (7) ______ (8) do you speak?

B. I ______ (9) Korean.

A. What ______ (10) ______ (11) do every day?

B. Every day I ______ (12) Korean food, and I ______ (13) Korean TV shows.

A. What ______ (14) your names?

B. ______ (15) ______ (16) are Carlos and Maria.

A. Where ______ (17) ______ (18) live?

B. ______ (19) ______ (20) in Madrid.

A. ______ (21) language ______ (22) ______ (23) speak?

B. We ______ (24) Spanish.

A. What ______ (25) you ______ (26) every day?

B. Every day ______ (27) ______ (28) Spanish songs, and we ______ (29) Spanish newspapers.

A. ________ 30 ________ 31 their names?

B. ________ 32 ________ 33 ________ 34 Yuko and Toshi.

A. ________ 35 ________ 36 they live?

B. ________ 37 ________ 38 in Kyoto.

A. ________ 39 ________ 40 ________ 41 ________ 42 speak?

B. They ________ 43 Japanese.

A. What ________ 44 they ________ 45 every day?

B. Every day ________ 46 ________ 47 Japanese food, and ________ 48 ________ 49 Japanese TV shows.

B LISTENING

Listen and choose the correct response.

1. (a.) My name is Kenji.
   b. I live in Tokyo.
2. a. They speak Italian.
   b. I speak Italian.
3. a. They watch Russian TV shows.
   b. I watch Russian TV shows.
4. a. We live in Seoul.
   b. They live in Seoul.
5. a. We eat French food.
   b. We speak French.
6. a. They live in Madrid.
   b. We sing Spanish songs.

C PEOPLE AROUND THE WORLD

My name is Jane. I live in Montreal. Every day I play the piano, and I listen to Canadian music.

1. What's her name? Her name is Jane.
2. Where does she live? ________
3. What does she do every day? ________

(continued)

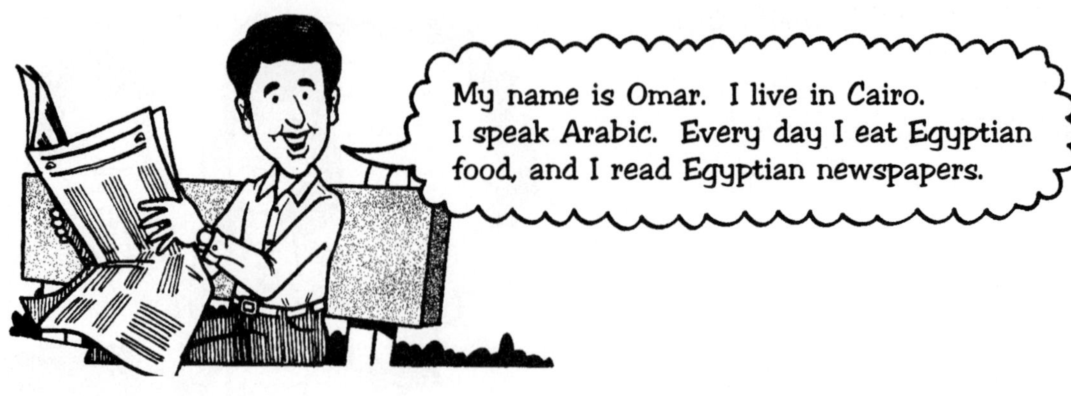

4. ______________________? His name is Omar.

5. ______________________? He lives in Cairo.

6. What language does he speak? ______________________

7. What ______________ every day? He ________ Egyptian food, and ________ ______________________.

My name is Sonia. I live in Sao Paolo. I speak Portuguese. Every day I do exercises, and I play soccer.

8. What's her name? ______________________

9. ______________________ she live? ______________________

10. What language ______________? ______________________

11. What ______________ every day? ______________________ ______________________

D WRITE ABOUT YOURSELF

1. What's your name? ....

2. Where do you live? ....

3. What language do you speak? ....

4. What do you do every day? ....
....

E GrammarRap: *People and Places*

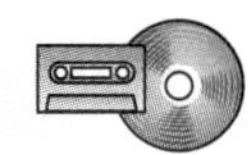

Listen. Then clap and practice.

A. What's his name?
B. His name is Joe.
A. Where does he live?
B. In Mexico.

A. What's his name?
B. His name is Lance.
A. Where does he live?
B. He lives in France.

A. What's her name?
B. Her name is Anne.
A. Where does she live?
B. She lives in Japan.

A. What's her name?
B. Her name is Anastasia.
A. Where does she live?
B. She lives in Malaysia.

A. What's her name?
B. Her name is Denise.
A. Where does she live?
B. She lives in Greece.

A. What's her name?
B. Her name is Maria.
A. Where does she live?
B. She lives in Korea.

F EDUARDO'S FAMILY

Fill in the correct form of the verb.

clean	cook	do	live	play	read	shop	speak	work
cleans	cooks	does	lives	plays	reads	shops	speaks	works

My name is Eduardo. I ___live___ 1 in Rio de Janeiro. I ___________ 2 English and Portuguese. My wife's name is Sonia. She ___________ 3 English, Portuguese, and Spanish. Our children, Fernando and Claudio, also ___________ 4 English and Portuguese. At school they ___________ 5 English and Portuguese books.

We ___________ 6 in a large apartment. Every day my wife ___________ 7 the newspaper and ___________ 8 in a bank. I ___________ 9 breakfast and ___________ 10 in an office.

Every weekend we ___________ 11 our apartment. I also ___________ 12 at the supermarket. Fernando ___________ 13 soccer with his friends, and Claudio and I ___________ 14 basketball.

What languages ___________ 15 YOU speak? What do YOU ___________ 16 every day?

G LISTENING 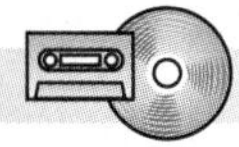

Listen and circle the word you hear.

1.	(live)	lives	4.	listen	listens	7.	sing	sings
2.	do	does	5.	watch	watches	8.	eat	eats
3.	do	does	6.	eat	eats	9.	read	reads

H WHAT'S THE WORD?

do does

cook	drive	live	paint	sell

1. A. Where ____does____ he live?
   B. He ____lives____ in San Francisco.

2. A. What ____________ they do?
   B. They ____________ houses.

3. A. What ____________ he do?
   B. He ____________ a bus.

4. A. Where ____________ you live?
   B. I ____________ in Sydney.

5. A. What ____________ you do?
   B. We ____________ in a restaurant.

6. A. What ________ he ________?
   B. He ____________ cars.

I WHAT'S THE DIFFERENCE?

1. I drive a bus. My friend Carla ____drives____ a taxi.
2. We ____________ in a bank. They work in an office.
3. Victor ____________ the violin. His children play the piano.
4. I sell cars. My wife ____________ computers.
5. I paint houses. My brother ____________ pictures.
6. We live in Los Angeles. Our son ____________ in London.

J LISTEN AND PRONOUNCE

Listen to each word and then say it.

1. chair	4. Chen	7. church	10. children	13. Sharp	16. Shirley	19. short
2. bench	5. kitchen	8. cheap	11. Richard	14. shirt	17. washing	20. English
3. Charlie	6. Chinese	9. watch	12. shoes	15. machine	18. station	21. French

K LOUD AND CLEAR

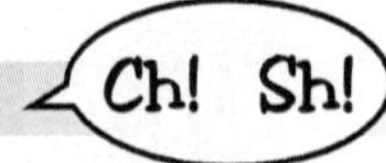

Fill in the words. Then read the sentences aloud.

chair   Charlie   kitchen   Chinese

1. ___Charlie___ is sitting in a ___chair___ in his ________ and eating ________ food.

Shirley   short   shoes

2. ________ isn't ________ in her new ________.

watch   Richard   cheap   French

3. ________ is looking for a ________ ________ ________.

shirt   washing   washing machine

4. He's ________ his ________ in his ________ ________.

bench   children   Chen   church

5. Mr. ________ and his ________ are sitting on a ________ in front of the ________.

Sharp   station   English

6. Mr. ________ is in London at an ________ train ________.

A WHAT'S THE DAY?

10

1. Monday ___Tuesday___ Wednesday
2. Friday __________ Sunday
3. Tuesday __________ Thursday
4. Saturday __________ Monday
5. Thursday __________ Saturday
6. Sunday __________ Tuesday

B WHAT ARE THEY SAYING?

Yes, {he / she / it} does.	No, {he / she / it} doesn't.

what kind of
when

1. ___Does___ your husband cook breakfast every day?
Yes, ___he does___.
3. ________ your son drive a car?
No, ________.
5. ________ that dog live in this neighborhood?
No, it ________.
7. ________ your sister work at the bank?
No, ________.

2. ________ your daughter study English in school?
Yes, ________.
4. ________ food does he cook?
He cooks Italian food.
6. ________ your grandfather shop at the grocery store in his neighborhood?
Yes, ________.
8. ________ does Robert visit his friends?
He visits his friends on Sunday.

C WHAT ARE THEY SAYING?

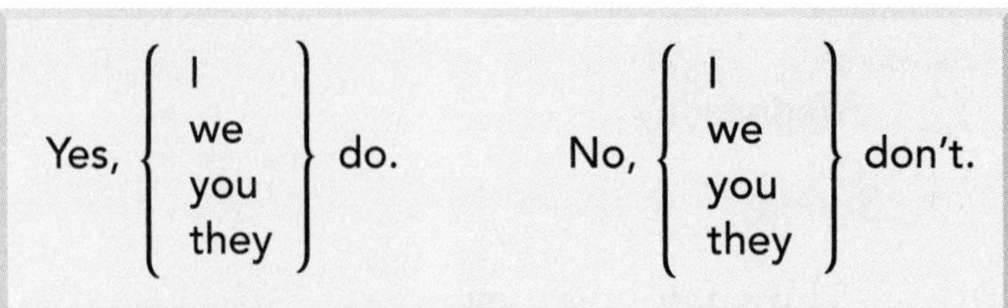

Yes, { I / we / you / they } do.
No, { I / we / you / they } don't.

1.

Do you sing in the shower?
Yes, I do.

2.

_____ your children speak French?
No, __________.

3.

_____ you and your husband live in this neighborhood?
Yes, __________.

4.

_____ you and your wife play cards?
No, __________.

5.

_____ you work on Saturday?
No, __________.

6.

_____ your neighbors make a lot of noise?
Yes, __________.

D LISTENING

Listen and choose the correct response.

1. a. Chinese music.
   (b.) French food.
   c. Every day.

2. a. Yes, he does.
   b. No, we don't.
   c. Yes, they do.

3. a. No, he doesn't.
   b. Because he likes the food.
   c. On Wednesday.

4. a. On Sunday.
   b. Yes, she does.
   c. In her house.

5. a. I go every day.
   b. I don't go there.
   c. Yes, I do.

6. a. In New York.
   b. On Thursday.
   c. They don't go there.

7. a. Because it's open.
   b. They play.
   c. He rides his bicycle.

8. a. No, they don't.
   b. In the city.
   c. Yes, she does.

9. a. Because it's near their house.
   b. On Central Avenue.
   c. Yes, they do.

E YES AND NO

1. My husband cooks Italian food. He _doesn't_ _cook_ Thai food.
2. Linda drives a taxi. She __________ __________ a bus.
3. Our children play the piano. They __________ __________ the guitar.
4. I work on Saturday. I __________ __________ on Sunday.
5. Tom lives in an apartment. He __________ __________ in a house.
6. My wife and I exercise in the park. We __________ __________ in a health club.
7. Every Saturday Mrs. Roberts __________ to the library. She doesn't go to the mall.
8. I __________ in large supermarkets. I don't shop in small grocery stores.
9. My mother __________ stockings. She doesn't wear socks.
10. Omar __________ Arabic. He doesn't speak Spanish.
11. Harry sings in the shower. He __________ __________ in the jacuzzi.

F WHAT'S THE WORD?

do does

1. Where _do_ they live?
2. When __________ your daughter do her homework?
3. What kind of books __________ you read?
4. Why __________ he call you every day?
5. What languages __________ they speak?
6. Where __________ your husband work?
7. __________ you visit your friends every week?
8. __________ he go to Stanley's Restaurant?
9. When __________ you go to the supermarket?
10. __________ your children wash the dishes?
11. What kind of music __________ she listen to?
12. What __________ he sell?
13. Why __________ they cry at weddings?

G WRITE ABOUT YOURSELF

1. I like .... I don't like ....
2. I play .... I don't play ....
3. I speak .... I don't speak ....
4. I eat .... I don't eat ....
5. I cook .... I don't cook ....

H YES OR NO?

1. Does Kathy take karate lessons?

Yes, she does.

2. Do Jim and Tom play tennis on Sunday?

No, they don't. They play volleyball.

3. Do you and Harry go dancing on Friday?

____

4. Does Miguel play in the orchestra?

____

5. Do you see a movie every weekend?

____

6. Do Mr. and Mrs. Kim go to a health club?

____

7. Does Richard jog in the park?

____

8. Do you and your wife watch TV every day?

____

I LISTENING

Listen and choose the correct response.

1. a. Yes, they do.
   (b.) Yes, I do.
2. a. Yes, he does.
   b. Yes, I do.
3. a. No, he doesn't.
   b. No, they don't.
4. a. No, she doesn't.
   b. No, I don't.
5. a. Yes, we do.
   b. Yes, he does.
6. a. Yes, we do.
   b. No, they don't.
7. a. No, I don't.
   b. Yes, he does.
8. a. Yes, they do.
   b. Yes, he does.
9. a. No, we don't.
   b. No, they don't.

J GRAMMARRAP: *They Do, They Don't*

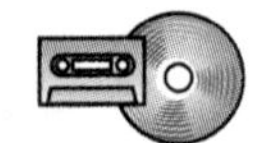

Listen. Then clap and practice.

Does he   Yes he   No he

A. Does he eat French bread?
B. Yes, he does.
A. Does she like Swiss cheese?
B. Yes, she does.

A. Do they cook Greek food?
B. Yes, they do.
A. Do they speak Chinese?
B. Yes, they do.

All. He eats French bread.
She likes Swiss cheese.
They cook Greek food.
And they speak Chinese.

A. Does he read the paper?
B. No, he doesn't.
A. Does she watch TV?
B. No, she doesn't.

A. Do they go to movies?
B. No, they don't.
A. Do they drink iced tea?
B. No, they don't.

All. He doesn't read the paper.
She doesn't watch TV.
They don't go to movies.
And they don't drink tea.

K A LETTER TO A PEN PAL

Read and practice.

Wednesday

Dear Peter,

My family and I live in San Juan. We speak Spanish. My mother is a music teacher. She plays the violin and the piano. My father works in an office.

My brother Ramon and I go to school every day. We study history, English, Spanish, science, and mathematics. My favorite school subject is science. I don't like history, but I like mathematics.

Do you like sports? Every day at school I play soccer. On Saturday I swim. What sports do you play? What kind of music do you like? I like rock music and country music very much, but I don't like jazz. What kind of movies do you like? I like adventure movies and comedies. I think science fiction movies are terrible.

Tell me about your family and your school.

Your friend,
Maria

L YOUR LETTER TO A PEN PAL

history
English
mathematics
science
music

baseball
football
hockey
golf
tennis
soccer

cartoons
dramas
comedies
westerns
adventure movies
science fiction movies

classical music
jazz
popular music
rock music
country music

Dear ....,

My family and I live in .... We speak .... At school, I study ...., ..., and .... My favorite subject is .... I don't like ....

What sports do you play? I play .... and .... I think .... is wonderful. I don't like ....

What kind of movies do you like? I like .... and ....

My favorite kind of music is ...., and I like .... I don't listen to ....

Tell me about your school and your city.

Your friend,

....

✓ CHECK-UP TEST: Chapters 9-10

A. Circle the correct answers.

Ex. We (live) / lives in Tokyo.

1. Tom play / plays in the park.

2. My wife and I shop / shops on Monday.

3. She don't / doesn't work on Saturday.

4. Where do / does your cousins live?

5. We stays / stay home every Sunday.

6. What activities do / does she do?

B. Fill in the blanks.

Ex. ___What___ is your address?

1. __________ does he live?
2. __________ kind of food do you like?
3. __________ Patty baby-sit for her neighbors?
4. __________ do you eat at that restaurant?
   Because we like the food.
5. __________ does Julie go to a health club?
   On Monday.
6. __________ does your family do on Sunday?

C. Fill in the blanks.

Mrs. Davis __________ 1 in Dallas. She's a very active person. She __________ 2 exercises every day. On Monday she __________ 3 her apartment, on Wednesday she __________ 4 tennis, on Friday she __________ 5 a karate lesson, on Saturday she __________ 6 her bicycle in the park, and on Sunday she __________ 7 to a museum and __________ 8 lunch in a restaurant.

D. Listen and choose the correct response.

Ex. a. We go to school.
(b.) They work in an office.
c. They're shy.

1. a. Yes, we do.
   b. We like dramas.
   c. On Thursday.

2. a. In a restaurant.
   b. Because we like it.
   c. Every day.

3. a. Yes, they do.
   b. Yes, he does.
   c. In Puerto Rico.

4. a. Short stories.
   b. News programs.
   c. I like golf.

5. a. Yes, they do.
   b. Because it's convenient.
   c. On Center Street.

A WHAT ARE THEY SAYING?

me	us
him	you
her	them
it	

1. Do you like me?
   Of course I like __you__.

2. Do you like your neighbors?
   Of course I like ________.

3. Do you like Helen?
   Of course I like ________.

4. Do you like George?
   Of course I like ________.

5. Do you like videos?
   Of course I like ________.

6. Do you like English?
   Of course I like ________.

7. Do your friends like you?
   Of course they like ________.

8. Do you like your new apartment?
   Of course I like ________.

9. Does your dog like you?
   Of course he likes ________.

B WHAT'S THE WORD?

it	her	him	them

1. She washes ___it___ every morning.
2. I think about ________ all the time.
3. We visit ________ every weekend.

4. I talk to ________ every night.
5. He uses ________ every day.
6. We feed ________ every afternoon.

C LISTENING

Listen and put a check (✓) under the correct picture.

1. ______ ___✓___
2. ______ ______
3. ______ ______

4. ______ ______
5. ______ ______
6. ______ ______

D WRITE ABOUT YOURSELF

1. I .... every day.
2. I .... every week.
3. I .... every month.
4. I .... every year.
5. I .... every weekend.
6. I .... every Sunday.
7. I .... every morning.
8. I .... all the time.

E WRITE IT AND SAY IT

Write the correct form of the word in parentheses and then say the sentence.

1. Carol sometimes (eat) ___eats___ Thai food.
2. My neighbor's dog always (bark) ________ in the afternoon.
3. My son never (clean) ________ his bedroom.
4. Ray always (wash) ________ his car on the weekend.
5. My brother sometimes (jog) ________ at night.
6. Amy usually (read) ________ poetry.
7. My mother rarely (shop) ________ at the grocery store around the corner.
8. Dan sometimes (watch) ________ videos on Saturday.
9. Omar usually (speak) ________ English at work.
10. Patty usually (play) ________ tennis in the park on Saturday.

F MATCHING

_c_	1. Walter always washes his car on Sunday.	a.	She usually watches dramas.
___	2. Jonathan never cooks dinner.	b.	He rarely jogs at night.
___	3. Carla rarely watches comedies.	c.	He never washes it during the week.
___	4. My grandmother rarely speaks English.	d.	She usually studies in the library.
___	5. Richard usually jogs in the morning.	e.	He always eats in a restaurant.
___	6. Larry never writes letters.	f.	He always writes e-mail messages.
___	7. Nancy rarely studies at home.	g.	She usually speaks Spanish.
___	8. Jane always fixes her computer.	h.	She never calls a repairperson.

G LISTENING 

Listen and choose the correct answer.

1. a. He usually washes it.
   (b.) He never washes it.
2. a. My husband sometimes cooks.
   b. My husband never cooks.
3. a. My neighbors are quiet.
   b. My neighbors are noisy.
4. a. They usually speak Spanish.
   b. They usually speak English.
5. a. Jane is shy.
   b. Jane is outgoing.
6. a. I usually study at home.
   b. I usually study in the library.

H WRITE ABOUT YOURSELF

always	usually	sometimes	rarely	never

1. I .... wear glasses.
2. I .... eat Italian food.
3. I .... listen to country music.
4. I .... go to English class.
5. I .... watch videos.
6. I .... read poetry.
7. I .... fix my car.
8. I .... visit my grandparents.
9. I .... watch game shows on TV.
10. I .... use a cell phone.
11. I .... clean my apartment.
12. I always ....
13. I usually ....
14. I sometimes ....
15. I rarely ....
16. I never ....

I GrammarRap: *I Always Get to Work on Time*

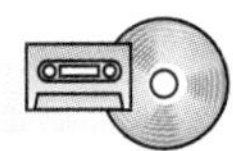

Listen. Then clap and practice.

A. I always get to work on time.
I'm usually here by eight.
I sometimes get here early.
I never get here late.
No, I never get here late.

B. He always gets to work on time.
He's usually here by eight.
He sometimes gets here early.
He rarely gets here late.

A. No! I NEVER get here late.

B. Right! He never gets here late.

J WHAT'S THE WORD?

have has

1. Do you ___have___ a bicycle?
2. My daughter __________ curly hair.
3. My parents __________ an old car.
4. Does your son __________ blond hair?
5. Our building __________ a satellite dish.
6. Do you __________ large sunglasses?
7. My sister __________ green eyes.
8. We __________ two dogs and a cat.

K WHAT ARE THEY SAYING?

have has do does don't doesn't

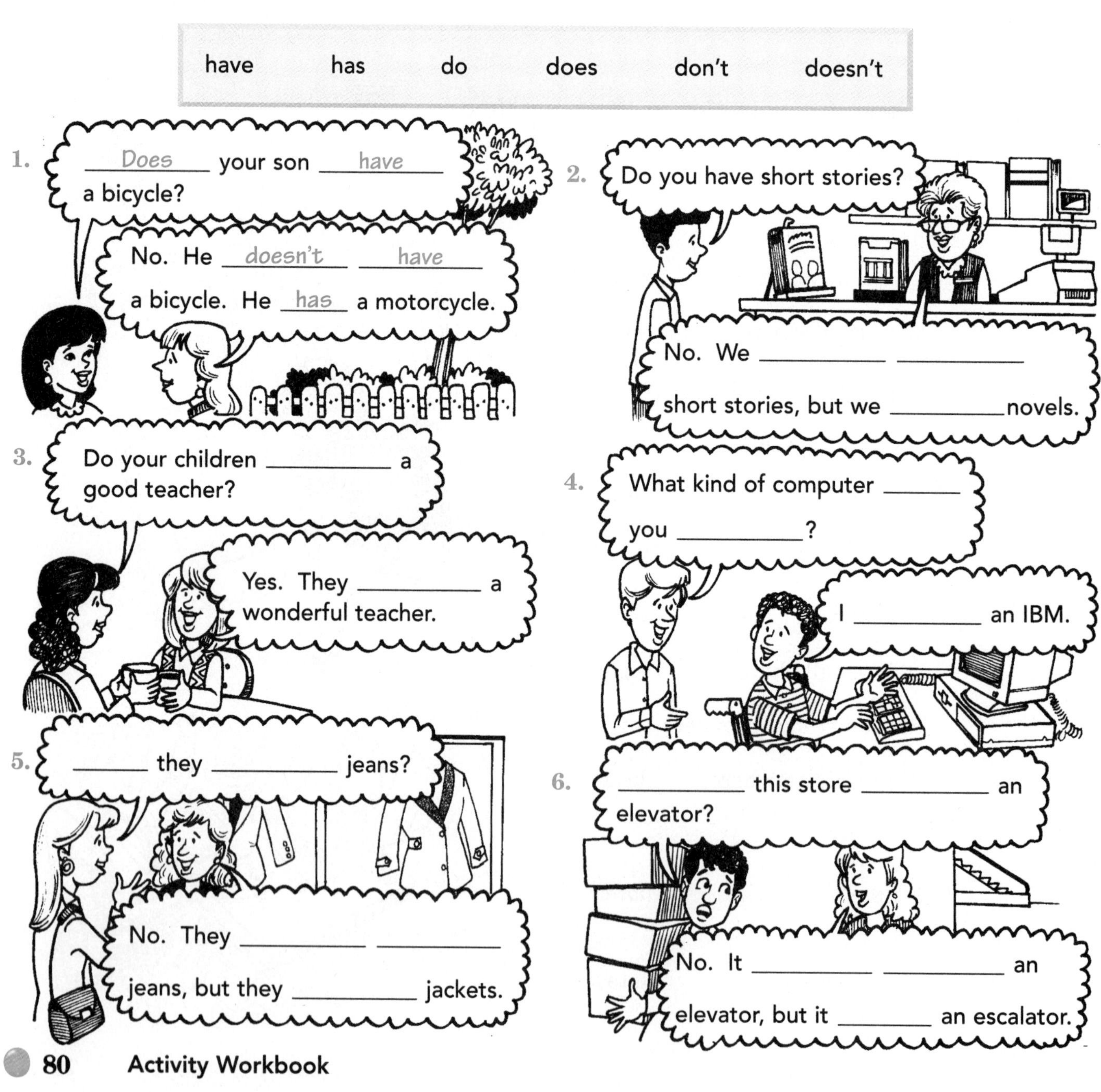

1.
___Does___ your son ___have___ a bicycle?
No. He ___doesn't___ ___have___ a bicycle. He ___has___ a motorcycle.
2.
Do you have short stories?
No. We __________ __________ short stories, but we __________ novels.
3.
Do your children __________ a good teacher?
Yes. They __________ a wonderful teacher.
4.
What kind of computer __________ you __________?
I __________ an IBM.
5.
__________ they __________ jeans?
No. They __________ __________ jeans, but they __________ jackets.
6.
__________ this store __________ an elevator?
No. It __________ __________ an elevator, but it __________ an escalator.

L WHAT'S THE WORD?

1. Tina doesn't have short hair. She has (long) / curly hair.

2. I don't have straight hair. I have thin / curly hair.

3. My brother isn't tall. He's heavy / short .

4. Albert isn't married. He's curly / single .

5. Your baby boy has beautiful blond eyes / hair .

6. His eyes aren't blue. They're brown / straight .

7. We don't live in the city. We live in the house / suburbs .

M TWO BROTHERS

My brother and I are very different. I'm tall, and he's short 1. I ______ 2 brown eyes, and he ______ 3 blue eyes. We both ______ 4 brown hair, but I have long, straight hair, and he has ______ 5, ______ 6 hair. I'm short and heavy. And he's ______ 7 and ______ 8. I'm a chef, and ______ 9 a doctor. I live in New York. He ______ 10 in San Diego. I have a small apartment in the city. He ______ 11 a large house ______ 12 the suburbs. I play tennis. He ______ 13 golf. I play the guitar. He doesn't ______ 14 a musical instrument. On the weekend, I usually ______ 15 to parties. He doesn't ______ 16 to parties. He ______ 17 TV and ______ 18 the newspaper.

N LISTENING

Listen and choose the correct response.

1. a. No. I have short hair.
   (b.) No. I have straight hair.
2. a. No. I'm single.
   b. No. I'm tall and thin.
3. a. No. He has black eyes.
   b. No. He has brown eyes.
4. a. No. This is my mother.
   b. No. I have a sister.
5. a. Yes. I go to parties.
   b. Yes. I stay home.
6. a. Yes. He's thin.
   b. No. He's thin.
7. a. No. I live in an apartment.
   b. No. I live in the suburbs.
8. a. No. I have long hair.
   b. No. I have curly hair.

O WHAT'S THE WORD?

Circle the correct word.

1. He watches TV [at / with / (in)] the evening.
2. The health club is [in / on / between] Main Street.
3. I'm playing a game [on / to / in] my computer.
4. Ann is sleeping [on / in / across] the yard.
5. He always talks [about / to / with] the weather.
6. I'm looking [from / for / to] a striped shirt.
7. Do you live [in / on / at] the suburbs?
8. Do your children go [to / at / in] school every day?
9. Tim is swimming [with / on / at] the beach.
10. My son is wearing a pair [from / for / of] new jeans.
11. Do you go [in / to / at] work [at / in / on] Saturday?
12. I listen [to / at / on] the radio in the morning.

A WHAT'S THE WORD?

angry	embarrassed	hot	nervous	scared	thirsty
cold	happy	hungry	sad	sick	tired

1. Howard is crying. He's ___sad___.

2. Helen is yawning. She's ______________.

3. Sam is perspiring. He's ______________.

4. Frank is shouting. He's ______________.

5. Mrs. Allen is going to the hospital.

   She's ______________.

6. Peter is looking at his paper and smiling.

   He's ______________.

7. Ben's cat is eating. It's ______________.

8. Irene is shivering. She's ______________.

9. Louise is biting her nails.

   She's ______________.

10. Jason is covering his eyes.

    He's ______________.

11. Pam is drinking milk.

    She's ______________.

12. Bobby is blushing.

    He's ______________.

B TELL ME WHY

1. A. Why are they yawning?

   B. They're yawning because they're tired.

   They always yawn when they're tired.

2. A. Why is she crying?

   B. ______________________ sad.

   She always ______________________.

3. A. Why is he shivering?

   B. ______________________ cold.

   He always ______________________.

4. A. Why are you perspiring?

   B. ______________________ hot.

   I always ______________________.

5. A. Why is she smiling?

   B. ______________________ happy.

   She always ______________________.

6. A. Why are they eating?

   B. ______________________ hungry.

   They always ______________________.

7. A. Why are you shouting?

   B. ______________________ angry.

   We always ______________________.

8. A. Why is he covering his eyes?

   B. ______________________ scared.

   He always ______________________.

C GrammarRap: *I Smile When I'm Happy*

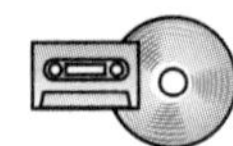

Listen. Then clap and practice.

A. I smile when I'm happy.
I frown when I'm sad.
I blush when I'm embarrassed.
And I shout when I'm mad.

B. Are you smiling?
A. Yes. I'm happy.
B. Are you frowning?
A. Yes. I'm sad.
B. Are you blushing?
A. I'm embarrassed.
B. Are you shouting?
A. Yes. I'm mad.

D GrammarRap: *Why Are You Doing That?*

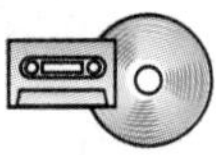

Listen. Then clap and practice.

A. What's Fran doing?
B. She's working late.
A. Working late?
Why's she doing that?
B. It's Monday.
She always works late on Monday.

A. What are you doing?
B. We're playing cards.
A. Playing cards?
Why are you doing that?
B. It's Tuesday.
We always play cards on Tuesday.

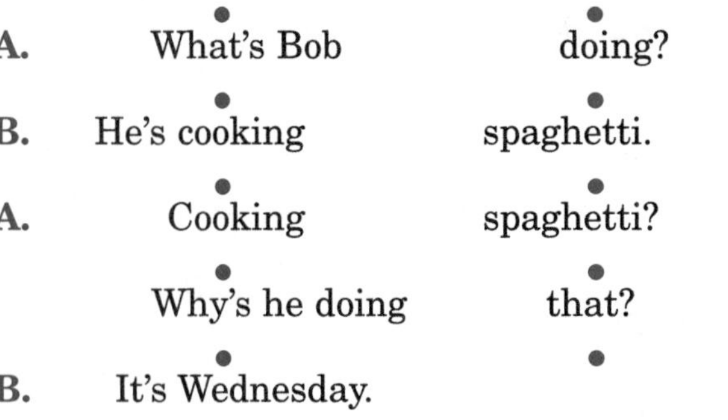

A. What's Bob doing?

B. He's cooking spaghetti.

A. Cooking spaghetti?

Why's he doing that?

B. It's Wednesday.

He always cooks spaghetti on Wednesday.

A. What's Maria doing?

B. She's dancing.

A. Dancing?

Why's she doing that?

B. It's Thursday.

She always dances on Thursday.

A. What's Gary doing?

B. He's bathing his cat.

A. Bathing his cat?

Why's he doing that?

B. It's Friday.

He always bathes his cat on Friday.

A. What are you doing?

B. I'm ________________ing.

A. ____________________?

Why are you doing that?

B. It's Saturday.

I always ________________ on Saturday.

E THAT'S STRANGE!

1. A. My sister is cooking dinner today.
   B. That's strange! She never cooks dinner.

2. A. Our children are studying with a flashlight.
   B. That's strange! They never __________ with a flashlight.

3. A. Victor is walking to work today.
   B. That's strange! He never __________ to work.

4. A. Ann is brushing her teeth in the kitchen.
   B. That's strange! She never __________ her teeth in the kitchen.

5. A. The dog is eating in the dining room today.
   B. That's strange! It never __________ in the dining room.

6. A. Nancy and Bob are dancing in the office.
   B. That's strange! They never __________ in the office.

7. A. Ruth __________ the carpet today.
   B. That's strange! She never sweeps the carpet.

8. A. My parents __________ poetry today.
   B. That's strange! They never read poetry.

9. A. __________ a typewriter today.
   B. That's strange! You never use a typewriter.

10. A. My cousins __________ in the yard.
    B. That's strange! They never sleep in the yard.

F WHAT'S THE QUESTION?

Choose the correct question word. Then write the question.

What	When	Where	Why	What kind of	How many

1. I'm blushing because I'm embarrassed. Why are you blushing?
2. They play tennis in the park. ______
3. She reads her e-mail at night. ______
4. I like Brazilian food. ______
5. We have ten cats. ______
6. He's using his cell phone. ______

What	How often	Where	Why	What kind of	How many

7. He watches game shows. ______
8. We call our grandchildren every week. ______
9. They play golf every weekend. ______
10. I'm smiling because I'm happy. ______
11. She's eating in the cafeteria today. ______
12. I'm wearing two sweaters. ______

G WHICH ONE DOESN'T BELONG?

1.	her	me	them	(we)
2.	noisy	usually	sometimes	rarely
3.	does	doesn't	has	don't
4.	angry	yoga	nervous	happy
5.	Wednesday	Why	What	When
6.	smiling	shivering	crying	outgoing
7.	clean	sweep	shy	wash
8.	year	evening	night	afternoon

H LISTENING

As you listen to each story, read the sentences and check *yes* or *no*.

Jennifer and Jason

1. yes ☐ no ☑ Jennifer and Jason are visiting their father.
2. yes ☐ no ☐ Jennifer and Jason are happy.
3. yes ☐ no ☐ Their grandfather isn't taking them to the park.

Our Boss

4. yes ☐ no ☐ Our boss usually smiles at the office.
5. yes ☐ no ☐ He's happy today.
6. yes ☐ no ☐ Everybody is thinking about the weekend.

On Vacation

7. yes ☐ no ☐ I like vacations.
8. yes ☐ no ☐ When the weather is nice, I watch videos.
9. yes ☐ no ☐ I'm swimming at the beach today because it's cold.

Timmy and His Brother

10. yes ☐ no ☐ Timmy is covering his eyes because he's sad.
11. yes ☐ no ☐ Timmy doesn't like science fiction movies.
12. yes ☐ no ☐ Timmy's brother is scared.

I LOUD AND CLEAR

sorry	hospital	sick	sister	Sally

scientist	speaking	What's	experiments

1. Sally is sorry her sister is sick in the hospital.

2. ________ the ________ doing? He's ________ about his new ________.

always cousin Athens busy is

3. My ________ in ________

____ ________ very

________.

doesn't Sally's clothes husband closet

4. ________ ________ ________

have any clean ________ in his

________.

Steven it's sweeping is because

5. ________ ____ ________

the floor ________ ____ dirty.

Sunday Mrs. newspaper Garcia reads

6. ____ ________ ________ the

________ every ________.

zoo students sometimes bus school

7. The ________ in our

________ ________ go

to the ____ on the ____.

plays soccer friends Tuesday son

8. My ____ Sam ________

________ with his ________

every ________.

✓ CHECK-UP TEST: Chapters 11–12

A. Fill in the blanks.

me	him	her	it	us	you	them

Ex. Do you like this book?
Of course I like __it__.

1. Do you look like your father?
   Yes. I look like ________.
2. When my cats are hungry, I always feed ________.
3. Sally rarely plays with her sister, but she's playing with ________ today.
4. I say "hello" to my boss every day, and he says "hello" to ________.
5. We're going to the park. Do you want to go with ______?

B. Fill in the blanks.

Ex. Betty never talks to her landlord, but she's __talking__ to him today.

1. We never feed the birds, but we're __________ them today.
2. Harriet never __________ to parties, but she's going to a party today.
3. My children never bake, but they're __________ today.
4. Tim never __________ his TV, but he's fixing it today.
5. Amy rarely __________ her kitchen windows, but she's washing them today.

C. Fill in the blanks.

do	does	is	are

Ex. a. What __do__ you usually do on the weekend?
b. What __is__ Tina doing today?

1. Why ______ the baby crying?
2. When ______ David and Pam go to the supermarket?
3. ________ Bob usually dance?
4. Do they work here? Yes, they ______.
5. ________ your parents cooking lunch?

D. Write the question.

Ex. I'm shivering <u>because I'm cold</u>. (Why?)
__Why are you shivering?__

1. They work <u>in a laboratory</u> every day. (Where?)
   ____
2. We get together <u>on Saturday</u>. (When?)
   ____
3. He's crying <u>because he's sad</u>. (Why?)
   ____
4. She has <u>three</u> children. (How many?)
   ____
5. I'm drinking <u>milk</u>. (What?)
   ____

E. Listen and choose the correct response.

Ex. (a.) They're playing soccer.
b. They play tennis.

1. a. They're delivering mail.
   b. They deliver mail.
2. a. We're going to the zoo.
   b. We go to the park.
3. a. I'm covering my eyes.
   b. I cover my eyes.
4. a. No, I don't.
   b. No, I'm not.
5. a. I'm studying in the library.
   b. I study in the library.

A CAN OR CAN'T?

cook	drive	play	skate	speak
dance	paint	sing	ski	use

1. Billy ___can't___ ___ski___.

   He ___can___ ___skate___.

2. Sally ________ ________.

   She ________ ________.

3. Edward ________ ________ pictures.

   He ________ ________ houses.

4. Carla ________ ________ Arabic.

   She ________ ________ Italian.

5. We ________ ________ Greek food.

   We ________ ________ Japanese food.

6. I ________ ________ a cash register.

   I ________ ________ a calculator.

7. They ________ ________ tennis.

   They ________ ________ baseball.

8. Harold ________ ________ a taxi.

   He ________ ________ a bus.

B WHAT CAN YOU DO?

Check the things you can do. Then ask other students.

Can you . . .?	*You*		*Student 1*		*Student 2*	
1. cook	❑ yes	❑ no	❑ yes	❑ no	❑ yes	❑ no
2. swim	❑ yes	❑ no	❑ yes	❑ no	❑ yes	❑ no
3. ski	❑ yes	❑ no	❑ yes	❑ no	❑ yes	❑ no
4. skate	❑ yes	❑ no	❑ yes	❑ no	❑ yes	❑ no
5. paint	❑ yes	❑ no	❑ yes	❑ no	❑ yes	❑ no
6. drive	❑ yes	❑ no	❑ yes	❑ no	❑ yes	❑ no
7. play tennis	❑ yes	❑ no	❑ yes	❑ no	❑ yes	❑ no
8. speak Chinese	❑ yes	❑ no	❑ yes	❑ no	❑ yes	❑ no
9. use a cash register	❑ yes	❑ no	❑ yes	❑ no	❑ yes	❑ no

C WHAT'S THE QUESTION?

1. ____Can he cook____?
Yes, he can.

2. ________________?
No, she can't.

3. ________________?
Yes, they can.

4. ________________?
Yes, I can.

5. ________________?
No, he can't.

6. ________________?
No, we can't.

D LISTENING

Listen and circle the word you hear.

1.	(can)	can't	4.	can	can't	7.	can	can't	10.	can	can't
2.	can	can't	5.	can	can't	8.	can	can't	11.	can	can't
3.	can	can't	6.	can	can't	9.	can	can't	12.	can	can't

E PUZZLE

actor actress baker chef dancer mechanic secretary singer teacher truck driver

Across

4. She fixes cars every day.
6. He teaches in a school.
7. She acts in the movies.
9. He dances every day.
10. He acts on TV.

Down

1. She drives a truck.
2. He types every day.
3. He cooks in a restaurant.
5. He bakes pies and cakes.
8. She sings on TV.

F *CAN* OR *CAN'T?*

1. My brother is a chef in a bakery. He ___can___ bake pies and cakes.
2. They ___can't___ sing. They aren't very good singers.
3. __________ Jane drive a truck? Of course she __________. She's a truck driver.
4. The chef in that restaurant __________ cook! The food is terrible!
5. Of course I __________ fix cars. I'm a mechanic.
6. That actor is terrible! He __________ act!
7. __________ they dance? Of course they __________. They're dancers on TV.
8. I'm a very good cashier. I __________ use a cash register.
9. My new secretary isn't very good. He __________ type, and he __________ speak on the telephone.
10. They're very athletic. They __________ skate, they __________ ski, and they __________ play soccer.
11. My friend George can only speak English. He __________ speak Spanish, and he __________ speak French.

G GrammarRap: *Of Course They Can!*

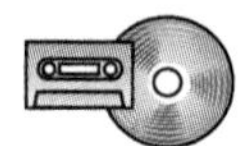

Listen. Then clap and practice.

> She can speak.
> He can speak.
> We can speak.
> They can speak.

A. Can Anne speak French?
B. Of course she can.
She can speak French very well.

A. Can the Browns play tennis?
B. Of course they can.
They can play tennis very well.

A. Can Peter bake pies?
B. Of course he can.
He can bake pies very well.

A. Can we speak English?
B. Of course we can.
We can speak English very well.

H WHAT ARE THEY SAYING?

have to	do	don't
has to	does	doesn't

1.
Can you play baseball with me?
I'm sorry. I can't. I __have__ __to__ do my homework.
2.
Why is Susie upset today?
She ________ ______ go to the dentist this afternoon.
3.
Can your husband fix the sink?
No, he can't. He ________ ______ call a plumber.
4.
Do I really __________ ______ get a haircut?
Yes, you do. You __________ ______ get a haircut today.
5.
________ Grandma ________ ______ go to the doctor often?
Yes, she ________. She ________ ______ go to the doctor every month.
6.
______ you __________ ______ work today?
No, I __________. I'm on vacation.
7.
Do you want to go skiing this weekend?
This weekend? Sorry. We can't. We __________ ______ clean our apartment.
8.
Are you bored?
No. I'm tired. I __________ ______ go to bed.

I A BUSY FAMILY

Mr. and Mrs. Lane, their son Danny, and their daughter Julie are very busy this week.

Monday: Dad – speak to the superintendent
Mom – meet with Danny's teacher
Tuesday: Danny and Julie–go to the doctor
Wednesday: Dad – fix the car

Thursday: Mom – go to the dentist
Friday: Julie – baby-sit
Saturday: Mom and Dad – clean the apartment
Danny and Julie – plant flowers in the yard

1. What does Mr. Lane have to do on Monday? He has to speak to the superintendent.
2. What does Mrs. Lane have to do on Monday? ______
3. What do Danny and Julie have to do on Tuesday? ______
4. What does Mr. Lane have to do on Wednesday? ______
5. What does Mrs. Lane have to do on Thursday? ______
6. What does Julie have to do on Friday? ______
7. What do Mr. and Mrs. Lane have to do on Saturday? ______
8. What do Danny and Julie have to do on Saturday? ______

J WRITE ABOUT YOURSELF

What do YOU have to do this week?

______

______

______

______

K LISTENING

Listen and circle the words you hear.

1.	has to	(have to)	4.	has to	have to	7.	can	can't
2.	has to	have to	5.	can	can't	8.	has to	have to
3.	can	can't	6.	has to	have to	9.	can	can't

L THEY'RE BUSY

can't	baby-sit	go swimming	have dinner
have to	clean the house	go to a movie	study
has to	go bowling	go to a soccer game	wash my clothes
	go dancing	go to the dentist	work

1. I ___can't go swimming___ today.
   I ___have to go the dentist___.

2. Patty ______________________ on Saturday.
   She ______________________.

3. Bob and Julie ______________________ today.
   They ______________________.

4. Tom ______________________ today.
   He ______________________.

5. We ______________________ on Saturday.
   We ______________________.

6. I ______________________ with you today.
   I ______________________.

M LISTENING

Listen and choose the correct answer.

1. (a.) She has to go to the dentist.
   b. She can go to the movies.
2. a. He has to wash his car.
   b. He can't go to the party.
3. a. She can have lunch with her friend.
   b. She can have dinner with her friend.
4. a. They have to paint their kitchen.
   b. They can go skiing.
5. a. He has to cook lunch.
   b. He has to go shopping today.
6. a. She has to baby-sit on Friday.
   b. She can't see a play on Saturday.

N GRAMMARRAP: *Where Is Everybody?*

Listen. Then clap and practice.

A. Where's Joe?
B. He has to go.
A. Where's Ray?
B. He can't stay.
A. Where's Kate?
B. She can't wait.
A. Where's Steve?
B. He has to leave.
A. Where's Murray?
B. He has to hurry.
A. What about you?
B. I have to go, too.

All. Oh, no!
Joe has to go.
Ray can't stay.
Kate can't wait.
Steve has to leave.
Murray has to hurry.
What can I do?
I have to go, too.

O GRAMMARRAP: *Can't Talk Now*

Listen. Then clap and practice.

A. I can't talk now.
I have to go to work.
B. I can't stop now.
I have to catch a train.
C. I can't leave now.
I have to make a call.
D. I can't stop now.
I have to catch a plane.

All. She can't stop now.
She has to catch a train.
She can't stop now.
She has to catch a plane.

A WHAT ARE THEY GOING TO DO?

1. What's Larry going to do tomorrow?

   He's going to cook.

2. What's Jane going to do tomorrow?

   ____

3. What are you going to do tomorrow?

   ____

4. What are they going to do tomorrow?

   ____

5. What are you and your friends going to do tomorrow?

   ____

6. What's William going to do tomorrow?

   ____

B WHAT ARE THEY SAYING?

1. What are you going to do tomorrow?
I'm going to clean my apartment.
3. ________ your mother ________ tomorrow?
________ plant flowers.

2. ________ your husband ________ tomorrow?

   ________ fix the kitchen sink.

4. ________ your cousins ________ tomorrow?

   ________ visit us.

C WHAT ARE THEY GOING TO DO?

are	is	going	go	to

1. We're ___going___ ___to___ ___go___ dancing tonight.
2. They're ___going___ swimming this afternoon.
3. I'm ________ ______ ______ shopping tomorrow.
4. Brian ______ ________ ______ the library this morning.
5. Rita ______ ________ ______ ______ ______ a party tomorrow night.
6. My friends and I ________ ________ to a baseball game tomorrow afternoon.
7. Mr. and Mrs. Lopez ________ ________ ______ ______ ______ a concert this evening.
8. I'm ________ ______ the supermarket tomorrow morning, and my husband ______ ________ ______ ______ ______ the bank.

D GRAMMARRAP: *What Are You Going to Do?*

Listen. Then clap and practice.

going to = gonna

All. What are you going to do tomorrow morning?
How about tomorrow afternoon?
What are you going to do tomorrow evening?
What are you going to do this June?

A. I'm going to vacuum all my rugs tomorrow morning.

B. I'm going to walk my dog tomorrow afternoon.

C. I'm going to visit all my friends tomorrow evening.

D. I'm going to dance at my wedding this June.

E WHICH WORD DOESN'T BELONG?

1.	January	May	(Monday)	April
2.	Tuesday	Saturday	Sunday	September
3.	autumn	at once	winter	summer
4.	Friday	February	March	October
5.	him	them	he	her
6.	right now	next week	at once	immediately

F WHAT'S NEXT?

1. June	July	August		4. summer	fall	________
2. Monday	Tuesday	________		5. Friday	Saturday	________
3. February	March	________		6. October	November	________

G MATCH THE SENTENCES

Are you going to . . .

c	1. call your friends on Thursday?	a. No. I'm going to visit them in October.
____	2. fix our doorbell this week?	b. No. I'm going to visit her next winter.
____	3. visit your aunt next summer?	c. No. I'm going to call them on Friday.
____	4. visit your cousins in April?	d. No. I'm going to fix them next month.
____	5. fix our windows this month?	e. No. I'm going to call him this July.
____	6. call your uncle this June?	f. No. I'm going to fix it next week.

H LISTENING

Listen and circle the words you hear.

1.	(this)	next	5.	Tuesday	Thursday	9.	autumn	August
2.	right now	right away	6.	November	December	10.	watch	wash
3.	Monday	Sunday	7.	spring	winter	11.	next	this
4.	wash	cut	8.	at once	next month	12.	number	plumber

I WHAT'S THE QUESTION?

1. We're going to do our exercises right now. What *are you going to do right now?*
2. She's going to baby-sit this Friday. When ______
3. We're going to Paris next April. Where ______
4. I'm going to clean it because it's dirty. Why ______
5. They're going to go to the beach today. What ______
6. I'm going to fix the doorbell next week. When ______
7. She's going to plant flowers in her yard. Where ______
8. He's going to read his e-mail right now. When ______
9. I'm going to bed now because I'm tired. Why ______

J LISTENING

Listen to the following weather forecasts and circle the correct answers.

Today's Weather Forecast

This afternoon:	hot	(cool)	sunny	(cloudy)
This evening:	foggy	clear	rain	warm

This Weekend's Weather Forecast

Tonight:	cool	cold	clear	warm
Saturday:	cloudy	sunny	foggy	hot
Sunday:	foggy	cool	snow	rain

Monday's Weather Forecast

Monday morning:	cold	cool	cloudy	nice
Monday afternoon:	cool	cold	foggy	snow
Tuesday morning:	sunny	cloudy	nice	warm

K WHAT DOES EVERYBODY WANT TO DO TOMORROW?

want to	wants to

1. I ___want to___ have a picnic tomorrow.
2. George ______________ work in his garden.
3. Karen ______________ take her children to a concert.
4. Mr. and Mrs. Sato ______________ go to the beach.
5. You ______________ see a movie.
6. I ______________ see a play.
7. My friends ______________ go to a basketball game.

L BAD WEATHER

go skiing	go sailing	snow	be cold
take her son to the zoo	go jogging	rain	be warm

1. What does Richard want to do tomorrow?

   ___He wants to go sailing.___

   What's the forecast?

   ___It's going to rain.___

2. What does Lucy want to do this afternoon?

   ____

   What's the forecast?

   ____

3. What do Carl and Betty want to do today?

   ____

   What's the forecast?

   ____

4. What does Jeff want to do tomorrow morning?

   ____

   What's the forecast?

   ____

M YES AND NO

doesn't want to
don't want to

YES! | NO!

1. My parents want to buy a new car. _They don't want to buy_ a motorcycle.
2. David wants to go to a baseball game. ______________ to a concert.
3. I want to wash my car. ______________ my clothes.
4. Nancy and Pam want to play baseball. ______________ soccer.
5. Michael wants to cook Italian food. ______________ American food.
6. We want to study English. ______________ history.
7. Margaret wants to dance with John. ______________ with Jim.
8. I want to work in the garden today. ______________ in the kitchen.

N YES AND NO

I'm	not	going to
He / She / It	isn't	
We / You / They	aren't	

1. Steven is going to go swimming. _He isn't going to go_ sailing.
2. I'm going to take a shower. ______________ a bath.
3. We're going to go bowling. ______________ shopping.
4. Barbara is going to go to the beach. ______________ to the mall.
5. My parents are going to clean the attic. ______________ the basement.
6. It's going to be warm. ______________ cool.
7. Robert is going to listen to the news. ______________ the forecast.
8. You're going to buy a used car. ______________ a new car.

O WHAT DO THEY WANT TO BE?

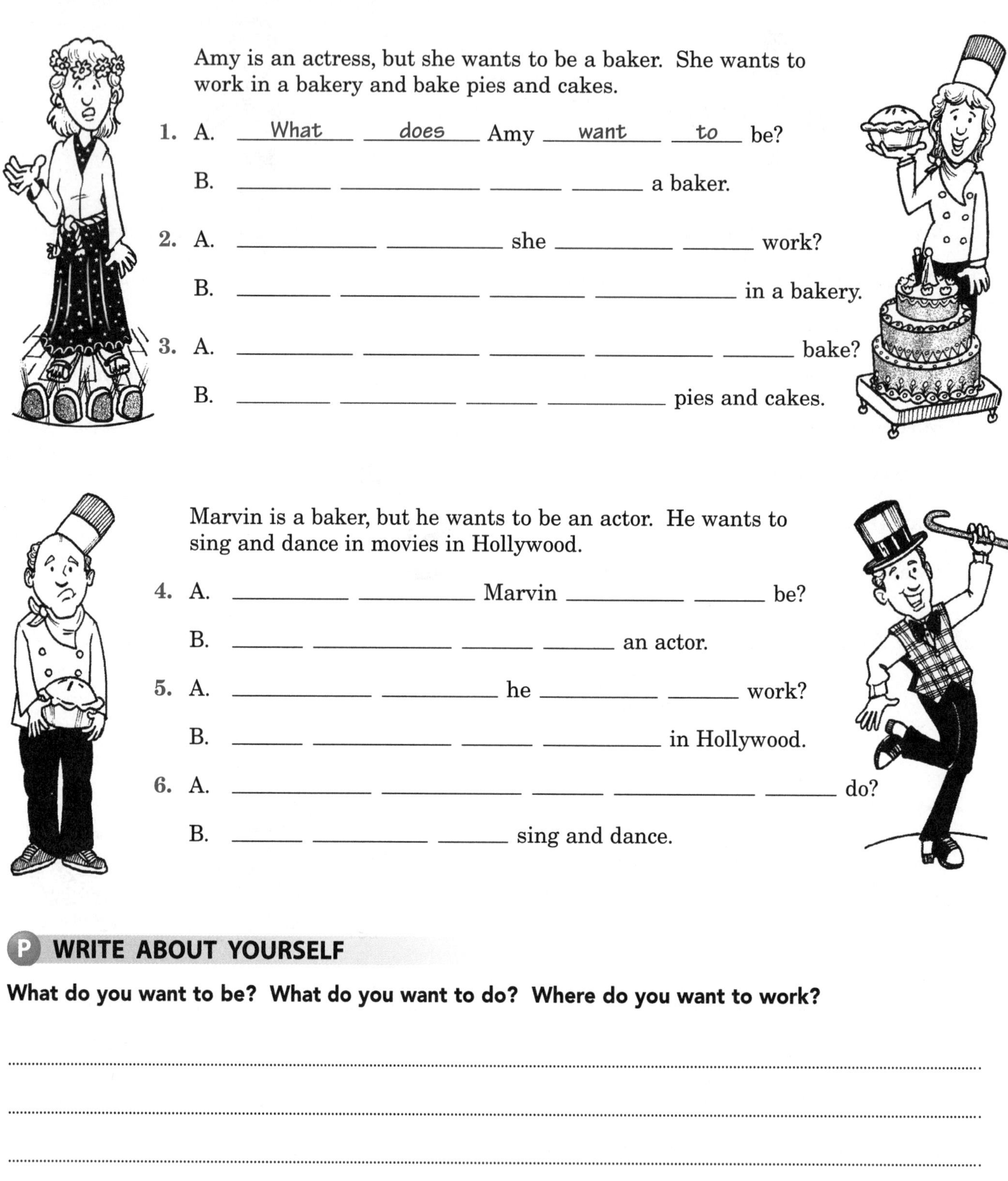

Amy is an actress, but she wants to be a baker. She wants to work in a bakery and bake pies and cakes.

1. A. What does Amy want to be?
   B. ______ ______ ______ ______ a baker.
2. A. ______ ______ she ______ ______ work?
   B. ______ ______ ______ ______ in a bakery.
3. A. ______ ______ ______ ______ ______ bake?
   B. ______ ______ ______ ______ pies and cakes.

Marvin is a baker, but he wants to be an actor. He wants to sing and dance in movies in Hollywood.

4. A. ______ ______ Marvin ______ ______ be?
   B. ______ ______ ______ ______ an actor.
5. A. ______ ______ he ______ ______ work?
   B. ______ ______ ______ ______ in Hollywood.
6. A. ______ ______ ______ ______ ______ do?
   B. ______ ______ ______ sing and dance.

P WRITE ABOUT YOURSELF

What do you want to be? What do you want to do? Where do you want to work?

....

....

....

....

....

....

Q GrammarRap: *What Do They Want to Do?* 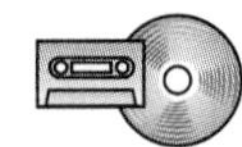

Listen. Then clap and practice.

want to = wanna
wants to = wantsta

He wants to go.
I want to stay.
He wants to work.
I want to play.

She wants to eat at a restaurant.
I want to eat at home.
She wants to eat with all our friends.
I want to eat alone.

We want to leave at seven.
They want to leave at eight.
We want to get there early.
They want to get there late.

Jack wants to take the eight o'clock plane.
Joe wants to take the bus.
Bob wants to take the six o'clock train.
Bill wants to come with us.

R WHAT TIME IS IT?

Draw the time on the clocks.

1. It's ten o'clock.

2. It's five fifteen.

3. It's nine thirty.

4. It's three forty-five.

5. It's noon.

6. It's half past eleven.

7. It's a quarter to one.

8. It's a quarter after two.

S WHICH TIMES ARE CORRECT?

Circle the correct times.

1. a. It's four o'clock.
   b. It's five o'clock.

2. a. It's eleven thirteen.
   b. It's eleven thirty.

3. a. It's a quarter after nine.
   b. It's three fifteen.

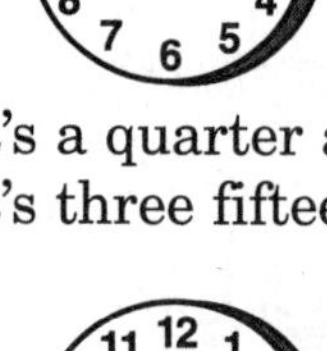

4. a. It's noon.
   b. It's midnight.

5. a. It's half past six.
   b. It's twelve thirty.

6. a. It's two fifteen.
   b. It's a quarter to three.

7. a. It's one thirty.
   b. It's one forty-five.

8. a. It's a quarter to seven.
   b. It's a quarter after seven.

9. a. It's six o'clock.
   b. It's midnight.

T LISTENING

Listen and write the time you hear.

1. 7:45
2. ______
3. ______
4. ______
5. ______
6. ______
7. ______
8. ______
9. ______
10. ______
11. ______
12. ______

U ALAN CHANG'S DAY

Alan Chang gets up every day at seven fifteen. He brushes his teeth and takes a shower. At seven forty-five he eats breakfast and reads his e-mail. At eight thirty he leaves the house and drives to work. Alan works at a computer company. He begins work at nine o'clock. Every day he uses business software on the computer and talks to people on the telephone. At twelve o'clock Alan is always hungry and thirsty. He eats lunch in the cafeteria. Alan leaves work at five thirty. He eats dinner at six o'clock and then at half past seven he watches videos on his new DVD player.

1. What time does Alan get up every day? He gets up at 7:15.
2. What time does he eat breakfast? ________________
3. What time does he leave the house? ________________
4. What time does he begin work? ________________
5. Where does Alan work? ________________
6. What does he do at noon? ________________
7. What does he do at half past five? ________________
8. What time does he eat dinner? ________________
9. What does he do at seven thirty? ________________

V YOUR DAY

Answer in complete sentences.

1. What time do you usually get up? ....
2. What do you do after you get up? ....
3. When do you usually leave for school or work? ....
4. What time do you usually have lunch? ....
5. When do you get home from school or work? ....
6. What time do you usually have dinner? ....
7. What do you usually do after dinner? ....
8. When do you usually go to bed? ....

W GrammarRap: *Time Flies*

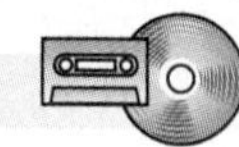

Listen. Then clap and practice.

Time flies.
The days go by.
Monday, Tuesday,
Wednesday, Thursday,
Friday, Saturday.
Time flies.
The days go by.

Time flies.
The months go by.
January, February, March, April,
May, June, July, August,
September, October, November, December.
Time flies.
The months go by.

The seasons come,
The seasons go.
Autumn, winter, spring, summer,
Autumn, winter, spring, summer.
Time flies.
The years go by.
Where do they go?
I don't know.

X GrammarSong: *To Be With You*

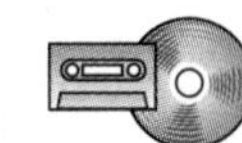

Listen and fill in the words to the song. Then listen again and sing along.

I'm	going	be	after	day	year	December	April	right
it's	wait	in	past	month	fall	February	July	
you	waiting	to	with	week	summer	September		

Any day, any ___week___[1], any month, any _______[2], I'm _______ _______[3] wait right here to be with you.

_______[4] the spring, in the _______[5], in the winter, or the _______[6], just call. I'm _______[7] here to be with you.

_______ _______[8] to wait from January, _______[9] March, _______[10], May, June and _______[11], August, _______[12], October, and November, and all of _______[13]. I'm going to wait . . .

_______[14] one o'clock, a quarter _______[15]. It's half _______[16] one, a quarter _______[17] two. And I'm going _______ _______[18] right here to be with you.

Any _______[19], any week, any _______[20], any year, I'm going to wait _______[21] here to be _______[22] you.

Yes, I'm going to wait right here _______ _______[23] with _______[24].

✓ CHECK-UP TEST: Chapters 13–14

A.

Ex. Ted wants to go skating, but he can't. He has to fix his car.

1. We ______, but ______. We ______.

2. Alice ______, but ______. She ______.

3. I ______, but ______. I ______.

B. Fill in the blanks.

is	are	do	does

Ex. When is Harry going to leave the house?

1. When ______ you going to call the mechanic?
2. ______ you have a bad cold?
3. What ______ they going to do this evening?
4. Where ______ you going skiing?
5. What ______ Carol have to do this Tuesday?
6. ______ your son going to take a bath today?

C. *Ex.* Tom wants to move next spring. He doesn't want to move this fall.

Dad is going to fix the sink. He isn't going to fix the car.

1. I want to teach French. ______ English.
2. We're going to bed at 10:00. ______ at 9:00.
3. Mrs. Miller can bake pies. ______ cakes.
4. Frank has to go to the dentist. ______ the doctor.
5. Jim and Julie can speak Japanese. ______ Spanish.
6. We have to do our homework. ______ our exercises.

D. Every day Helen gets up at 7:30. At 8:00 she eats breakfast, and at 8:30 she goes to work. At noon she has lunch, and at 5:00 she takes the bus home. What's Helen going to do tomorrow?

Tomorrow Helen ___*is going to get up*___ at 7:30. At 8:00 she's ______ 1 breakfast, and at 8:30 ______ 2 to work. At noon ______ 3 lunch, and at 5:00 ______ 4 home.

E. Write the question.

What	When	Where

Ex. I'm going to clean my house <u>this evening</u>. ___*When are you going to clean your house?*___

1. She's going to <u>fix her sink</u> tomorrow. ______
2. He's going to play tennis <u>in the park</u>. ______
3. I'm going to go to the zoo <u>this weekend</u>. ______
4. They're going to study <u>Spanish</u> next year. ______

F. What time is it?

Ex. It's ten o'clock.

1. It's five fifteen.
2. It's nine thirty.
3. It's noon.
4. It's two forty-five.
5. It's a quarter after eleven.

G. Listen to the story. Fill in the correct times.

English	______	Chinese	______	lunch	______
mathematics	______	science	______	music	______

A WHAT'S THE MATTER?

backache	cough	fever	sore throat	toothache
cold	earache	headache	stomachache	

1. He has a cold ____________________.

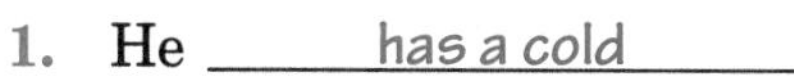

2. She ____________________.

3. I ____________________.

4. She ____________________.

5. I ____________________.

6. He ____________________.

7. She ____________________.

8. You ____________________.

9. He ____________________.

B LISTENING

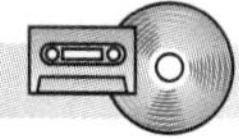

Listen to the story. Put the number under the correct picture.

______

1

______

______

______

______

______

______

C GrammarRap: *What's the Matter?* 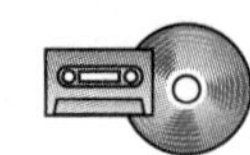

Listen. Then clap and practice.

A. What's the matter with you?
B. I have a headache.
What's the matter with YOU?
A. I have a cold.

A. What's the matter with him?
B. He has a toothache.
What's the matter with HER?
A. She has a cold.

A. What's the matter with Mary?
B. She has an earache.
What's the matter with BILL?
A. He has a very bad cold.

A. What's the matter with Fred?
B. He has a backache.
What's the matter with ANNE?
A. She has an awful cold.

A. What's the matter with Jane?
B. She has a stomachache.
What's the matter with PAUL?
A. He has a terrible cold.

A. What's the matter with the students?
B. They have sore throats.
What's the matter with the teachers?
A. They have terrible colds.
They have terrible terrible colds!

D WHAT DID YOU DO YESTERDAY?

bake	cook	dance	rest	shout	study
clean	cry	paint	shave	smile	type

1. I ___cooked___.
2. I ______________.
3. I ______________.

4. I ______________.
5. I ______________.
6. I ______________.

7. I ______________.
8. I ______________.
9. I ______________.

10. I ______________.
11. I ______________.
12. I ______________.

E WHAT'S THE WORD?

brush	cook	paint	plant	play	study	wait	watch	work

1. I ___work___ in an office every day. 
2. I ___played___ the guitar yesterday. 
3. I __________ my teeth every day. 
4. I __________ flowers yesterday. 
5. I __________ dinner every day. 
6. I __________ English yesterday. 
7. I __________ my fence yesterday. 
8. I __________ TV every day. 
9. I __________ for the bus yesterday.

F LISTENING

Listen and circle the correct answer.

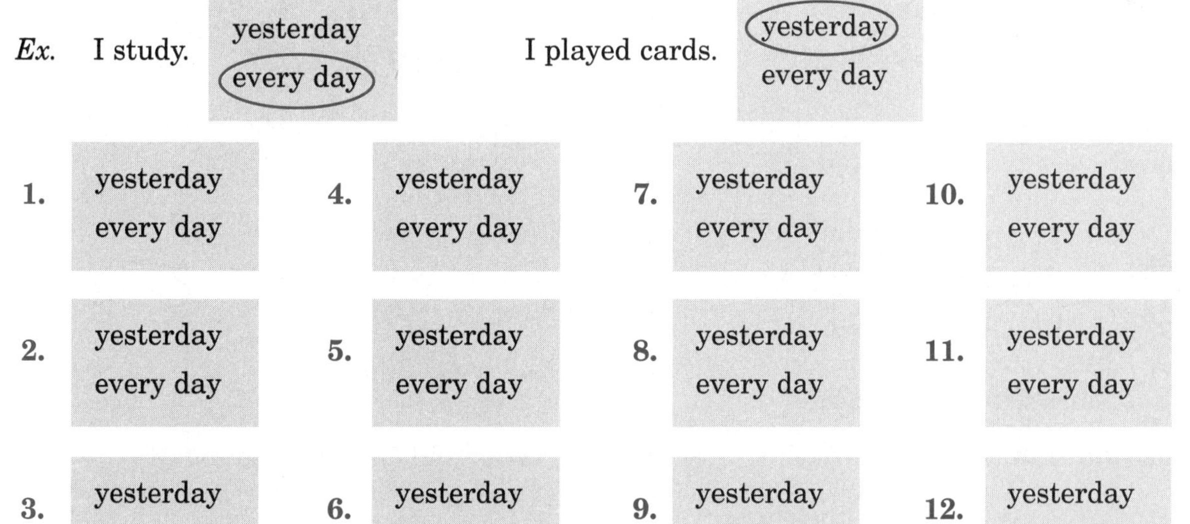

Ex. I study. yesterday / (every day) I played cards. (yesterday) / every day

1.	yesterday every day	4.	yesterday every day	7.	yesterday every day	10.	yesterday every day
2.	yesterday every day	5.	yesterday every day	8.	yesterday every day	11.	yesterday every day
3.	yesterday every day	6.	yesterday every day	9.	yesterday every day	12.	yesterday every day

G WHAT DID EVERYBODY DO?

bark	clean	cry	drink	eat	ride	sing	sit	skate	write

1. A. What did James do today?

   B. ___He cleaned___ his apartment all day.

2. A. What did your sister do today?

   B. ______________ letters all morning.

3. A. What did Mr. and Mrs. Porter do yesterday?

   B. ______________ songs all evening.

4. A. What did you and your friends do today?

   B. ______________ in the park all afternoon.

5. A. What did Linda do yesterday?

   B. ______________ lemonade all morning.

6. A. What did Jimmy do today?

   B. ______________ candy and cookies all day.

7. A. What did Mrs. Mason's children do today?

   B. ______________ all afternoon.

8. A. What did the neighbors' dogs do yesterday?

   B. ______________ all night.

9. A. What did Howard do yesterday?

   B. ______________ in the clinic all evening.

10. A. What did Grandma do today?

    B. ______________ her bicycle all afternoon.

H PUZZLE

Across

3. ride
4. study
6. eat

Down

1. cry
2. work
4. sit
5. drink

I PETER'S DAY AT HOME

bake	cook	fix	paint	plant	rest	wash

1. Thank you, Peter. This is a very good dinner.
3. Look at the car! It's really clean. Thank you.
5. The kitchen looks beautiful. Yellow is my favorite color.

2. This is a wonderful cake, Peter.

4. The new flowers in the garden are beautiful.

6. The sink isn't broken! I can brush my teeth in the bathroom now!

What did Peter do today?

1. He cooked dinner.
2. ______________________
3. ______________________
4. ______________________
5. ______________________
6. ______________________

What did Peter do after dinner?

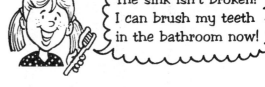

7. ______________________

J GrammarRap: *What Did They Do?*

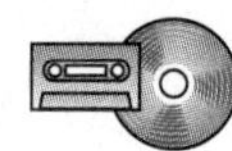

Listen. Then clap and practice.

washed [t]	cleaned [d]	painted [ɪd]

A. What did you do today?
B. I washed my floors.
A. Your floors? B. Yes!
B. I washed my floors all day!

A. What did Mark do today?
B. He cleaned his house.
A. His house? B. Yes!
B. He cleaned his house all day!

A. What did Pam do today?
B. She painted her porch.
A. Her porch? B. Yes!
B. She painted her porch all day!

A. What did they do today?
B. They sang some songs.
A. Some songs? B. Yes!
They sang some songs all day!

A. What did you do today?
B. I ______________________.
A. ____________? B. Yes!
B. I ______________________ all day!

K MY GRANDFATHER'S BIRTHDAY PARTY

At my grandfather's birthday party last night, everybody (listen) ___listened___[1] to Mexican music and (dance) __________[2]. My sister Gloria (sing) __________[3] my grandfather's favorite songs all evening, and my brother Daniel (play) __________[4] the guitar.

Everybody (sit) __________[5] in the living room with my grandmother and grandfather and (look) __________[6] at old photographs. We (laugh) __________[7], we (smile) __________[8], we (cry) __________[9], and we (talk) __________[10] about "the good old days." What did I do at my grandfather's birthday party? I (drink) __________[11] lemonade and (eat) __________[12] a lot of food!

L MATCHING

_e_	1. At the party my brother played ______.	a.	drank lemonade all night
____	2. Everybody sat and talked about ______.	b.	Mexican music
____	3. My sister has a sore throat today because ______.	c.	"the good old days"
____	4. We all looked at ______.	d.	ate a lot of food
____	5. We listened to ______.	e.	the guitar
____	6. I have a toothache today because I ______.	f.	old photographs
____	7. I also have a stomachache because I ______.	g.	she sang all evening

A CORRECT THE SENTENCE

1. Jennifer brushed her teeth last night.

   She didn't brush her teeth.

   She brushed her hair.

2. Kevin played the violin yesterday afternoon.

   ____

   ____

3. Harold and Betty listened to the news yesterday evening.

   ____

   ____

4. Mrs. Martinez waited for the train this afternoon.

   ____

   ____

5. Frank fixed his fence yesterday morning.

   ____

   ____

6. Mr. and Mrs. Park cleaned their attic today.

   ____

   ____

7. Marvin baked a pie yesterday evening.

   ____

   ____

8. Patty called her grandmother last night.

   ____

   ____

B ALAN AND HIS SISTER

Alan and his sister Ellen did very different things yesterday. Alan (rest) ___rested___[1] all day. He didn't (work) ________[2], and he didn't (study) ________[3]. He (listen) ________[4] to music yesterday morning. He (watch) ________[5] game shows on TV yesterday afternoon. And yesterday evening he (talk) ________[6] to his friends on the telephone and (play) ________[7] games on his computer.

Ellen didn't (listen) ________[8] to music. She didn't (watch) ________[9] game shows on TV, and she didn't (play) ________[10] games on her computer What did she do? She (study) ________[11] English yesterday morning. She (clean) ________[12] the yard yesterday afternoon. And she (cook) ________[13] dinner for her family last night.

C YES AND NO

1. Did Alan rest all day yesterday? ___Yes, he did.___
2. Did Ellen rest all day yesterday? ___No, she didn't.___
3. Did Ellen study yesterday morning? ________________
4. Did Alan study yesterday morning? ________________
5. Did Alan watch TV yesterday afternoon? ________________

6. ___Did Ellen clean___ the yard yesterday afternoon? Yes, she did.
7. ________________ to his friends yesterday evening? Yes, he did.
8. ________________ dinner for his family last night? No, he didn't.
9. ________________ to music yesterday morning? No, she didn't.
10. ________________ game shows yesterday afternoon? No, she didn't.
11. ________________ English yesterday afternoon? No, he didn't.

D WHAT DID THEY DO?

1. I didn't buy a car. I __bought__ a motorcycle.
2. Michael didn't have a headache. He __________ a toothache.
3. Alice didn't write to her uncle. She __________ to her cousin.
4. We didn't do our homework last night. We __________ yoga.
5. They didn't take the bus to work today. They __________ the train.
6. Barbara didn't get up at 7:00 this morning. She __________ up at 6:00.
7. My friend and I didn't go swimming yesterday. We __________ bowling.
8. Martha didn't read the newspaper last night. She __________ a book.
9. My children didn't make breakfast this morning. They __________ lunch.

E THEY DIDN'T DO WHAT THEY USUALLY DO

1. Robert usually writes to his friends.	He __didn't__ __write__ to his friends yesterday.	He __wrote__ to his grandparents.
2. I usually have a cold in January.	I _________ _________ a cold last January.	I _________ a cold last July.
3. We usually eat at home on Friday night.	We _________ _________ at home last Friday night.	We _________ at a very nice restaurant.
4. Bill usually gets up 7:00 o'clock.	He _________ _________ up at 7:00 this morning.	He _________ up at 10:00.
5. Tom and Tina usually go dancing every week.	They _________ _________ dancing this week.	They _________ sailing.
6. Susie usually drinks milk every afternoon.	She _________ _________ milk this afternoon.	She _________ lemonade.
7. My brother usually makes lunch on Sunday.	He _________ _________ lunch last Sunday.	He _________ dinner.
8. Mr. Lee usually takes his wife to the movies.	He _________ _________ his wife to the movies last night.	He _________ his daughter and his son-in-law.
9. We usually buy food at a large supermarket.	We _________ _________ food at a supermarket today.	We _________ food at a small grocery store.
10. I usually sit next to Maria in English class.	I _________ _________ next to Maria yesterday.	I _________ next to her sister Carmen.

F GRAMMARRAP RHYMING GAME: *No, They Didn't*

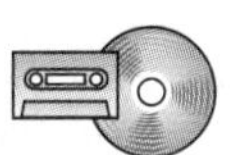

A. Did she wash her skirt?
B. No, she didn't.
A. What did she wash?
B. She washed her __shirt__.

A. Did they paint the door?
B. No, they didn't.
A. What did they paint?
B. They painted the ________.

A. Did he call his mother?
B. No, he didn't.
A. Who did he call?
B. He called his ________.

A. Did you buy new suits?
B. No, we didn't.
A. What did you buy?
B. We bought new ________.

A. Did you get up at seven?

B. No, I didn't.
A. When did you get up?
B. I got up at ________.

G WHAT'S THE ANSWER?

1. Did Henry ride his bicycle to work this morning? Yes, he did.
2. Did you get up at 6:00 this morning? No, ________.
3. Did your sister call you last night? Yes, ________.
4. Did Mr. and Mrs. Chen clean their apartment last weekend? No, ________.
5. Did you and your friends go to the library yesterday afternoon? Yes, ________.
6. Did your father make spaghetti for dinner last night? No, ________.
7. Excuse me. Did I take your gloves? Yes, ________.
8. Bob, did you do your exercises today? No, ________.

H WHAT'S THE QUESTION?

1. Did she buy a car? — No, she didn't. She bought a truck.
2. ________ a headache? — No, he didn't. He had a backache.
3. ________ a shower? — No, I didn't. I took a bath.
4. ________ to the supermarket? — No, they didn't. They went to the bank.
5. ________ in the living room? — No, we didn't. We sat in the kitchen.
6. ________ a right turn? — No, you didn't. You made a left turn.

I LISTENING

Listen and choose the correct response.

1. a. I write to her every day.
   (b.) I wrote to her this morning.
2. a. He washes it every weekend.
   b. He washed it last weekend.
3. a. They visit my aunt and my uncle.
   b. They visited my aunt and my uncle.
4. a. She did yoga in the park.
   b. She does yoga in the park.
5. a. He went to sleep at 8:00.
   b. He goes to sleep at 8:00.
6. a. We clean it every weekend.
   b. We cleaned it last weekend.
7. a. We take them to the zoo.
   b. We took them to the zoo.
8. a. I make spaghetti.
   b. I made spaghetti.
9. a. She reads it every afternoon.
   b. She read it this afternoon.
10. a. I get up at 7:00.
    b. I got up at 7:00.

J I'M SORRY I'M LATE!

forget	go	have to	miss
get up	have	meet	steal

1. I ___missed___ the train.

2. I ______________ a headache.

3. I ______________ my lunch.

4. I ______________ my girlfriend on the way to work.

5. I ______________ late.

6. A thief ______________ my bicycle.

7. I ______________ go to the bank.

8. I ______________ to sleep on the bus.

K MATCHING

_d_ 1. buy	a. wrote		____ 7. get	g. had
____ 2. steal	b. did		____ 8. eat	h. drove
____ 3. do	c. went		____ 9. have	i. made
____ 4. see	d. bought		____ 10. forget	j. got
____ 5. go	e. saw		____ 11. make	k. forgot
____ 6. write	f. stole		____ 12. drive	l. ate

L GrammarRap: *Old Friends*

Listen. Then clap and practice.

We walked and talked
And talked and walked.
Walked and talked,
Talked and walked.

We sat in the garden
And looked at the flowers.
We talked and talked
For hours and hours.

He drank milk,
And I drank tea.
We talked and talked
From one to three.

We talked about him.
We talked about us.
Then we walked to the corner
To get the bus.

We waited and waited.
The bus was late.
So we stood and talked
From four to eight.

M GrammarRap: *Gossip*

Listen. Then clap and practice.

I told Jack.
Jack told Jill.
Jill told Fred.
Fred told Bill.
Bill called Anne.
Anne called Sue.
Sue told Jim.
But who told you?

A A TERRIBLE DAY AND A WONDERFUL DAY!

17

was	were

We ___*were*___ [1] very upset at work last Friday. Our computers __________ [2] broken, our boss __________ [3] angry because he __________ [4] tired, and my friends and I __________ [5] sick. Outside it __________ [6] cloudy and it __________ [7] very cold. And then in the afternoon all the trains __________ [8] late. I __________ [9] hungry when I got home, and my children __________ [10] very noisy. It __________ [11] a terrible day!

We ___*were*___ [12] very happy at work on Monday. Our computers __________ [13] fine, our boss __________ [14] happy, and my friends and I __________ [15] energetic. Outside it __________ [16] sunny, it __________ [17] warm, and all the trains __________ [18] early. My children __________ [19] very quiet when I got home. We ate a big dinner, and I __________ [20] very full. It was a wonderful day!

B LISTENING

Listen and circle the word you hear.

1. (is) / was
2. is / was
3. are / were
4. is / was
5. is / was
6. are / were
7. are / were
8. are / were
9. is / was
10. is / was
11. are / were
12. are / were

C BEFORE AND AFTER

clean	enormous	happy	shiny	thin
comfortable	full	healthy	tall	

1. Before I took A-1 Vitamins, I __was__ always sick. Now __I'm__ __healthy__.

2. Before Harold met Gertrude, he ________ sad. Now ________ ______________ all the time.

3. Before we ate a big breakfast today, we __________ hungry. Now __________ __________.

4. Before Helen got her new sofa, she ________ uncomfortable. Now ________ very ________________.

5. Before you drank A-1 Skim Milk, you __________ heavy. Now __________ __________.

6. Before Charlie used A-1 Car Wax, his car __________ dull. Now ________ ______________.

7. Before these children used A-1 soap, they __________ dirty. Now ____________ ____________.

8. When I __________ young, I __________ very short. Now __________ __________.

9. Before we bought A-1 Bird Food, our birds __________ very tiny. Now ____________ ________________.

D WHAT'S THE WORD?

1. A. ___Were___ you at a concert last night?

   B. No, I ___wasn't___. I ___was___ at a play.

2. A. __________ your neighbors quiet last Saturday night?

   B. No, they __________. They __________ very noisy.

3. A. __________ your boss in the office yesterday?

   B. No, she __________. She __________ on vacation.

4. A. __________ we at home last Tuesday?

   B. No, we __________. We __________ at the mall.

5. A. __________ the questions on the examination easy?

   B. No, they __________. They __________ very difficult.

6. A. __________ Timothy on time for his wedding?

   B. No, he __________. He __________ late.

E LISTENING

Listen and circle the word you hear.

1.	was (wasn't)	3.	were weren't	5.	was wasn't	7.	were weren't
2.	were weren't	4.	was wasn't	6.	were weren't	8.	was wasn't

F WHAT'S THE WORD?

did	was	were
didn't	wasn't	weren't

A. Why ___did___ [1] Victor leave the party early?

B. He ________ [2] like the party. It ________ [3] noisy, the food ________ [4] very good, and his friends ________ [5] there.

A. Where ________ [6] you last week? You ________ [7] at work.

B. That's right. I ________ [8].

A. ________ [9] you sick?

B. Yes, I ________ [10]. I ________ [11] very sick. I had an earache and a cold.

A. ________ [12] you also have a headache?

B. No. I ________ [13] have a headache, but I had a sore throat. I ________ [14] go to work all week. I ________ [15] really sick!

A. How ________ [16] your vacation?

B. It ________ [17] terrible!

A. That's too bad. ________ [18] you like the hotel?

B. No, we ________ [19]. The bathroom sink ________ [20] broken, the hotel room ________ [21] clean, and we ________ [22] sleep well at night because the people in the next room ________ [23] very loud.

A. ________ [24] you swim at the beach?

B. No, we ________ [25]. The weather ________ [26] very cold!

A. ________ [27] your grandchildren visit you last weekend?

B. No, they ________ [28].

A. That's too bad. ________ [29] they busy?

B. My grandson ________ [30] feel well, and my granddaughter ________ [31] on a business trip. We ________ [32] sad because we ________ [33] see them.

G GrammarRap: *Were You Late This Morning?*

Listen. Then clap and practice.

A.	Were you late this	morning?
B.	No, I wasn't. I was	early.
A.	Was he sick last	night?
B.	No, he wasn't. He was	fine.
A.	Was her hair very	straight?
B.	No, it wasn't. It was	curly.
A.	Were there eight new	lessons?
B.	No, there weren't. There were	nine.

A.	Was the movie	short?
B.	No, it wasn't. It was	long.
A.	Was the food	expensive?
B.	No, it wasn't. It was	free.
A.	Was I right?	
B.	No, you weren't. You were	wrong.
A.	Were the tickets two	dollars?
B.	No, they weren't. They were three.	

H WHAT ARE THEY SAYING?

basketball	did	freckles	short	subjects	wasn't	weren't
curly	didn't	hobby	sports	was	were	

A. Tell me, what ___did___ 1 you look like when you _________ 2 young? _________ 3 you tall?

B. No, I _________ 4. I _________ 5 _________ 6.

A. _________ 7 you have straight hair?

B. No, I _________ 8. I had _________ 9 hair.

A. Oh. And _________ 10 you have dimples?

B. No, I _________ 11, but I had _________ 12.

A. I'm sure you _________ 13 very cute!

What _________ 14 you do with your friends?

B. We played sports.

A. Oh. What _________ 15 you play?

B. We played _________ 16 and tennis.

A. Tell me, _________ 17 you like school?

B. Yes. I liked school a lot.

A. What _________ 18 your favorite _________ 19?

B. English and mathematics.

A. _________ 20 you have a _________ 21?

B. Yes, I _________ 22. I played chess.

I LISTENING 

Listen and choose the correct response.

1. a. I was born last week.
   (b.) I was born in Japan.
2. a. Yes, I did.
   b. I grew up in Tokyo.
3. a. English.
   b. No, I didn't.
4. a. In Los Angeles.
   b. Last year.

5. a. I was tall and thin.
   b. I didn't look.
6. a. No. I had straight hair.
   b. No. I had dimples.
7. a. I played sports.
   b. I play chess.
8. a. Yes. I'm here.
   b. Yes. My father.

J GrammarRap: *The Teacher Was There* 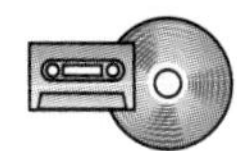

Listen. Then clap and practice.

A.	The teacher was	there,
	But where were the	students?
B.	The students were	there.
All.	Where?	

A.	The teacher was	there,
	The students were	there,
	But where were the	books?
B.	The books were	there.
All.	Where?	

A.	The teacher was	there,
	The students were	there,
	The books were	there,
	But where was the	chalk?
B.	The chalk was	there.
All.	Where?	

A.	The teacher was	there,
	The students were	there,
	The books were	there,
	The chalk was	there,
	But where were the	chairs?
B.	The chairs were	there.
All.	Where?	
B.	There.	
All.	Where?	
B.	Right there!	
	Right	there!

✓ CHECK-UP TEST: Chapters 15–17

A. Fill in the blanks.

was	were	wasn't	weren't

1. A. ___Was___ Barbara at work yesterday?

   B. No, she __________. She __________ sick.

2. A. Why __________ you late today?

   B. I __________ late because I __________ on time for the bus.

3. A. Where __________ Grandma and Grandpa last night? They __________ at home.

   B. They __________ at a concert.

B. Complete the sentences.

Ex. Before we washed our car, it ___was___ dirty. Now ___it's___ ___clean___.

1. Before I ate dinner, I __________ hungry. Now __________ __________.
2. When I got my cats, they __________ tiny. Now __________ __________.
3. When we __________ in college, we __________ thin. Now __________ __________.
4. When I was young, I __________ energetic. Now __________ __________.

C. Complete the sentences.

Ex.	a. Carla usually studies English.	She ___didn't___ ___study___ English yesterday.	She ___studied___ mathematics.
	b. Paul usually writes to his friends.	He ___didn't___ ___write___ to his friends yesterday.	He ___wrote___ to his cousins.
1.	I usually drive to the park on Saturday.	I __________ __________ to the park last Saturday.	I __________ to the mall.
2.	We usually arrive late.	We __________ __________ late today.	We __________ on time.
3.	My husband and my son usually shave in the morning.	They __________ __________ in the morning today.	They __________ in the afternoon.
4.	Bob usually goes jogging in the evening.	He __________ __________ jogging yesterday evening.	He __________ dancing.
5.	Margaret usually reads the newspaper in the morning.	She __________ __________ the newspaper yesterday morning.	She __________ a magazine.

D. Write the question.

Ex. Did they get up at 8:00? — No, they didn't. They got up at 10:00.

1. ______________ his brother? — No, he didn't. He met his sister.
2. ______________ her bicycle? — No, she didn't. She rode her motorcycle.
3. ______________ a good time? — No, we didn't. We had a terrible time.
4. ______________ lunch? — No, they didn't. They made dinner.
5. ______________ a movie? — No, I didn't. I saw a play.

E. Read the story and then write about yesterday.

Every morning I get up early. I brush my teeth, and I do my exercises. Then I sit in the kitchen and I eat breakfast. At 8:00 I go to work. I walk to the drug store and I buy a newspaper. Then I take the train to my office. I don't take the bus, and I don't drive my car.

Yesterday I got up early. I ________[1] my teeth, and I ________[2] my exercises. Then I ________[3] in the kitchen and I ________[4] breakfast. At 8:00 I ________[5] to work. I ________[6] to the drug store and I ________[7] a newspaper. Then I ________[8] the train to my office. I ________ ________[9] the bus, and I ________ ________[10] my car.

F. Listen and circle the word you hear.

Ex. (is) / was

1. is / was
2. are / were
3. is / was
4. are / were
5. is / was
6. are / were
7. is / was
8. are / were

ACHIEVEMENT TESTS

Name ______________________________

Date ____________________ Class ____________________

A PERSONAL INFORMATION & FORMS

Name: (1) ______________________________

Street: (2) ______________________ Apartment: (3) __________

City: (4) ______________ State: (5) ________ Zip Code: (6) ________

Telephone: (7) ____________ E-Mail: (8) ____________ Age: (9) ______

Social Security Number: (10) ____________ Country of Origin: (11) ____________

Look at the information. Choose the correct line on the form.

Example:

062-41-9275

Ⓐ Line 2
Ⓑ Line 3
Ⓒ Line 9
Ⓓ Line 10

Ⓐ Ⓑ Ⓒ ●

1. Mexico

Ⓐ Line 1
Ⓑ Line 6
Ⓒ Line 8
Ⓓ Line 11

2. Los Angeles

Ⓐ Line 2
Ⓑ Line 3
Ⓒ Line 4
Ⓓ Line 7

3. 6-A

Ⓐ Line 3
Ⓑ Line 6
Ⓒ Line 9
Ⓓ Line 10

4. 90021

Ⓐ Line 2
Ⓑ Line 6
Ⓒ Line 7
Ⓓ Line 9

5. 840 Central Avenue

Ⓐ Line 1
Ⓑ Line 2
Ⓒ Line 4
Ⓓ Line 8

1 Ⓐ Ⓑ Ⓒ Ⓓ   3 Ⓐ Ⓑ Ⓒ Ⓓ   5 Ⓐ Ⓑ Ⓒ Ⓓ

2 Ⓐ Ⓑ Ⓒ Ⓓ   4 Ⓐ Ⓑ Ⓒ Ⓓ

Go to the next page

B INFORMATION ON AN ENVELOPE

Sally Grant
360 Lake Street, Apt. 4-D
Los Angeles, California 90016

Choose the correct answer.

Example:

last name

Ⓐ Sally
Ⓑ Lake
Ⓒ Grant
Ⓓ Los Angeles

Ⓐ Ⓑ ● Ⓓ

6. state

Ⓐ Street
Ⓑ Grant
Ⓒ Los Angeles
Ⓓ California

7. first name

Ⓐ Lake
Ⓑ Sally
Ⓒ Grant
Ⓓ Street

8. address

Ⓐ 360 Lake Street
Ⓑ Sally Grant
Ⓒ 90016
Ⓓ California

9. apartment number

Ⓐ 360
Ⓑ 4-D
Ⓒ 90016
Ⓓ 4

10. city

Ⓐ California
Ⓑ Grant
Ⓒ Lake Street
Ⓓ Los Angeles

C COMMON ABBREVIATIONS IN ADDRESSES

Look at the abbreviation. Choose the correct answer.

Example:

W.

Ⓐ East
Ⓑ West
Ⓒ North
Ⓓ South

Ⓐ ● Ⓒ Ⓓ

11. N.

Ⓐ East
Ⓑ West
Ⓒ North
Ⓓ South

12. Ave.

Ⓐ Apartment
Ⓑ Avenue
Ⓒ Street
Ⓓ East

13. St.

Ⓐ South
Ⓑ West
Ⓒ Street
Ⓓ East

6 Ⓐ Ⓑ Ⓒ Ⓓ   8 Ⓐ Ⓑ Ⓒ Ⓓ   10 Ⓐ Ⓑ Ⓒ Ⓓ   12 Ⓐ Ⓑ Ⓒ Ⓓ
7 Ⓐ Ⓑ Ⓒ Ⓓ   9 Ⓐ Ⓑ Ⓒ Ⓓ   11 Ⓐ Ⓑ Ⓒ Ⓓ   13 Ⓐ Ⓑ Ⓒ Ⓓ

Go to the next page

Name ______________________________ Date ______________

D GRAMMAR IN CONTEXT: Asking About & Giving Personal Information

Choose the correct answer to complete the conversation.

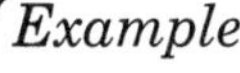

Example:

What's your _____?

- (A) address
- (●) name
- (C) city
- (D) state

My name is David Chen.

14. What's your _____?

- (A) name
- (B) city
- (C) state
- (D) address

427 Central Street.

15. What's your _____?

- (A) address
- (B) phone number
- (C) social security number
- (D) apartment number

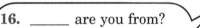

963-2434.

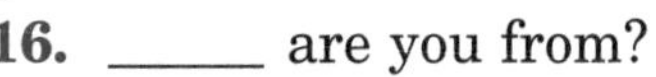

16. _____ are you from?

- (A) What's
- (B) What's your
- (C) Where
- (D) Where are

I'm from China.

17. _____ do you spell your last name?

- (A) How
- (B) Where
- (C) What's
- (D) Who

C–H–E–N.

E LISTENING ASSESSMENT

Read and listen to the questions. Then listen to the interview, and answer the questions.

18. What's her last name?

- (A) Sally
- (B) Susan
- (C) Keller
- (D) Geller

19. What's her phone number?

- (A) 68 Central Avenue
- (B) 86 Central Avenue
- (C) 681-2394
- (D) 861-2394

20. What's her address?

- (A) 68 Central Avenue
- (B) 86 Central Avenue
- (C) 681-2394
- (D) 861-2394

14 (A) (B) (C) (D) 16 (A) (B) (C) (D) 18 (A) (B) (C) (D) 20 (A) (B) (C) (D)

15 (A) (B) (C) (D) 17 (A) (B) (C) (D) 19 (A) (B) (C) (D)

Go to the next page

F WRITING ASSESSMENT: Fill Out the Form

Name: ______________________________

Street: ______________________ Apartment: __________

City: ______________ State: __________ Zip Code: __________

Telephone: ______________ Social Security Number: ______________

Age: __________ Country of Origin: ______________

G WRITING ASSESSMENT: Address the Envelope

Address the envelope to Mr. Peter Black. His address is 378 Main Street in Waterville, Florida. His zip code is 33068. Put your return address on the envelope.

____

____

____

____

____

____

H SPEAKING ASSESSMENT

I can ask and answer these questions:

Ask	Answer	
☐	☐	What's your name?
☐	☐	What's your address?
☐	☐	What's your telephone number?
☐	☐	What's your social security number?
☐	☐	What's your age?
☐	☐	Where are you from?

Ask	Answer	
☐	☐	Who is the president of the United States?
☐	☐	Who is the president or prime minister of your native country?
☐	☐	Who is the mayor of our city?
☐	☐	Who is the governor of our state?

STOP

Name ______________________________

Date ________________ Class ________________

2

A CLASSROOM ITEMS & SIMPLE COMMANDS

Choose the correct answer.

Example:

Open your _____.

- (A) chair
- (B) desk
- (C) book
- ● notebook

1. Go to the _____.

- (A) book
- (B) bookshelf
- (C) board
- (D) globe

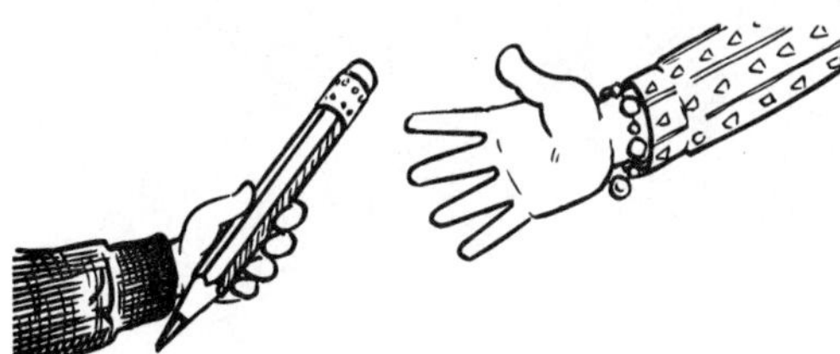

2. Give me the _____.

- (A) ruler
- (B) pencil
- (C) clock
- (D) wall

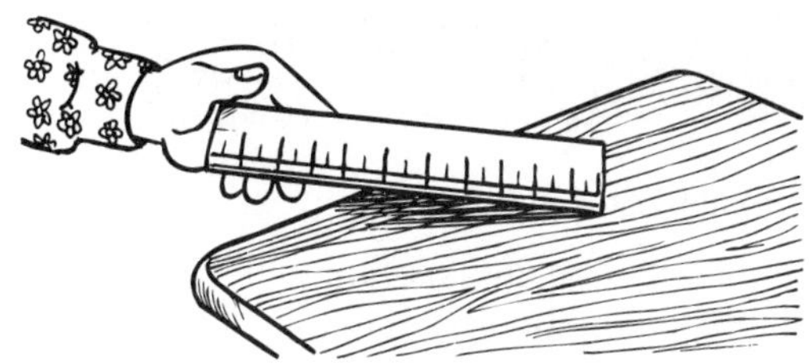

3. Put the _____ on the desk.

- (A) dictionary
- (B) computer
- (C) pen
- (D) ruler

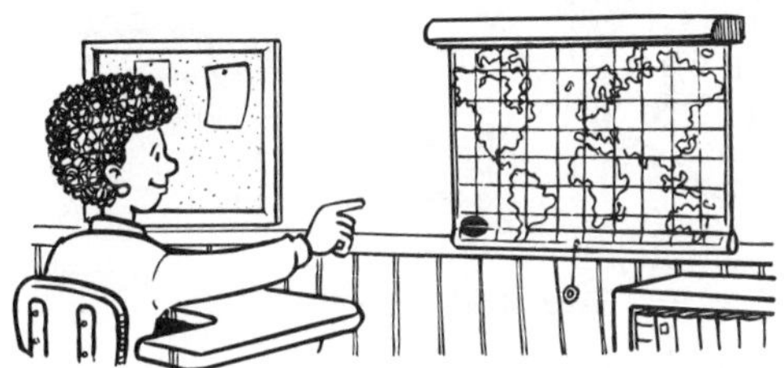

4. Point to the _____.

- (A) table
- (B) map
- (C) globe
- (D) bulletin board

5. Close your _____.

- (A) book
- (B) wall
- (C) table
- (D) pen

1 (A) (B) (C) (D)   3 (A) (B) (C) (D)   5 (A) (B) (C) (D)

2 (A) (B) (C) (D)   4 (A) (B) (C) (D)

Go to the next page

B SCHOOL PERSONNEL & LOCATIONS

Choose the correct answer.

Example:

Where's the principal?

- Ⓐ It's in the classroom.
- Ⓑ She's in the classroom.
- Ⓒ He's in the principal's office.
- ● She's in the principal's office.

6. Where are the teachers?

- Ⓐ She's in the hall.
- Ⓑ They're in the hall.
- Ⓒ He's in the classroom.
- Ⓓ They're in the classroom.

7. Where's the clerk?

- Ⓐ They're in the classroom.
- Ⓑ It's on the desk.
- Ⓒ She's in the hall.
- Ⓓ He's in the office.

8. Where's the security officer?

- Ⓐ She's on the wall.
- Ⓑ It's on the wall.
- Ⓒ She's in the hall.
- Ⓓ It's in the hall.

9. Where's the custodian?

- Ⓐ He's in the cafeteria.
- Ⓑ He's in the classroom.
- Ⓒ He's in the hall.
- Ⓓ He's in the office.

10. Where's the librarian?

- Ⓐ She's in the bookshelf.
- Ⓑ She's in the library.
- Ⓒ It's in the school.
- Ⓓ She's in the hospital.

6 Ⓐ Ⓑ Ⓒ Ⓓ 8 Ⓐ Ⓑ Ⓒ Ⓓ 10 Ⓐ Ⓑ Ⓒ Ⓓ

7 Ⓐ Ⓑ Ⓒ Ⓓ 9 Ⓐ Ⓑ Ⓒ Ⓓ

Go to the next page

Name ______________________ Date ____________

C GRAMMAR IN CONTEXT: Greeting • Locating Classroom Items

Choose the correct answer to complete the conversation.

Example:
Hi. __________
(A) Fine.
(B) Fine, thanks.
(C) And you?
● How are you?

11. __________
(A) Bye.
(B) Goodbye.
(C) Fine. And you?
(D) How are you?

12. _____ the pencils?
(A) Where's
(B) What's
(C) What are
(D) Where are

13. _____ on the desk.
(A) They're
(B) I'm
(C) We're
(D) It's

14. Where's the _____?
(A) clock
(B) computer
(C) dictionary
(D) ruler

15. The monitor and the _____ are on the table.
(A) board
(B) notebook
(C) keyboard
(D) bulletin board

16. _____ the floppy disk?
(A) What's
(B) Where's
(C) What are
(D) Where are

17. It's in the _____.
(A) dictionary
(B) keyboard
(C) disk drive
(D) desk

11 (A) (B) (C) (D)
12 (A) (B) (C) (D)
13 (A) (B) (C) (D)
14 (A) (B) (C) (D)
15 (A) (B) (C) (D)
16 (A) (B) (C) (D)
17 (A) (B) (C) (D)

Go to the next page

D LISTENING ASSESSMENT

Read and listen to the questions. Then listen to the conversation, and answer the questions.

18. What's the principal's name?
    - Ⓐ Rosa.
    - Ⓑ Mr. Wilson.
    - Ⓒ Mr. Lane.
    - Ⓓ Mrs. Lane.

19. Where's the teacher?
    - Ⓐ He's in the hospital.
    - Ⓑ He's in the classroom.
    - Ⓒ He's at the dentist.
    - Ⓓ He's the principal.

20. Which student is absent today?
    - Ⓐ Mr. Wilson.
    - Ⓑ Rosa.
    - Ⓒ Mrs. Wilson.
    - Ⓓ Mrs. Lane.

E WRITING ASSESSMENT: Classroom Objects

Write about the objects in your classroom. What are they, and where are they?

....

....

....

F WRITING ASSESSMENT: School Personnel

Write about the people in your school — your teacher, the principal, the security guard, and other people. What are their names? Where are they now?

....

....

....

....

G SPEAKING ASSESSMENT

I can give and respond to these commands:

Give	Respond	
☐	☐	Stand up.
☐	☐	Go to the board.
☐	☐	Write your name.
☐	☐	Erase your name.
☐	☐	Sit down.

Give	Respond	
☐	☐	Raise your hand.
☐	☐	Open the door.
☐	☐	Close the door.
☐	☐	Turn on the lights.
☐	☐	Turn off the lights.

Give	Respond	
☐	☐	Open your book.
☐	☐	Close your book.
☐	☐	Give me a pen/pencil.
☐	☐	Point to the door.
☐	☐	Point to the board.

I can ask and answer these questions about my classroom and my school:

Ask	Answer	
☐	☐	What objects are in our classroom?
☐	☐	Where's the *object* ?
☐	☐	What's on your desk?

Ask	Answer	
☐	☐	What's our teacher's name?
☐	☐	What's the principal's name?
☐	☐	Where's the principal?

....

18 Ⓐ Ⓑ Ⓒ Ⓓ   19 Ⓐ Ⓑ Ⓒ Ⓓ   20 Ⓐ Ⓑ Ⓒ Ⓓ

STOP

Name ______________________________

Date ____________________ Class ____________________

3

A COMMON CLASSROOM & HOME ACTIVITIES

Choose the correct answer.

Example:

What's Ms. Jenner doing?

- Ⓐ She's reading.
- Ⓑ He's cooking.
- Ⓒ She's cooking.
- ● She's eating.

1. What's Mr. Gray doing?
   - Ⓐ He's studying.
   - Ⓑ She's watching TV.
   - Ⓒ He's watching TV.
   - Ⓓ He's playing cards.

2. What's Miss Lewis doing?
   - Ⓐ She's reading.
   - Ⓑ I'm reading.
   - Ⓒ He's reading.
   - Ⓓ It's reading.

3. What are your friends doing?
   - Ⓐ He's playing the guitar.
   - Ⓑ They're playing the guitar.
   - Ⓒ She's playing baseball.
   - Ⓓ They're playing baseball.

4. What's your dog doing?
   - Ⓐ I'm sleeping.
   - Ⓑ It's sleeping.
   - Ⓒ We're sleeping.
   - Ⓓ They're sleeping.

5. What are you and Carla doing?
   - Ⓐ I'm studying English.
   - Ⓑ They're studying English.
   - Ⓒ We're studying English.
   - Ⓓ She's studying English.

6. What's Mrs. Carter doing?
   - Ⓐ He's teaching.
   - Ⓑ She's teaching.
   - Ⓒ He's playing.
   - Ⓓ She's planting.

7. What's Jimmy doing?
   - Ⓐ He's playing the piano.
   - Ⓑ He's playing baseball.
   - Ⓒ He's playing with the dog.
   - Ⓓ He's playing the guitar.

8. What are Mr. and Mrs. Lu doing?
   - Ⓐ We're eating.
   - Ⓑ They're eating.
   - Ⓒ They're cooking.
   - Ⓓ We're cooking.

9. What are the students doing?
   - Ⓐ They're studying English.
   - Ⓑ We're studying English.
   - Ⓒ I'm studying mathematics.
   - Ⓓ He's studying mathematics.

10. What am I doing?
    - Ⓐ She's reading a book.
    - Ⓑ He's reading the newspaper.
    - Ⓒ You're reading a book.
    - Ⓓ I'm reading the newspaper.

11. What are your friends doing?
    - Ⓐ We're singing.
    - Ⓑ You're singing.
    - Ⓒ I'm singing.
    - Ⓓ They're singing.

1 Ⓐ Ⓑ Ⓒ Ⓓ	4 Ⓐ Ⓑ Ⓒ Ⓓ	7 Ⓐ Ⓑ Ⓒ Ⓓ	10 Ⓐ Ⓑ Ⓒ Ⓓ
2 Ⓐ Ⓑ Ⓒ Ⓓ	5 Ⓐ Ⓑ Ⓒ Ⓓ	8 Ⓐ Ⓑ Ⓒ Ⓓ	11 Ⓐ Ⓑ Ⓒ Ⓓ
3 Ⓐ Ⓑ Ⓒ Ⓓ	6 Ⓐ Ⓑ Ⓒ Ⓓ	9 Ⓐ Ⓑ Ⓒ Ⓓ	

Go to the next page

B GRAMMAR IN CONTEXT: Asking About Home Activities • Checking Understanding

Choose the correct answer to complete the conversation.

12. Where are _____?
   - (A) I
   - (B) she
   - (C) he
   - (D) you

13. _____ in the kitchen.
   - (A) I'm
   - (B) She's
   - (C) They're
   - (D) It's

14. In the _____?
   - (A) hospital
   - (B) park
   - (C) kitchen
   - (D) classroom

15. Yes. I'm _____.
   - (A) kitchen
   - (B) in the kitchen
   - (C) the kitchen
   - (D) doing

16. What _____ you doing?
   - (A) am
   - (B) are
   - (C) is
   - (D) I

17. _____ cooking.
   - (A) You're
   - (B) They're
   - (C) I'm
   - (D) She's

C LISTENING ASSESSMENT

Read and listen to the questions. Then listen to the story, and answer the questions.

18. What are Mr. and Mrs. Baker doing?
   - (A) They're eating.
   - (B) They're swimming.
   - (C) He's reading.
   - (D) They're reading.

19. What's Tommy doing?
   - (A) He's swimming.
   - (B) He's reading.
   - (C) He's listening to music.
   - (D) She's listening to music.

20. Where are they today?
   - (A) It's a beautiful day.
   - (B) They're very happy.
   - (C) They're at home.
   - (D) They're at the beach.

D WRITING ASSESSMENT

What are you doing now? What are your friends doing?

....

....

E SPEAKING ASSESSMENT

I can ask and answer these questions:

Ask	Answer	
☐	☐	Where are you?
☐	☐	What are you doing?
☐	☐	What are other students doing?
☐	☐	What are your friends doing?

12 (A) (B) (C) (D)	15 (A) (B) (C) (D)	18 (A) (B) (C) (D)	
13 (A) (B) (C) (D)	16 (A) (B) (C) (D)	19 (A) (B) (C) (D)	
14 (A) (B) (C) (D)	17 (A) (B) (C) (D)	20 (A) (B) (C) (D)	STOP

Name ______________________

Date ______________ Class ______________

A COMMON CLASSROOM & HOME ACTIVITIES

Choose the best answer.

Example:

He's brushing _____ teeth.

Ⓐ my
Ⓑ our
Ⓒ his
Ⓓ your

Ⓐ Ⓑ ● Ⓓ

1. She's doing _____ homework.
   Ⓐ my
   Ⓑ its
   Ⓒ our
   Ⓓ her

2. They're opening _____ books.
   Ⓐ my
   Ⓑ their
   Ⓒ her
   Ⓓ his

3. I'm brushing _____ teeth.
   Ⓐ their
   Ⓑ my
   Ⓒ its
   Ⓓ his

4. He's raising _____ hand.
   Ⓐ our
   Ⓑ her
   Ⓒ his
   Ⓓ their

5. We're doing _____ exercises.
   Ⓐ our
   Ⓑ their
   Ⓒ his
   Ⓓ her

6. What's Mr. Sharp doing?
   Ⓐ She's cleaning her kitchen.
   Ⓑ We're cleaning our kitchen.
   Ⓒ He's cleaning his kitchen.
   Ⓓ I'm cleaning my kitchen.

7. What are Mr. and Mrs. Lee doing?
   Ⓐ He's washing his car.
   Ⓑ She's washing her car.
   Ⓒ We're washing our car.
   Ⓓ They're washing their car.

8. Is Ms. Harris busy?
   Ⓐ Yes, he is.
   Ⓑ Yes, I am.
   Ⓒ Yes, she is.
   Ⓓ Yes, it is.

9. Are you busy?
   Ⓐ Yes, you are.
   Ⓑ Yes, I am.
   Ⓒ Yes, they are.
   Ⓓ Yes, it is.

10. Are the students studying?
    Ⓐ Yes, they are.
    Ⓑ Yes, you are.
    Ⓒ Yes, I am.
    Ⓓ Yes, he is.

11. What are your friends doing?
    Ⓐ We're painting our apartment.
    Ⓑ She's painting her apartment.
    Ⓒ I'm painting my apartment.
    Ⓓ They're painting their apartment.

1 Ⓐ Ⓑ Ⓒ Ⓓ	4 Ⓐ Ⓑ Ⓒ Ⓓ	7 Ⓐ Ⓑ Ⓒ Ⓓ	10 Ⓐ Ⓑ Ⓒ Ⓓ
2 Ⓐ Ⓑ Ⓒ Ⓓ	5 Ⓐ Ⓑ Ⓒ Ⓓ	8 Ⓐ Ⓑ Ⓒ Ⓓ	11 Ⓐ Ⓑ Ⓒ Ⓓ
3 Ⓐ Ⓑ Ⓒ Ⓓ	6 Ⓐ Ⓑ Ⓒ Ⓓ	9 Ⓐ Ⓑ Ⓒ Ⓓ	

Go to the next page

B GRAMMAR IN CONTEXT: Getting Someone's Attention • Asking About Home Activities

Choose the correct answer to complete the conversation.

12. Excuse me. Alex? _____ you busy?
    - (A) Am
    - (B) Is
    - (C) Are
    - (D) I

13. Yes, _____.
    - (A) we are
    - (B) they are
    - (C) he is
    - (D) I am

14. What _____ doing?
    - (A) are they
    - (B) are you
    - (C) am I
    - (D) is she

15. I'm _____.
    - (A) doing their homework
    - (B) doing its exercises
    - (C) doing my homework
    - (D) doing their exercises

16. _____ Bob doing?
    - (A) What
    - (B) What are
    - (C) Where's
    - (D) What's

17. _____ washing _____ car.
    - (A) He's . . his
    - (B) They're . . their
    - (C) We're . . our
    - (D) I'm . . my

C LISTENING ASSESSMENT

Read and listen to the questions. Then listen to the telephone conversation, and answer the questions.

18. What's Lisa doing?
    - (A) She's washing her car.
    - (B) She's washing her cat.
    - (C) She's watching her windows.
    - (D) She's washing her windows.

19. What's Richard doing?
    - (A) He's doing his homework.
    - (B) He's cooking breakfast.
    - (C) He's cooking dinner.
    - (D) He's cooking lunch.

20. What are the children doing?
    - (A) They're cooking.
    - (B) They're doing their exercises.
    - (C) They're cleaning.
    - (D) They're doing their homework.

D LEARNING SKILL ASSESSMENT: Alphabetizing

Alphabetize the list of names. Write the names in alphabetical (ABC) order.

Molina ____*Chang*____

Chang __________

Williams __________

Lopez __________

Gomez __________

E WRITING ASSESSMENT

Write a paragraph about the picture on page 31 of *Side by Side* Book 1. What are the people doing? (Use a separate sheet of paper.)

F SPEAKING ASSESSMENT

I can ask and answer these questions:

Ask	Answer	
☐	☐	Are you busy?
☐	☐	What are you doing now?
☐	☐	What are your neighbors doing?

12 (A) (B) (C) (D) 15 (A) (B) (C) (D) 18 (A) (B) (C) (D)

13 (A) (B) (C) (D) 16 (A) (B) (C) (D) 19 (A) (B) (C) (D)

14 (A) (B) (C) (D) 17 (A) (B) (C) (D) 20 (A) (B) (C) (D)

STOP

Name ______________________________

Date ______________ Class ______________

5

A DESCRIBING PEOPLE, THINGS, & WEATHER

Choose the best answer.

Example:

Is his car new or _____?

Ⓐ small
Ⓑ easy
Ⓒ old
Ⓓ thin

Ⓐ Ⓑ ● Ⓓ

1. Is her dog big or _____?
   Ⓐ new
   Ⓑ difficult
   Ⓒ noisy
   Ⓓ little

2. Is your brother single or _____?
   Ⓐ tall
   Ⓑ married
   Ⓒ young
   Ⓓ old

3. Are your neighbors quiet or _____?
   Ⓐ noisy
   Ⓑ cheap
   Ⓒ large
   Ⓓ expensive

4. Is your computer old or _____?
   Ⓐ small
   Ⓑ young
   Ⓒ new
   Ⓓ pretty

5. Is it sunny or _____?
   Ⓐ cold
   Ⓑ cloudy
   Ⓒ cool
   Ⓓ hot

6. _____ is pretty.
   Ⓐ Jill cat
   Ⓑ Cat Jill
   Ⓒ Jill's cat
   Ⓓ Jill's cats

7. _____ is large.
   Ⓐ Mr. Grant's car's
   Ⓑ Mr. Grant's cars
   Ⓒ Mr. Grant car
   Ⓓ Mr. Grant's car

8. The questions in our book _____.
   Ⓐ is difficult
   Ⓑ are difficult
   Ⓒ am difficult
   Ⓓ not difficult

9. Is it raining?
   Ⓐ Yes, he is.
   Ⓑ Yes, I am.
   Ⓒ No, it isn't.
   Ⓓ No, we aren't.

10. Are you married?
   Ⓐ No, you aren't.
   Ⓑ No, they aren't.
   Ⓒ No, he isn't.
   Ⓓ No, I'm not.

11. How's the weather?
   Ⓐ It's cool.
   Ⓑ It's cheap.
   Ⓒ It's short.
   Ⓓ It's thin.

1 Ⓐ Ⓑ Ⓒ Ⓓ	4 Ⓐ Ⓑ Ⓒ Ⓓ	7 Ⓐ Ⓑ Ⓒ Ⓓ	10 Ⓐ Ⓑ Ⓒ Ⓓ
2 Ⓐ Ⓑ Ⓒ Ⓓ	5 Ⓐ Ⓑ Ⓒ Ⓓ	8 Ⓐ Ⓑ Ⓒ Ⓓ	11 Ⓐ Ⓑ Ⓒ Ⓓ
3 Ⓐ Ⓑ Ⓒ Ⓓ	6 Ⓐ Ⓑ Ⓒ Ⓓ	9 Ⓐ Ⓑ Ⓒ Ⓓ	

Go to the next page

B GRAMMAR IN CONTEXT: Using the Telephone • Weather

Choose the correct answer to complete the conversation.

Example:

____

(A) Yes, it is.
(B) I'm calling.
● Hello.
(D) Goodbye.

12. Hi, Ann. ______________
I'm calling from Honolulu.
(A) Hello.
(B) Is this Jim?
(C) Am I Jim?
(D) This is Jim.

13. ______________
How's the weather in Honolulu?
(A) Hello. This is Ann.
(B) Hello. Is this Jim?
(C) Hi, Jim.
(D) Yes, it is.

14. The weather is beautiful. It's hot and _____.
(A) snowing
(B) sunny
(C) cold
(D) cool

C INTERPRETING A THERMOMETER

°F	°C	
100	38	(A)
70	21	(B)
50	10	(C)
32	0	(D)

For each weather expression, choose the correct temperature on the thermometer.

Example:
It's warm. (A) ● (C) (D)

15. It's cold.

16. It's hot.

17. It's cool.

D LISTENING ASSESSMENT: Weather Report

Read and listen to the questions. Then listen to the weather report, and answer the questions.

18. How's the weather in Miami?
(A) It's cool.
(B) It's raining.
(C) It's snowing.
(D) It's sunny.

19. What's the temperature in Los Angeles?
(A) 40°F.
(B) 95°F.
(C) 80°F.
(D) It's hot.

20. How's the weather in New York?
(A) It's hot.
(B) It's cold.
(C) It's snowing.
(D) It's warm.

E WRITING ASSESSMENT: Form

Name: ______________________

Social Security Number: ______________________

Marital Status: ______________________

F SPEAKING ASSESSMENT

I can ask and answer these questions:

Ask	Answer	
☐	☐	What's your marital status?
☐	☐	Are you married or single?
☐	☐	How's the weather today?

12 (A) (B) (C) (D)	15 (A) (B) (C) (D)	18 (A) (B) (C) (D)
13 (A) (B) (C) (D)	16 (A) (B) (C) (D)	19 (A) (B) (C) (D)
14 (A) (B) (C) (D)	17 (A) (B) (C) (D)	20 (A) (B) (C) (D)

STOP

Name ______________________________

Date ________________ Class ________________

A FAMILY RELATIONS

Look at the picture. Choose the correct answer.

Example:

John is Kate's _____.

Ⓐ wife
Ⓑ husband
Ⓒ daughter
Ⓓ son

Ⓐ ● Ⓒ Ⓓ

1. Billy is John and Kate's _____.
   Ⓐ brother
   Ⓑ father
   Ⓒ uncle
   Ⓓ son

2. Ann is Billy's _____.
   Ⓐ daughter
   Ⓑ cousin
   Ⓒ sister
   Ⓓ mother

3. John and Kate are Billy and Ann's _____.
   Ⓐ children
   Ⓑ parents
   Ⓒ grandparents
   Ⓓ aunt and uncle

Look at the picture. Choose the correct answer.

4. Henry is Billy and Ann's _____.
   Ⓐ grandson
   Ⓑ granddaughter
   Ⓒ grandfather
   Ⓓ grandmother

5. Ann is Peggy and Henry's _____.
   Ⓐ granddaughter
   Ⓑ daughter
   Ⓒ mother
   Ⓓ sister

6. Henry and Peggy are Billy and Ann's _____.
   Ⓐ children
   Ⓑ parents
   Ⓒ grandparents
   Ⓓ grandchildren

7. Ann and Billy are Henry and Peggy's _____.
   Ⓐ children
   Ⓑ grandparents
   Ⓒ parents
   Ⓓ grandchildren

1 Ⓐ Ⓑ Ⓒ Ⓓ   3 Ⓐ Ⓑ Ⓒ Ⓓ   5 Ⓐ Ⓑ Ⓒ Ⓓ   7 Ⓐ Ⓑ Ⓒ Ⓓ

2 Ⓐ Ⓑ Ⓒ Ⓓ   4 Ⓐ Ⓑ Ⓒ Ⓓ   6 Ⓐ Ⓑ Ⓒ Ⓓ

Go to the next page

B FAMILY RELATIONS & COMMON ACTIVITIES

Choose the correct answer.

Example:

My _____ is feeding his cat.

Ⓐ daughter
Ⓑ wife
Ⓒ uncle
Ⓓ mother

Ⓐ Ⓑ ● Ⓓ

8. My _____ is doing her homework.

Ⓐ brother
Ⓑ son
Ⓒ nephew
Ⓓ niece

9. My _____ is washing his hair.

Ⓐ niece
Ⓑ nephew
Ⓒ aunt
Ⓓ cousins

10. My _____ are brushing their teeth.

Ⓐ aunt
Ⓑ uncle
Ⓒ cousins
Ⓓ sister

11. My _____ is painting her living room.

Ⓐ aunt
Ⓑ uncle
Ⓒ father
Ⓓ brother

12. My _____ are doing their exercises.

Ⓐ sisters
Ⓑ parents
Ⓒ aunts
Ⓓ nieces

13. _____ her windows.

Ⓐ My brother is watching
Ⓑ My sister is watching
Ⓒ My brother is washing
Ⓓ My sister is washing

14. _____ TV.

Ⓐ My parents are washing
Ⓑ My uncles are washing
Ⓒ My aunt and uncle are watching
Ⓓ My aunts are watching

8 Ⓐ Ⓑ Ⓒ Ⓓ 10 Ⓐ Ⓑ Ⓒ Ⓓ 12 Ⓐ Ⓑ Ⓒ Ⓓ 14 Ⓐ Ⓑ Ⓒ Ⓓ

9 Ⓐ Ⓑ Ⓒ Ⓓ 11 Ⓐ Ⓑ Ⓒ Ⓓ 13 Ⓐ Ⓑ Ⓒ Ⓓ

Go to the next page

Name ________________________________ Date ______________

C GRAMMAR IN CONTEXT: Greeting & Introducing

Choose the correct answer to complete the conversation.

Example:
Hello. __________
Ⓐ Is this Brenda?
Ⓑ How are you?
Ⓒ Who are you?
Ⓓ How's the weather?
15. Fine. __________
Ⓐ Where are you?
Ⓑ What are you doing?
Ⓒ And you?
Ⓓ Yes, I am.
16. Fine, thanks.
_____ my sister.
Ⓐ I'm
Ⓑ Nice to meet
Ⓒ Her name is
Ⓓ I'd like to introduce
17. __________
Ⓐ Fine, thanks.
Ⓑ And you?
Ⓒ Nice to meet you.
Ⓓ Nice to meet you, too.

D LISTENING ASSESSMENT

Read and listen to the questions. Then listen to the story, and answer the questions.

18. What day is it?
- Ⓐ It's a beautiful day.
- Ⓑ He's happy.
- Ⓒ It's his wedding day.
- Ⓓ It's his birthday.

19. What are his parents doing?
- Ⓐ They're eating cake.
- Ⓑ They're sitting in the living room.
- Ⓒ They're dancing.
- Ⓓ They're taking photographs.

20. What's his grandfather doing?
- Ⓐ He's dancing.
- Ⓑ He's taking photographs.
- Ⓒ He's eating cake.
- Ⓓ He's old.

E LEARNING SKILL: Categorizing

Write each word in the correct column.

aunt	daughter	husband	sister	uncle
brother	father	mother	son	wife

Male	**Female**
brother	aunt
______________	______________
______________	______________
______________	______________
______________	______________

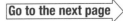

15 Ⓐ Ⓑ Ⓒ Ⓓ 17 Ⓐ Ⓑ Ⓒ Ⓓ 19 Ⓐ Ⓑ Ⓒ Ⓓ

16 Ⓐ Ⓑ Ⓒ Ⓓ 18 Ⓐ Ⓑ Ⓒ Ⓓ 20 Ⓐ Ⓑ Ⓒ Ⓓ

Go to the next page

F EYE CONTACT & GESTURES

For each sentence, choose the correct picture.

A

B

C

D

1. "Patty, this is Mr. Fisher." ________
2. "I'd like to introduce my sister." ________
3. "May I ask a question?" ________
4. "Hello. My name is Peter." ________

G WRITING ASSESSMENT

Write about the people in your family—sisters, brothers, parents, children, grandparents. What are their names? (Use a separate sheet of paper.)

H SPEAKING ASSESSMENT

I can introduce myself and others:

Say Respond

☐ ☐ I'm ________.
☐ ☐ I'd like to introduce ________.

I can ask and answer these questions:

Ask Answer

☐ ☐ Who is in your family? Who are the people in your family?
☐ ☐ What are their names?

I can talk about a photograph:

Ask Answer

☐ ☐ Who is he/she? Who are they?
☐ ☐ What's his/her name? What are their names?
☐ ☐ What's he/she doing? What are they doing?

STOP

Name ______________________________

Date ______________________ Class ______________________

A IDENTIFYING & LOCATING PLACES IN THE COMMUNITY

Choose the correct answer.

1. The _____ is next to the park.
   - (A) clinic
   - (B) hotel
   - (C) school
   - (D) supermarket

2. The laundromat is _____ the bakery and the bookstore.
   - (A) across from
   - (B) around the corner from
   - (C) next
   - (D) between

3. The _____ is around the corner from the hospital.
   - (A) restaurant
   - (B) department store
   - (C) cafeteria
   - (D) supermarket

4. The library is _____ the gas station.
   - (A) across from
   - (B) around the corner from
   - (C) next
   - (D) between

B IDENTIFYING ROOMS, FURNITURE, & FIXTURES IN A RESIDENCE

5. There's a new _____ in the _____.
   - (A) closet . . bedroom
   - (B) refrigerator . . bathroom
   - (C) stove . . kitchen
   - (D) refrigerator . . kitchen

6. Is there a _____ in the _____?
   - (A) window . . bathroom
   - (B) closet . . bedroom
   - (C) closet . . living room
   - (D) basement . . bedroom

7. There's a very nice _____ in the _____.
   - (A) sofa . . living room
   - (B) bed . . bedroom
   - (C) window . . living room
   - (D) TV . . living room

8. How many _____ are there in the _____?
   - (A) closets . . floor
   - (B) floors . . apartment
   - (C) elevators . . building
   - (D) apartments . . building

1 (A) (B) (C) (D)　4 (A) (B) (C) (D)　7 (A) (B) (C) (D)

2 (A) (B) (C) (D)　5 (A) (B) (C) (D)　8 (A) (B) (C) (D)

3 (A) (B) (C) (D)　6 (A) (B) (C) (D)

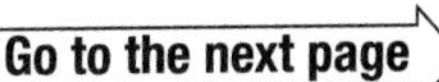

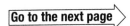

C GRAMMAR IN CONTEXT: Inquiring About Residences, Rentals, & Neighborhoods

Choose the correct answer to complete each conversation.

Example:

Excuse me. _____ a bank in this neighborhood?

Ⓐ There
Ⓑ Where
Ⓒ Are there
● Is there

9. Yes. _____ a bank on State Street.

Ⓐ There
Ⓑ There's
Ⓒ There are
Ⓓ It's

10. _____

Ⓐ Thank.
Ⓑ Thanks you.
Ⓒ Thank you.
Ⓓ Yes.

11. _____

Ⓐ Welcome.
Ⓑ Yes, there is.
Ⓒ Thanks.
Ⓓ You're welcome.

12. How many bedrooms _____ in the house?

Ⓐ is there
Ⓑ are there
Ⓒ there is
Ⓓ there are

13. _____ three bedrooms.

Ⓐ There
Ⓑ There's
Ⓒ They are
Ⓓ There are

14. _____ condominiums _____ in the complex?

Ⓐ How . . are there
Ⓑ How . . there are
Ⓒ How many . . are there
Ⓓ How many . . there are

15. _____ fifty condos.

Ⓐ Are
Ⓑ There
Ⓒ There are
Ⓓ Are there

16. Is there a _____ in the apartment building?

Ⓐ cockroach
Ⓑ mailbox
Ⓒ satellite dish
Ⓓ superintendent

17. Yes. His apartment is in the _____.

Ⓐ basement
Ⓑ window
Ⓒ wall
Ⓓ roof

9	Ⓐ Ⓑ Ⓒ Ⓓ	12	Ⓐ Ⓑ Ⓒ Ⓓ	15	Ⓐ Ⓑ Ⓒ Ⓓ
10	Ⓐ Ⓑ Ⓒ Ⓓ	13	Ⓐ Ⓑ Ⓒ Ⓓ	16	Ⓐ Ⓑ Ⓒ Ⓓ
11	Ⓐ Ⓑ Ⓒ Ⓓ	14	Ⓐ Ⓑ Ⓒ Ⓓ	17	Ⓐ Ⓑ Ⓒ Ⓓ

Go to the next page

Name ______________________ Date ____________

D LISTENING ASSESSMENT

Read and listen to the questions. Then listen to the conversation, and answer the questions.

18. How many bedrooms are there in the apartment?
   - Ⓐ Six.
   - Ⓑ Three.
   - Ⓒ One.
   - Ⓓ Two.

19. How many bathrooms are there?
   - Ⓐ Six.
   - Ⓑ Three.
   - Ⓒ One.
   - Ⓓ Two.

20. Where's the laundromat?
   - Ⓐ It's next to the building.
   - Ⓑ It's next to the supermarket.
   - Ⓒ It's across from the building.
   - Ⓓ It's across from the post office.

E SPEAKING ASSESSMENT: Information Gap (Part A)

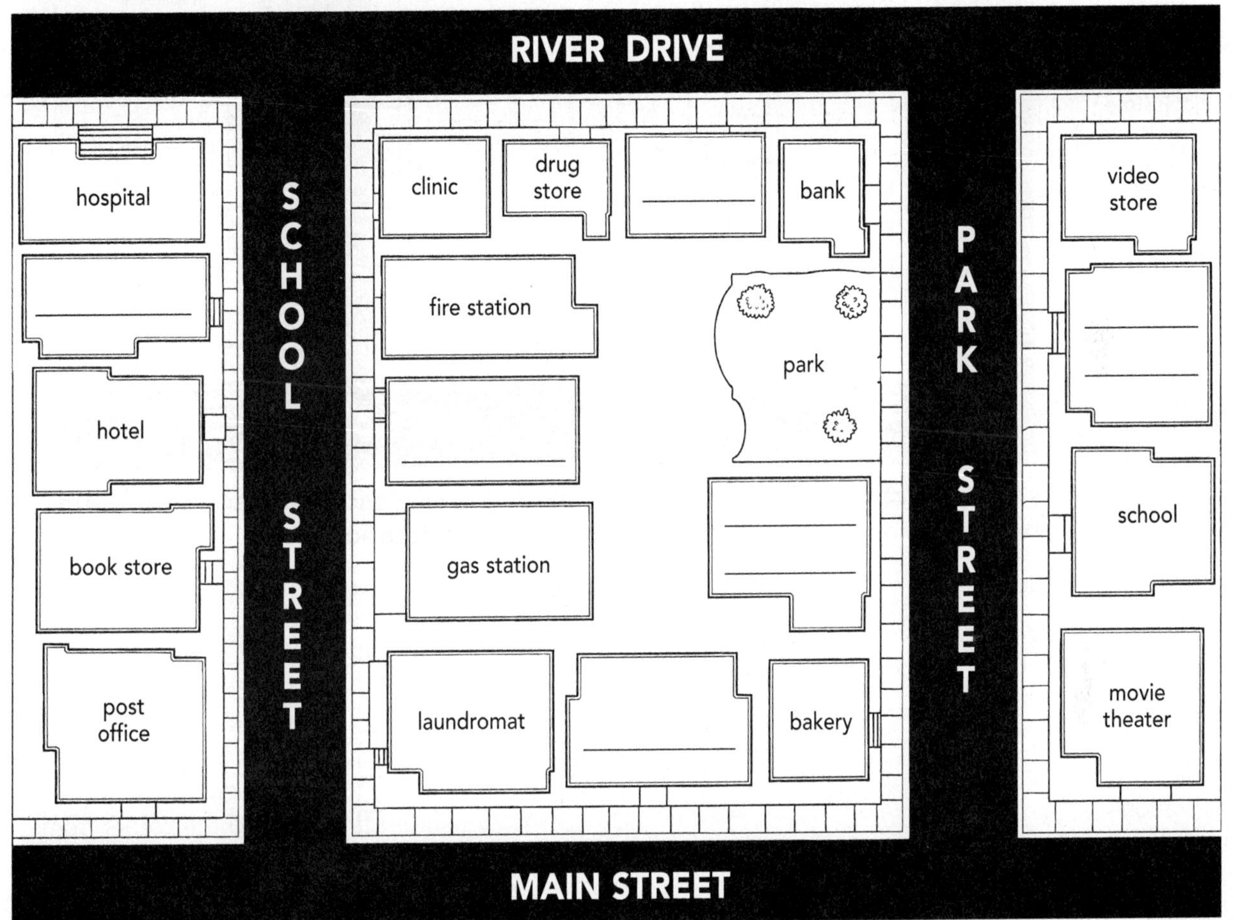

There are two maps for this activity. This is Map A. Work with a student with Map B. Ask and answer questions about the maps. Write the places in the correct locations.

Ask about these places:

- ☐ bus station
- ☐ library
- ☐ cafeteria
- ☐ department store
- ☐ supermarket
- ☐ hair salon
- ☐ restaurant

Use these expressions:

- ☐ Is there a ________ in this neighborhood?
  - ☐ Yes, there is.
  - ☐ No, there isn't.
- ☐ Where's the ________?
  - ☐ It's on *street*.
  - ☐ It's next to ________.
  - ☐ It's across from ________.
  - ☐ It's between ________.
  - ☐ It's around the corner from ________.

18 Ⓐ Ⓑ Ⓒ Ⓓ 19 Ⓐ Ⓑ Ⓒ Ⓓ 20 Ⓐ Ⓑ Ⓒ Ⓓ

Go to the next page

E SPEAKING ASSESSMENT: Information Gap (Part B)

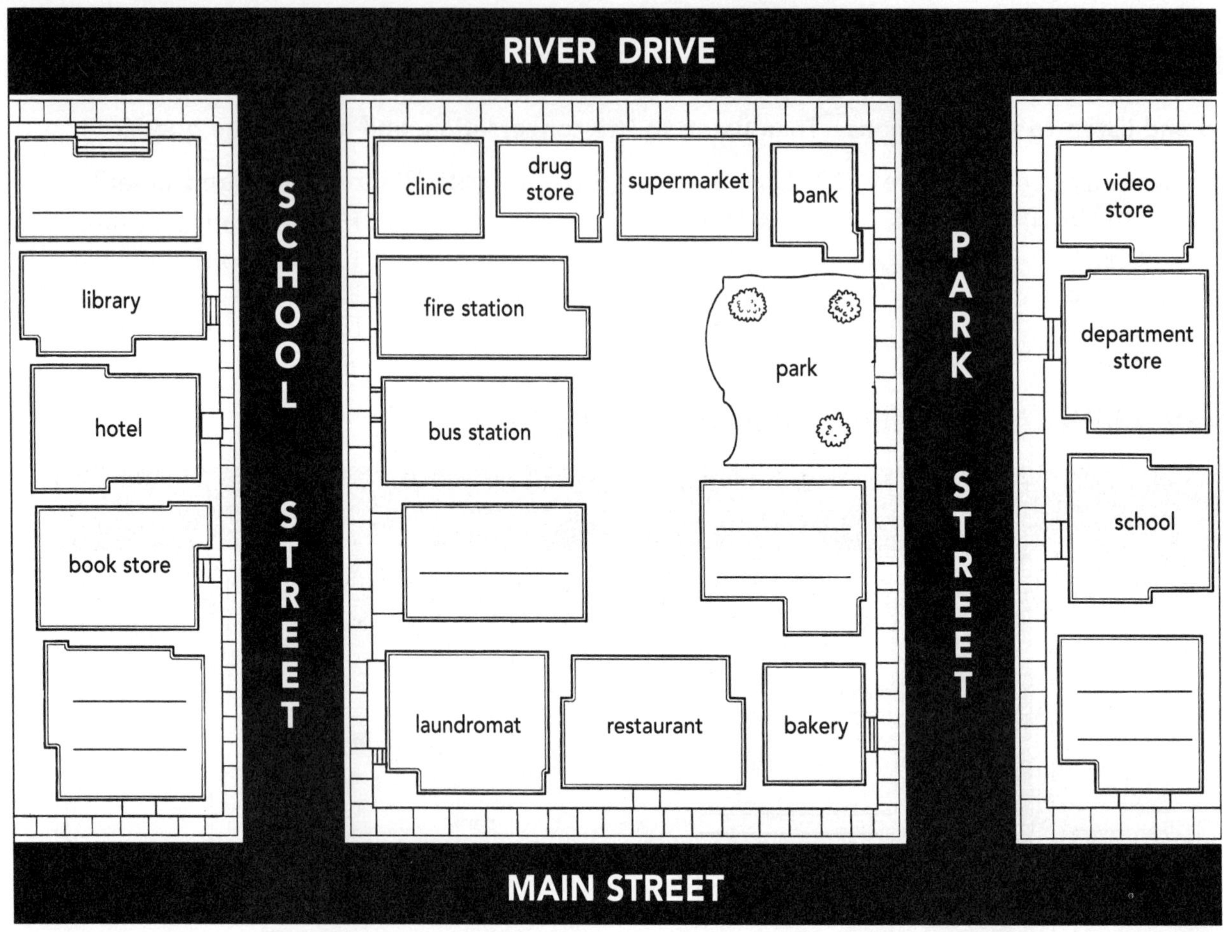

There are two maps for this activity. This is Map B. Work with a student with Map A. Ask and answer questions about the maps. Write the places in the correct locations.

Ask about these places:

- ☐ post office
- ☐ police station
- ☐ barber shop
- ☐ hospital
- ☐ health club
- ☐ gas station
- ☐ movie theater

Use these expressions:

- ☐ Is there a _______ in this neighborhood?
  - ☐ Yes, there is.
  - ☐ No, there isn't.

- ☐ Where's the _______?
  - ☐ It's on _street_.
  - ☐ It's next to _______.
  - ☐ It's across from _______.
  - ☐ It's between _______.
  - ☐ It's around the corner from _______.

F WRITING ASSESSMENT

Write a paragraph about your neighborhood.

....

....

....

....

STOP

Name ____________________

Date ______________ Class ______________

A CLOTHING

Choose the correct answer.

Example:

I'm looking for _____.

- (A) pants
- (B) a blouse
- ● a dress
- (D) a suit

1. I'm looking for _____.
   - (A) a sock
   - (B) a suit
   - (C) a skirt
   - (D) a shirt

2. I need _____.
   - (A) a shoe
   - (B) a pair of shoe
   - (C) a pair of shoes
   - (D) pairs of shoe

3. Here's a nice _____.
   - (A) tie
   - (B) belt
   - (C) watch
   - (D) necklace

4. _____ your watch?
   - (A) Are these
   - (B) Are those
   - (C) Is this
   - (D) I think

5. _____ jeans are blue.
   - (A) Those
   - (B) That
   - (C) This
   - (D) Here's

6. Excuse me. I think that's my _____.
   - (A) boots
   - (B) coat
   - (C) gloves
   - (D) shoes

7. _____ are over there.
   - (A) Sweater
   - (B) Sweaters
   - (C) A sock
   - (D) A pair of socks

8. _____ your glasses?
   - (A) Is this
   - (B) Is that
   - (C) Are these
   - (D) Are you sure

9. _____ very nice hat!
   - (A) This
   - (B) That's
   - (C) These are
   - (D) That's a

10. Is this your jacket?
    - (A) Yes, they are.
    - (B) No, they aren't.
    - (C) No, I'm not.
    - (D) No, it isn't.

11. Excuse me. I'm looking for a gray suit.
    - (A) Gray shirts are very popular.
    - (B) I'm sorry. All our suits are gray.
    - (C) Suits are over there.
    - (D) I think this is my suit.

1 (A) (B) (C) (D)	4 (A) (B) (C) (D)	7 (A) (B) (C) (D)	10 (A) (B) (C) (D)
2 (A) (B) (C) (D)	5 (A) (B) (C) (D)	8 (A) (B) (C) (D)	11 (A) (B) (C) (D)
3 (A) (B) (C) (D)	6 (A) (B) (C) (D)	9 (A) (B) (C) (D)	

Go to the next page

B GRAMMAR IN CONTEXT: Asking for Help • Identifying Clothing Needs

Choose the correct answer to complete the conversation.

Example:

May I help ____?

- (A) me
- (B) my
- ● you
- (D) your

12. Yes, please. I need ____.
- (A) a pair of
- (B) glove
- (C) a pair of glove
- (D) a pair of gloves

13. Excuse me. ____ a brown umbrella.
- (A) I'm looking
- (B) I'm looking for
- (C) You're looking
- (D) You're looking for

14. I'm sorry. All our ____ black.
- (A) umbrella is
- (B) umbrellas is
- (C) umbrella are
- (D) umbrellas are

15. Can you help ____?
- (A) me
- (B) my
- (C) I
- (D) you

Yes.

16. How much ____ coat?
- (A) are these
- (B) are those
- (C) is this
- (D) is it

17. It's very ____. It's 25 dollars.
- (A) clean
- (B) brown
- (C) over there
- (D) inexpensive

C LISTENING ASSESSMENT

Read and listen to the questions. Then listen to the conversation, and answer the questions.

18. Where is the conversation taking place?
- (A) In a closet.
- (B) In a laundromat.
- (C) In a store.
- (D) In a restaurant.

19. What's the person looking for?
- (A) Her raincoat.
- (B) Her husband.
- (C) A raincoat for a man.
- (D) A raincoat for a woman.

20. What size is the raincoat?
- (A) He's tall.
- (B) It's large.
- (C) He's short.
- (D) It's small.

12 (A) (B) (C) (D)   15 (A) (B) (C) (D)   18 (A) (B) (C) (D)
13 (A) (B) (C) (D)   16 (A) (B) (C) (D)   19 (A) (B) (C) (D)
14 (A) (B) (C) (D)   17 (A) (B) (C) (D)   20 (A) (B) (C) (D)

Go to the next page

Name ______________________________ Date ______________

D MONEY: Coins

penny
1¢
$.01

nickel
5¢
$.05

dime
10¢
$.10

quarter
25¢
$.25

half-dollar
50¢
$.50

Choose the correct amount and write it.

3¢	$.05	6¢	$.10	15¢	$.20	35¢	$.50	$.61

1. $.10

2. ______________

3. ______________

4. ______________

5. ______________

6. ______________

7. ______________

8. ______________

9. ______________

Write the amount two ways.

10. three nickels 15¢ or $.15
11. two pennies ________ or ________
12. four dimes ________ or ________
13. a quarter and a penny ________ or ________
14. two dimes and a nickel ________ or ________
15. a half-dollar and a dime ________ or ________

Go to the next page

E MONEY: Bills

one dollar
$1.00

five dollars
$5.00

ten dollars
$10.00

twenty dollars
$20.00

fifty dollars
$50.00

one hundred dollars
$100.00

Write the correct amount.

1. $25.00

2. ______________

3. ______________

4. ______________

5. ______________

6. ______________

7.   ______________

8. ______________

9.   ______________

10.   ______________

Go to the next page

Name ______________________________ Date ______________

F CLOTHING LABELS: Sizes, Prices, Colors

Clothing Sizes & Abbreviations

S	Small	M	Medium	L	Large	XL	Extra

Look at the clothing labels. Answer the questions.

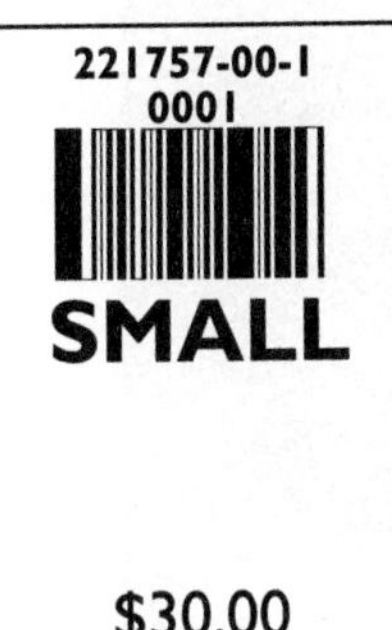

1. What size is this? ______________
2. How much is it? ______________

30 DEPT. 27 CLASS 05 SUB
277665-700066 SKU 449
SIZE L
OUR PRICE $8.99

3. How much is this? ______________
4. What's the size? ______________

107883
H4001
WHITE
SIZE
36
$18.00
~~$24.00~~

5. This is on sale. What's the price? ______________
6. What size is it? ______________
7. What color is it? ______________

REGULAR FIT
BOYS
100% COTTON
CLR: BLUE
SIZE: M
$21.99

8. How big is this? ______________
9. What's the color? ______________
10. What's the cost? ______________

Go to the next page

G CLOTHING ADS: Regular Prices, Sale Prices, Sizes

Look at the advertisement for clothing. Answer the questions.

1. What's the regular price of the jeans? ______________________
2. What's the sale price of the jeans? ______________________
3. How much are the children's sneakers now? ______________________
4. What are the sizes of the women's blouses? ______________________
5. What's the regular price of the men's shirts? ______________________
6. What's the sale price of the men's shirts? ______________________
7. How much are the women's blouses on sale? ______________________

H WRITING ASSESSMENT

What are you wearing today? Tell about the clothing and the colors. Write about it on a separate sheet of paper.

I SPEAKING ASSESSMENT

I can ask and answer these questions:

Ask	Answer	
☐	☐	What are you wearing today?
☐	☐	What color is your *clothing item*?
☐	☐	What's your favorite color?

Name ______________________________

Date ____________________ Class ____________________

9

A COMMON ACTIVITIES

Choose the correct answer.

Example:

I ______.

● read
Ⓑ reads
Ⓒ sing
Ⓓ sings

1. She ______ Spanish.
   Ⓐ call
   Ⓑ calls
   Ⓒ speak
   Ⓓ speaks

2. He ______ every day.
   Ⓐ cook
   Ⓑ cooks
   Ⓒ eat
   Ⓓ eats

3. They ______ in an office.
   Ⓐ live
   Ⓑ lives
   Ⓒ work
   Ⓓ works

4. He ______ TV every day.
   Ⓐ watch
   Ⓑ watches
   Ⓒ listen
   Ⓓ listens

5. She ______ to school.
   Ⓐ goes
   Ⓑ visits
   Ⓒ go
   Ⓓ visit

6. Where ______ he live?
   Ⓐ are
   Ⓑ is
   Ⓒ do
   Ⓓ does

7. What languages ______ you speak?
   Ⓐ are
   Ⓑ is
   Ⓒ do
   Ⓓ does

8. What ______ every day?
   Ⓐ do you
   Ⓑ you do
   Ⓒ do
   Ⓓ do you do

9. ______ she work?
   Ⓐ What does
   Ⓑ Where does
   Ⓒ What do
   Ⓓ Where do

10. ______ she do at the office?
    Ⓐ What does
    Ⓑ What do
    Ⓒ Where does
    Ⓓ Where do

11. ______ your parents live?
    Ⓐ What does
    Ⓑ What do
    Ⓒ Where does
    Ⓓ Where do

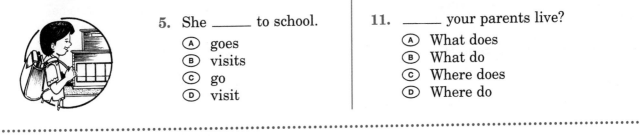

1 Ⓐ Ⓑ Ⓒ Ⓓ	4 Ⓐ Ⓑ Ⓒ Ⓓ	7 Ⓐ Ⓑ Ⓒ Ⓓ	10 Ⓐ Ⓑ Ⓒ Ⓓ
2 Ⓐ Ⓑ Ⓒ Ⓓ	5 Ⓐ Ⓑ Ⓒ Ⓓ	8 Ⓐ Ⓑ Ⓒ Ⓓ	11 Ⓐ Ⓑ Ⓒ Ⓓ
3 Ⓐ Ⓑ Ⓒ Ⓓ	6 Ⓐ Ⓑ Ⓒ Ⓓ	9 Ⓐ Ⓑ Ⓒ Ⓓ	

Go to the next page

B GRAMMAR IN CONTEXT: Social Interactions

Choose the correct answer to complete the conversation.

12. _____ you speak?
    - (A) Where do
    - (B) Where does
    - (C) What language do
    - (D) What language does

13. I speak _____.
    - (A) Mexico
    - (B) Mexican
    - (C) Mexico City
    - (D) Spanish

14. _____ your son live?
    - (A) Where do
    - (B) Where does
    - (C) What do
    - (D) What does

15. _____ in Las Vegas.
    - (A) I live
    - (B) He lives
    - (C) She lives
    - (D) They live

16. _____ he do?
    - (A) What does
    - (B) Where does
    - (C) What do
    - (D) Where do

17. He _____ in a hotel.
    - (A) work
    - (B) works
    - (C) visit
    - (D) visits

C LISTENING ASSESSMENT

Read and listen to the questions. Then listen to the conversation, and answer the questions.

18. Where does she live?
    - (A) In Greece.
    - (B) In Dallas.
    - (C) In a restaurant.
    - (D) At work.

19. What does she do at work?
    - (A) She watches TV.
    - (B) She reads.
    - (C) She cooks.
    - (D) She plays the piano.

20. What does she do at home?
    - (A) She plays the violin.
    - (B) She reads the newspaper.
    - (C) She watches TV.
    - (D) She works.

D WRITING ASSESSMENT: Daily Activities

What do you do at home every day? What do you do at school or at work? Write about your daily activities. (Use a separate sheet of paper.)

E SPEAKING ASSESSMENT

I can ask and answer these questions:

Ask	Answer	
☐	☐	What's your name?
☐	☐	Where do you live?
☐	☐	What languages do you speak?
☐	☐	What do you do every day?

Ask	Answer	
☐	☐	What's his/her name?
☐	☐	Where does he/she live?
☐	☐	What languages does he/she speak?
☐	☐	What does he/she do every day?

12 (A) (B) (C) (D)
13 (A) (B) (C) (D)
14 (A) (B) (C) (D)
15 (A) (B) (C) (D)
16 (A) (B) (C) (D)
17 (A) (B) (C) (D)
18 (A) (B) (C) (D)
19 (A) (B) (C) (D)
20 (A) (B) (C) (D)

STOP

Name ______________________________

Date ____________________ Class ____________________

10

A COMMON ACTIVITIES: DAILY LIFE, SPORTS, & RECREATION

Choose the best answer.

Example:

Tom _____ basketball on Saturday. He plays basketball on Friday.

- (A) play
- (B) doesn't play
- (C) don't play
- (D) not play

(A) ● (C) (D)

1. My wife and I _____ on Sunday. We go to a restaurant.
   - (A) don't cook
   - (B) doesn't cook
   - (C) don't we cook
   - (D) not cook

2. _____ Janet play tennis on Monday?
   - (A) Is
   - (B) Do
   - (C) Don't
   - (D) Does

3. _____ your parents watch TV?
   - (A) Does
   - (B) Are
   - (C) Do
   - (D) What

4. Does Mr. Lee ride his bike to work?
   - (A) Yes, they do.
   - (B) Yes, it does.
   - (C) Yes, I do.
   - (D) Yes, he does.

5. Do you and your friends play baseball?
   - (A) Yes, we do.
   - (B) Yes, they do.
   - (C) Yes, he does.
   - (D) Yes, it does.

6. Do you play a musical instrument?
   - (A) Yes, they do.
   - (B) Yes, you do.
   - (C) No, I don't.
   - (D) No, it doesn't.

7. What do your friends do on the weekend?
   - (A) Yes, we do.
   - (B) Yes, they do.
   - (C) They play football.
   - (D) I play football.

8. _____ movies do you like?
   - (A) What kind
   - (B) What kind of
   - (C) What's your favorite
   - (D) Who's your favorite

9. My parents _____ go to concerts because my father _____ like classical music.
   - (A) don't . . don't
   - (B) doesn't . . doesn't
   - (C) doesn't . . don't
   - (D) don't . . doesn't

10. My brother _____ very popular. He _____ to a lot of parties.
    - (A) is . . go
    - (B) does . . go
    - (C) is . . goes
    - (D) does . . goes

11. I _____ comedies, and my sister _____ dramas.
    - (A) like . . like
    - (B) like . . likes
    - (C) likes . . likes
    - (D) likes . . like

1 (A) (B) (C) (D) 4 (A) (B) (C) (D) 7 (A) (B) (C) (D) 10 (A) (B) (C) (D)

2 (A) (B) (C) (D) 5 (A) (B) (C) (D) 8 (A) (B) (C) (D) 11 (A) (B) (C) (D)

3 (A) (B) (C) (D) 6 (A) (B) (C) (D) 9 (A) (B) (C) (D)

Go to the next page

B GRAMMAR IN CONTEXT: Ordering in a Fast Food Restaurant

Read the story. Then choose the correct answer to complete each conversation.

Fran's Fast Food Restaurant is a very special place. Every day Fran cooks a different kind of fast food. On Monday she cooks hamburgers. On Tuesday she cooks cheeseburgers. On Wednesday she makes tacos. On Thursday she makes pizza. On Friday she cooks chicken. On Saturday she cooks hot dogs. And on Sunday she makes sandwiches.

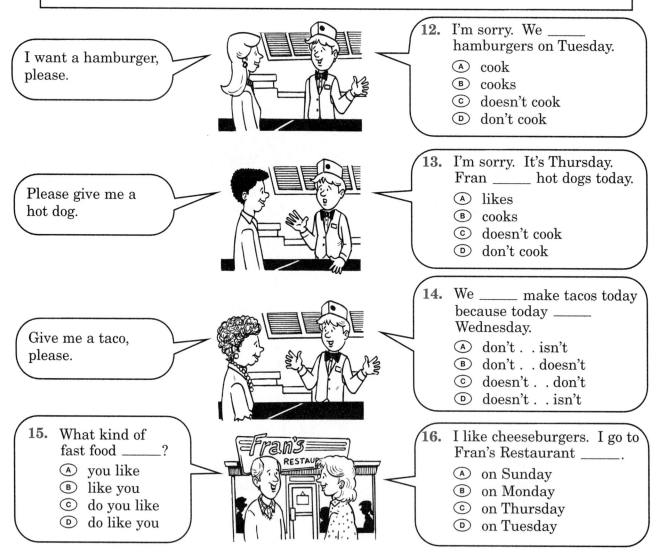

I want a hamburger, please.

12. I'm sorry. We _____ hamburgers on Tuesday.

Ⓐ cook
Ⓑ cooks
Ⓒ doesn't cook
Ⓓ don't cook

Please give me a hot dog.

13. I'm sorry. It's Thursday. Fran _____ hot dogs today.

Ⓐ likes
Ⓑ cooks
Ⓒ doesn't cook
Ⓓ don't cook

Give me a taco, please.

14. We _____ make tacos today because today _____ Wednesday.

Ⓐ don't . . isn't
Ⓑ don't . . doesn't
Ⓒ doesn't . . don't
Ⓓ doesn't . . isn't

15. What kind of fast food _____?

Ⓐ you like
Ⓑ like you
Ⓒ do you like
Ⓓ do like you

Fran's RESTAU

16. I like cheeseburgers. I go to Fran's Restaurant _____.

Ⓐ on Sunday
Ⓑ on Monday
Ⓒ on Thursday
Ⓓ on Tuesday

12 Ⓐ Ⓑ Ⓒ Ⓓ 14 Ⓐ Ⓑ Ⓒ Ⓓ 16 Ⓐ Ⓑ Ⓒ Ⓓ
13 Ⓐ Ⓑ Ⓒ Ⓓ 15 Ⓐ Ⓑ Ⓒ Ⓓ

Go to the next page

Name ______________________________ Date ______________

C LISTENING ASSESSMENT

Read and listen to the questions. Then listen to the story, and answer the questions.

17. What do they do on Tuesday?
    - (A) They jog.
    - (B) They play tennis.
    - (C) They play golf.
    - (D) They play basketball.

18. Do they ride their bikes on Wednesday?
    - (A) Yes, he does.
    - (B) Yes, she does.
    - (C) Yes, they do.
    - (D) No, they don't.

19. What do they do on Friday?
    - (A) They play golf.
    - (B) They play basketball.
    - (C) He plays golf, and she plays basketball.
    - (D) She plays golf, and he plays basketball.

20. What do they do on the weekend?
    - (A) She does yoga, and he swims.
    - (B) They jog.
    - (C) They go to a health club.
    - (D) They're very athletic people.

D WRITING & GRAMMAR ASSESSMENT

Write the correct words to complete the sentences.

1.  I ___live___ in New York.  He ___lives___ in Los Angeles.

2.  I __________ in a bank.  She __________ in an office.

3.  I __________ a taxi.  He __________ a bus.

4.  I __________ the piano.  She __________ the violin.

5.  I __________ the newspaper.  He __________ books.

6.  I __________ to movies.  She __________ to concerts.

7.  I __________ English. 

He __________ Spanish.

8.  I __________ TV.  She __________ videos.

17 (A) (B) (C) (D)   19 (A) (B) (C) (D)

18 (A) (B) (C) (D)   20 (A) (B) (C) (D)

Go to the next page

E WRITING ASSESSMENT: Days of the Week

Look at the abbreviation. Write the correct day of the week.

MON ____Monday____ THU ______________

FRI ______________ SUN ______________

TUE ______________ WED ______________

SAT ______________

F WRITING ASSESSMENT: Recreation & Entertainment Activities

What do you do on the weekend? How do you spend your time? Write a paragraph about it.

....

....

....

....

....

....

G SPEAKING ASSESSMENT

I can ask and answer these questions:

Ask Answer

☐ ☐ What do you do during the week?
☐ ☐ What do you do on the weekend?

☐ ☐ Do you like Italian/ Greek / Chinese / Puerto Rican / Japanese / Mexican / American food?
☐ ☐ What kind of food do you like?

☐ ☐ Do you like comedies / dramas / westerns / adventure movies / science fiction movies / cartoons?
☐ ☐ What kind of movies do you like?

☐ ☐ Do you like novels / poetry / short stories / non-fiction / biographies?
☐ ☐ What kind of books do you like?

☐ ☐ Do you like comedies / dramas / cartoons / game shows / news programs?
☐ ☐ What kind of TV programs do you like?

☐ ☐ Do you like classical music / popular music / jazz / rock music / country music?
☐ ☐ What kind of music do you like?

☐ ☐ Do you like football / baseball / soccer / golf / hockey / tennis?
☐ ☐ What kind of sports do you like?

STOP

Name ____________________

Date ____________ Class ____________

11

A FAMILY RELATIONS

Choose the correct answer.

1. My grandparents live in Chicago. We call _____ every Sunday.
   - (A) him
   - (B) her
   - (C) us
   - (D) them

2. My uncle is in the hospital. My aunt visits _____ there every day.
   - (A) him
   - (B) her
   - (C) me
   - (D) them

3. Our son's wife is very nice. We like _____ very much.
   - (A) it
   - (B) him
   - (C) her
   - (D) them

4. My father usually washes his car on Thursday. He rarely washes _____ on Friday.
   - (A) her
   - (B) him
   - (C) it
   - (D) them

5. We talk to our daughter every weekend. She always calls _____ on Saturday.
   - (A) him
   - (B) us
   - (C) we
   - (D) her

6. You're my very close friend. I think about _____ all the time.
   - (A) me
   - (B) your
   - (C) you
   - (D) them

7. My sister always studies in the library. She _____ studies in her room.
   - (A) always
   - (B) usually
   - (C) sometimes
   - (D) never

8. My parents _____ a small apartment.
   - (A) has
   - (B) live
   - (C) in
   - (D) have

9. Their son _____ brown hair.
   - (A) has
   - (B) have
   - (C) is
   - (D) his

10. Our neighbors _____ a new satellite dish.
    - (A) are
    - (B) never
    - (C) has
    - (D) have

11. I _____ one sister. My sister _____ blue eyes.
    - (A) have . . have
    - (B) has . . have
    - (C) have . . has
    - (D) have . . is

12. My brother _____ curly hair. My sisters _____ straight hair.
    - (A) have . . have
    - (B) has . . have
    - (C) have . . has
    - (D) has . . has

1	(A) (B) (C) (D)	4	(A) (B) (C) (D)	7	(A) (B) (C) (D)	10	(A) (B) (C) (D)
2	(A) (B) (C) (D)	5	(A) (B) (C) (D)	8	(A) (B) (C) (D)	11	(A) (B) (C) (D)
3	(A) (B) (C) (D)	6	(A) (B) (C) (D)	9	(A) (B) (C) (D)	12	(A) (B) (C) (D)

Go to the next page

B GRAMMAR IN CONTEXT: Asking for Tableware • Describing Oneself

Choose the correct answer to complete the conversation.

Excuse me. I need a fork and knife, please.

13. Here you are. _____ eat pizza with a fork and knife?
   - Ⓐ You usually
   - Ⓑ You do usually
   - Ⓒ Do you usually
   - Ⓓ Do usually

14. Yes. _____ a spoon for my granddaughter?
   - Ⓐ You have
   - Ⓑ Do you have
   - Ⓒ You do have
   - Ⓓ Do have

15. Yes. _____ eat spaghetti with a spoon?
   - Ⓐ Always
   - Ⓑ She always
   - Ⓒ Is she always
   - Ⓓ Does she always

Yes. Always.

16. _____ look like?
   - Ⓐ Who you
   - Ⓑ Who do you
   - Ⓒ Do you
   - Ⓓ How often do you

17. I look like my brother. We both have _____ hair.
   - Ⓐ tall
   - Ⓑ heavy
   - Ⓒ brown
   - Ⓓ different

C LISTENING ASSESSMENT

Read and listen to the questions. Then listen to the story, and answer the questions.

18. How does this person look like her sister?
   - Ⓐ They're both short.
   - Ⓑ They both have brown eyes.
   - Ⓒ They both have long hair.
   - Ⓓ They both have brown hair.

19. Where does the teacher live?
   - Ⓐ In the suburbs.
   - Ⓑ In the city.
   - Ⓒ In a small apartment.
   - Ⓓ In a school.

20. What do they do every day?
   - Ⓐ They watch videos.
   - Ⓑ They talk on the telephone.
   - Ⓒ They go to parties.
   - Ⓓ They're very different.

D WRITING ASSESSMENT

Write about yourself and another person. Do you look like this person? Describe how you and this person are different. (Use a separate sheet of paper.)

E SPEAKING ASSESSMENT

I can ask and answer these questions:

Ask	Answer	
☐	☐	Do you have any brothers or sisters?
☐	☐	Tell me about your family. (I have . . .)
☐	☐	Tell me about a family member or a friend:
☐	☐	What's his/her name?
☐	☐	What does he/she look like?
☐	☐	What does he/she do?

13 Ⓐ Ⓑ Ⓒ Ⓓ　15 Ⓐ Ⓑ Ⓒ Ⓓ　17 Ⓐ Ⓑ Ⓒ Ⓓ　19 Ⓐ Ⓑ Ⓒ Ⓓ

14 Ⓐ Ⓑ Ⓒ Ⓓ　16 Ⓐ Ⓑ Ⓒ Ⓓ　18 Ⓐ Ⓑ Ⓒ Ⓓ　20 Ⓐ Ⓑ Ⓒ Ⓓ

STOP

Name ______________________________

Date ______________ Class ______________

12

A DESCRIBING STATES OF BEING

1. Is he happy?
   - (A) No. He's tired.
   - (B) No. He's angry.
   - (C) No. He's sad.
   - (D) No. He's nervous.

2. Is she hungry?
   - (A) No. She's happy.
   - (B) No. She's thirsty.
   - (C) No. She's cold.
   - (D) No. She's scared.

3. Is he tired?
   - (A) No. He's scared.
   - (B) No. He's sick.
   - (C) No. He's hungry.
   - (D) No. He's angry.

4. Are they cold?
   - (A) Yes. They cry.
   - (B) Yes. They're crying.
   - (C) Yes. They shiver.
   - (D) Yes. They're shivering.

5. Why are you perspiring?
   - (A) I'm cold.
   - (B) I'm happy.
   - (C) I'm hot.
   - (D) I'm angry.

6. What do you do when you're tired?
   - (A) I yawn.
   - (B) I'm yawning.
   - (C) We're smiling.
   - (D) You shout.

7. _____ when I'm nervous.
   - (A) I'm blushing
   - (B) I'm perspiring
   - (C) I'm biting my nails
   - (D) I always bite my nails

8. _____ because she's happy today.
   - (A) She smiles
   - (B) She's smiling
   - (C) She always smiles
   - (D) She never smiles

B GRAMMAR IN CONTEXT: Asking About Home Activities

9. _____ doing?
   - (A) What do you
   - (B) What are you
   - (C) Why do you
   - (D) Why are you

10. _____ the rug with a broom.
   - (A) I sweep
   - (B) I walk
   - (C) I'm sweeping
   - (D) I'm walking

11. _____ the rug with a broom?
   - (A) Are you usually walking
   - (B) Are you usually sleeping
   - (C) Do you usually walk
   - (D) Do you usually sweep

12. No. My _____ is broken.
   - (A) vacuum
   - (B) flashlight
   - (C) hammer
   - (D) computer

1 (A) (B) (C) (D)	4 (A) (B) (C) (D)	7 (A) (B) (C) (D)	10 (A) (B) (C) (D)
2 (A) (B) (C) (D)	5 (A) (B) (C) (D)	8 (A) (B) (C) (D)	11 (A) (B) (C) (D)
3 (A) (B) (C) (D)	6 (A) (B) (C) (D)	9 (A) (B) (C) (D)	12 (A) (B) (C) (D)

Go to the next page

C READING

Read the story. Then answer the questions.

It isn't a typical Monday morning at the Lane family's apartment. Mr. Lane usually takes the train to his laboratory, but he isn't taking the train today. Mrs. Lane usually drives to her office, but she isn't driving there today. Jimmy and Jennifer Lane usually take the bus to school, but they aren't taking the bus today. And Julie Lane usually rides her bicycle to her job at the shopping mall, but she isn't riding her bicycle there today. It's snowing very hard this morning. The streets are empty, and the city is quiet. Everybody in town is staying home.

13. Who usually goes to work in a car?
   - Ⓐ Mr. Lane.
   - Ⓑ Mrs. Lane.
   - Ⓒ Jimmy Lane.
   - Ⓓ Julie Lane.

14. How do the young children in the family usually go to school?
   - Ⓐ They take the train.
   - Ⓑ They're taking the train.
   - Ⓒ They take the bus.
   - Ⓓ They're taking the bus.

15. Who works in a store?
   - Ⓐ Mr. Lane.
   - Ⓑ Mrs. Lane.
   - Ⓒ Jennifer Lane.
   - Ⓓ Julie Lane.

16. Why is everybody in town staying home this morning?
   - Ⓐ The streets are empty.
   - Ⓑ The city is quiet.
   - Ⓒ It's snowing.
   - Ⓓ It's cold.

D LISTENING ASSESSMENT

Read and listen to the questions. Then listen to the conversation, and answer the questions.

17. What does Wanda do at the office?
   - Ⓐ She answers the telephone.
   - Ⓑ She sorts the mail.
   - Ⓒ She cleans the office.
   - Ⓓ She types all the letters.

18. Who cleans the office?
   - Ⓐ Ken.
   - Ⓑ Mrs. Kent.
   - Ⓒ George.
   - Ⓓ Nancy.

19. What's Nancy's job?
   - Ⓐ She's sick today.
   - Ⓑ She's at home with the flu.
   - Ⓒ She usually types letters.
   - Ⓓ She's typing letters today.

20. Where's Mrs. Kent?
   - Ⓐ She's with the president.
   - Ⓑ She's at home with the flu.
   - Ⓒ She's the boss.
   - Ⓓ She's at the dentist.

E WRITING ASSESSMENT: States of Being

What do you usually do when you're happy? sad? tired? hungry? thirsty? Write about it on a separate sheet of paper.

F SPEAKING ASSESSMENT

I can ask and answer these questions:

Ask	Answer	
☐	☐	Are you hungry?
☐	☐	Are you thirsty?
☐	☐	Are you happy/sad/tired?
☐	☐	Why are you happy/sad/tired?

Ask	Answer	
☐	☐	How do you go to school?
☐	☐	Do you drive a car?
☐	☐	Do you take a bus/train?
☐	☐	Do you walk?
☐	☐	Do you ride a bicycle?

13 Ⓐ Ⓑ Ⓒ Ⓓ 15 Ⓐ Ⓑ Ⓒ Ⓓ 17 Ⓐ Ⓑ Ⓒ Ⓓ 19 Ⓐ Ⓑ Ⓒ Ⓓ

14 Ⓐ Ⓑ Ⓒ Ⓓ 16 Ⓐ Ⓑ Ⓒ Ⓓ 18 Ⓐ Ⓑ Ⓒ Ⓓ 20 Ⓐ Ⓑ Ⓒ Ⓓ

Name ______________________________

Date ____________________ Class ____________________

13

A OCCUPATIONS, ABILITIES, & SKILLS

1. What's his job?
   - (A) He's a teacher.
   - (B) He's a singer.
   - (C) He's a baker.
   - (D) He's an actor.

2. What's her occupation?
   - (A) She's a dancer.
   - (B) She's a chef.
   - (C) She's a secretary.
   - (D) She's a mechanic.

3. Can he type?
   Yes. He's _____.
   - (A) a superintendent
   - (B) a secretary
   - (C) a salesperson
   - (D) a computer

4. What can you do?
   I can _____.
   - (A) use a cash register
   - (B) use a calculator
   - (C) use business software
   - (D) use a computer

5. I can cook.
   - (A) I'm a construction worker.
   - (B) I'm a chef.
   - (C) I'm a mechanic.
   - (D) I'm a driver.

6. She can talk to customers.
   - (A) She's a teacher.
   - (B) She's a singer.
   - (C) She's a salesperson.
   - (D) She's a dancer.

7. He can build things.
   - (A) He's a mechanic.
   - (B) He's a salesperson.
   - (C) He's a building superintendent.
   - (D) He's a construction worker.

8. Tell me about your skills.
   - (A) I'm looking for work.
   - (B) I'm looking for a job as a secretary.
   - (C) I can file and type.
   - (D) I'm a salesperson.

B GRAMMAR IN CONTEXT: Requesting Permission to Leave Work • Calling to Explain Absence

9. May I leave work early today? _____ go to the doctor.
   - (A) You have
   - (B) You have to
   - (C) I have
   - (D) I have to

10. Okay. _____ leave early.
    - (A) You have to
    - (B) You can
    - (C) I have to
    - (D) I can

11. I'm sorry. _____ come to work today. I'm sick.
    - (A) You can
    - (B) I can
    - (C) I can't
    - (D) I have to

12. That's okay. _____ come to work.
    - (A) Don't have to
    - (B) You don't have to
    - (C) I have to
    - (D) I don't have to

1 (A) (B) (C) (D)	4 (A) (B) (C) (D)	7 (A) (B) (C) (D)	10 (A) (B) (C) (D)
2 (A) (B) (C) (D)	5 (A) (B) (C) (D)	8 (A) (B) (C) (D)	11 (A) (B) (C) (D)
3 (A) (B) (C) (D)	6 (A) (B) (C) (D)	9 (A) (B) (C) (D)	12 (A) (B) (C) (D)

Go to the next page

C READING: "Help Wanted" Sign

Read the sign. Then answer the questions.

NOW HIRING!

- Looking for new employees.
- Days or eves
- FT & PT
- $9.00 / hr.

Ask cashier in store for application form

13. What's the salary?
    - Ⓐ Nine dollars per week.
    - Ⓑ Nine dollars per month.
    - Ⓒ Nine dollars per hour.
    - Ⓓ Nine dollars per year.

14. What kind of jobs are there?
    - Ⓐ Only jobs during the day.
    - Ⓑ Only jobs during the evening.
    - Ⓒ Only jobs for cashiers.
    - Ⓓ Full-time jobs and part-time jobs.

15. What does a person have to do to apply for a job there?
    - Ⓐ Fill out an application form.
    - Ⓑ Work days and evenings.
    - Ⓒ Look for new employees.
    - Ⓓ Talk with the president of the company.

D READING: Classified Ads

Read the job advertisements. Then answer the questions.

HELP WANTED

BAKER
Small bakery. M–F. Full-time. Apply in person. G&R Pastry Shop. 700 Central Ave.

Secretary
Large office. Call Mary at 262-7910.

CASHIERS
Large supermarket. FT & PT. Days & eves. 420 Main St. Apply in person. Ask for Ray.

16. Chet can type and file. He's applying for a job. What does he have to do?
    - Ⓐ He has to go to 700 Central Avenue.
    - Ⓑ He has to go to 420 Main Street.
    - Ⓒ He has to talk with Ray.
    - Ⓓ He has to call 262-7910.

17. Sheila can use a cash register. She's applying for a job. What does she have to do?
    - Ⓐ She has to work full-time.
    - Ⓑ She has to go to 420 Main Street.
    - Ⓒ She has to call Mary.
    - Ⓓ She has to work part-time.

E LISTENING ASSESSMENT

Read and listen to the questions. Then listen to the job interview, and answer the questions.

18. Where is the job interview taking place?
    - Ⓐ In a restaurant.
    - Ⓑ In a bank.
    - Ⓒ In a store.
    - Ⓓ In a computer company.

19. What can David do?
    - Ⓐ He can paint.
    - Ⓑ He can take inventory.
    - Ⓒ He can teach.
    - Ⓓ He can use tools.

20. David doesn't have one skill. What can't he do?
    - Ⓐ Take inventory.
    - Ⓑ Use a cash register.
    - Ⓒ Talk to customers.
    - Ⓓ Operate business software.

13 Ⓐ Ⓑ Ⓒ Ⓓ 15 Ⓐ Ⓑ Ⓒ Ⓓ 17 Ⓐ Ⓑ Ⓒ Ⓓ 19 Ⓐ Ⓑ Ⓒ Ⓓ

14 Ⓐ Ⓑ Ⓒ Ⓓ 16 Ⓐ Ⓑ Ⓒ Ⓓ 18 Ⓐ Ⓑ Ⓒ Ⓓ 20 Ⓐ Ⓑ Ⓒ Ⓓ

Go to the next page

Name ______________________ Date __________

F WRITING: Job Application Form

Complete this form about yourself.

Name: ______________________ Social Security No. ______________

Street: ______________________ Apartment: __________

City: ______________________ State: ______ Zip Code: __________

Telephone: ______________________

Skills and Abilities:

What can you do? Describe your skills and abilities:

____

____

____

Work Experience:

Job	Company	From	To

Education:

School	City, State	From	To

Date: ______________ Signature: ______________________

Go to the next page

G POLICE/SAFETY COMMANDS & SIGNS

For each command, choose the correct sign.

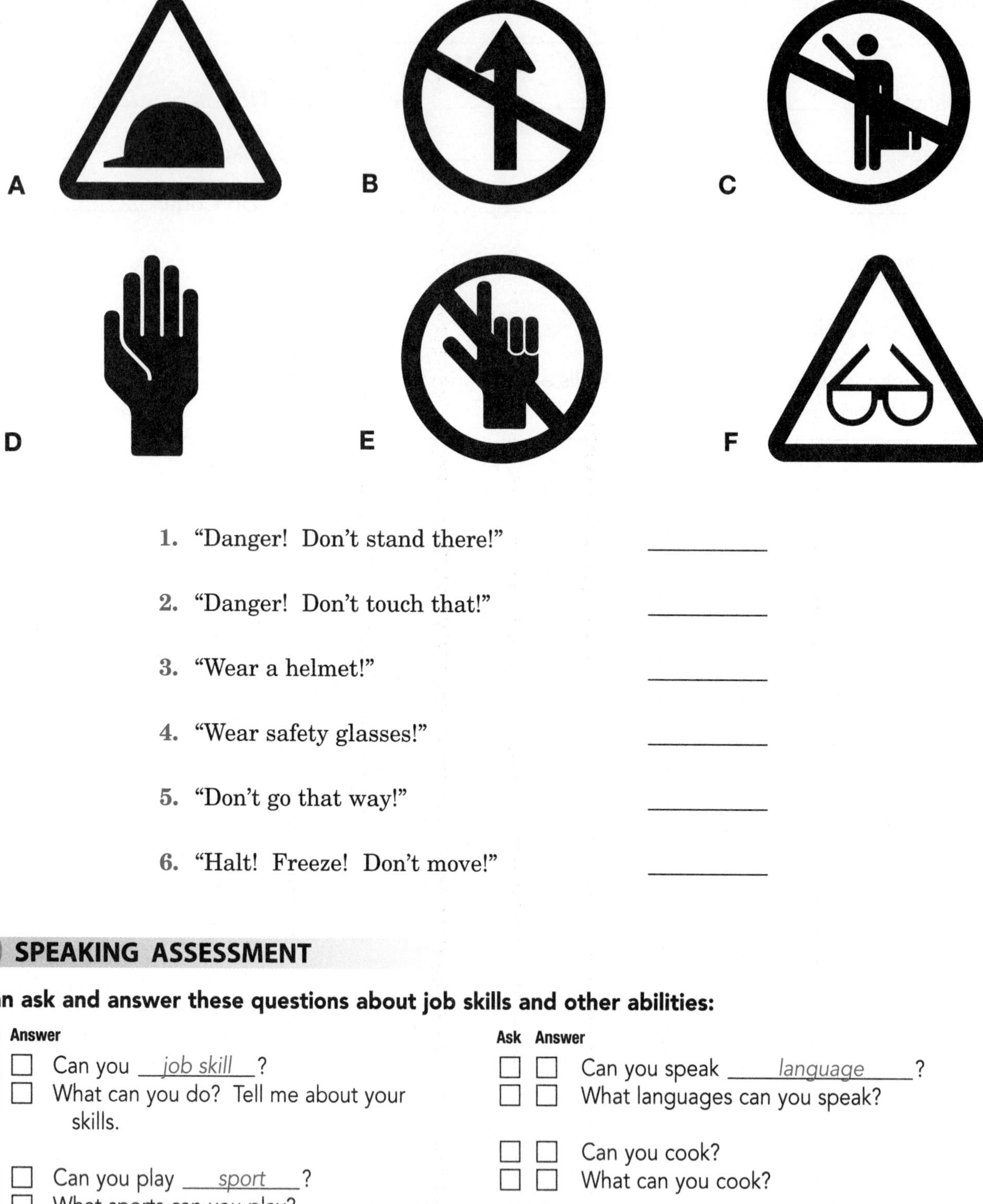

1. "Danger! Don't stand there!" ________
2. "Danger! Don't touch that!" ________
3. "Wear a helmet!" ________
4. "Wear safety glasses!" ________
5. "Don't go that way!" ________
6. "Halt! Freeze! Don't move!" ________

H SPEAKING ASSESSMENT

I can ask and answer these questions about job skills and other abilities:

Ask	Answer	
☐	☐	Can you *job skill* ?
☐	☐	What can you do? Tell me about your skills.
☐	☐	Can you play *sport* ?
☐	☐	What sports can you play?
☐	☐	Can you play *musical instrument* ?
☐	☐	What musical instrument can you play?

Ask	Answer	
☐	☐	Can you speak *language* ?
☐	☐	What languages can you speak?
☐	☐	Can you cook?
☐	☐	What can you cook?

STOP

Name ______________________________

Date ______________ Class ______________

14

A TIME

1. It's ____.
   - (A) 7:00
   - (B) 8:00
   - (C) 6:30
   - (D) 7:30

2. It's ____.
   - (A) 11:15
   - (B) 11:45
   - (C) 9:00
   - (D) 9:45

3. It's ____.
   - (A) a quarter to five
   - (B) half past six
   - (C) half past five
   - (D) a quarter to six

4. The time is ____.
   - (A) a quarter to three
   - (B) a quarter to four
   - (C) half past three
   - (D) half past four

5. What's the weather forecast for tomorrow?
   - (A) It rains.
   - (B) It's raining.
   - (C) It's going to rain.
   - (D) I'm going to go to the beach.

6. What are you going to do tomorrow?
   - (A) We're going to clean our apartment.
   - (B) He's going to cook.
   - (C) It's going to be cloudy.
   - (D) They're going to have a picnic.

7. What time does the train leave?
   - (A) It begins at 6:00.
   - (B) It's 6:00.
   - (C) It's going to leave.
   - (D) At 6:00.

8. What's the date?
   - (A) It's 4:00.
   - (B) It's Thursday.
   - (C) It's April 10th.
   - (D) It's spring.

B GRAMMAR IN CONTEXT: Asking & Telling Time • Congratulating

9. ____ is it?
   - (A) What time
   - (B) What's the time
   - (C) Tell the time
   - (D) Tell me the time

10. ______________
   - (A) It's sunny and warm.
   - (B) It's two o'clock.
   - (C) I'm going to study.
   - (D) It's November 4th.

11. ____ August 31st. Today is my birthday!
   - (A) Today
   - (B) It
   - (C) It's
   - (D) I'm

12. Congratulations! ______
   - (A) Oh no!
   - (B) Happy New Year!
   - (C) Happy Thanksgiving!
   - (D) Happy Birthday!

AUG 31

1 (A) (B) (C) (D)	4 (A) (B) (C) (D)	7 (A) (B) (C) (D)	10 (A) (B) (C) (D)
2 (A) (B) (C) (D)	5 (A) (B) (C) (D)	8 (A) (B) (C) (D)	11 (A) (B) (C) (D)
3 (A) (B) (C) (D)	6 (A) (B) (C) (D)	9 (A) (B) (C) (D)	12 (A) (B) (C) (D)

Go to the next page

C READING: National Holidays in the United States & Canada

Read the story. Then answer the questions.

Some holidays in the United States and Canada are on the same date every year. New Year's Day is always on January 1st. Christmas Day is always on December 25th. Canadians always celebrate Canada Day on July 1st, and people in the United States always celebrate Independence Day on July 4th. Veterans Day in the U.S. and Remembrance Day in Canada are always on November 11th.

Other holidays are on different dates every year because these holidays are on certain days of the week. For example, in the U.S. and Canada, Labor Day is always on the first Monday in September. Thanksgiving Day in the U.S. is always on the fourth Thursday in November. In Canada, Thanksgiving Day is on the second Monday in October. Many other U.S. holidays are always on Monday: Martin Luther King, Jr. Day in January, Presidents' Day in February, Memorial Day in May, and Columbus Day in October.

13. Which holiday is in September?

- Ⓐ Presidents' Day.
- Ⓑ Memorial Day.
- Ⓒ Columbus Day.
- Ⓓ Labor Day.

14. Which holiday is always on the same date every year?

- Ⓐ Thanksgiving Day.
- Ⓑ Labor Day.
- Ⓒ New Year's Day.
- Ⓓ Memorial Day.

15. Which sentence is correct?

- Ⓐ New Year's Day is always on Monday.
- Ⓑ Memorial Day in the U.S. is always on Monday.
- Ⓒ Canada Day is in June.
- Ⓓ Christmas Day is on December 24th.

16. Which sentence is <u>not</u> correct?

- Ⓐ Canada and the U.S. celebrate Labor Day on the same day.
- Ⓑ Canada and the U.S. have a holiday on November 11th.
- Ⓒ New Year's Day is on the first day of January.
- Ⓓ Canada and the U.S. celebrate Thanksgiving on the same day.

D LISTENING ASSESSMENT

Read and listen to the questions. Then listen to the story, and answer the questions.

17. What's he going to do in March?

- Ⓐ He's going to start a new job.
- Ⓑ He's going to move.
- Ⓒ He's going to get married.
- Ⓓ He's going to have a birthday party.

18. When is he going to begin to study at a computer school?

- Ⓐ In January.
- Ⓑ In June.
- Ⓒ In September.
- Ⓓ In December.

19. Where is he going to work?

- Ⓐ In an office.
- Ⓑ In a new apartment building.
- Ⓒ In a computer school.
- Ⓓ In Honolulu.

20. How old is he going to be in June?

- Ⓐ 13 years old.
- Ⓑ 23 years old.
- Ⓒ 30 years old.
- Ⓓ 40 years old.

13	Ⓐ Ⓑ Ⓒ Ⓓ	16	Ⓐ Ⓑ Ⓒ Ⓓ	19	Ⓐ Ⓑ Ⓒ Ⓓ
14	Ⓐ Ⓑ Ⓒ Ⓓ	17	Ⓐ Ⓑ Ⓒ Ⓓ	20	Ⓐ Ⓑ Ⓒ Ⓓ
15	Ⓐ Ⓑ Ⓒ Ⓓ	18	Ⓐ Ⓑ Ⓒ Ⓓ		

Go to the next page

Name ______________________ Date ______________

E THE CALENDAR

2009

January

S	M	T	W	T	F	S
			1	2	3	4
5	6	7	8	9	10	11
12	13	14	15	16	17	18
19	20	21	22	23	24	25
26	27	28	29	30	31	

February

S	M	T	W	T	F	S
						1
2	3	4	5	6	7	8
9	10	11	12	13	14	15
16	17	18	19	20	21	22
23	24	25	26	27	28	

March

S	M	T	W	T	F	S
						1
2	3	4	5	6	7	8
9	10	11	12	13	14	15
16	17	18	19	20	21	22
23/30	24/31	25	26	27	28	29

April

S	M	T	W	T	F	S
		1	2	3	4	5
6	7	8	9	10	11	12
13	14	15	16	17	18	19
20	21	22	23	24	25	26
27	28	29	30			

May

S	M	T	W	T	F	S
				1	2	3
4	5	6	7	8	9	10
11	12	13	14	15	16	17
18	19	20	21	22	23	24
25	26	27	28	29	30	31

June

S	M	T	W	T	F	S
1	2	3	4	5	6	7
8	9	10	11	12	13	14
15	16	17	18	19	20	21
22	23	24	25	26	27	28
29	30					

July

S	M	T	W	T	F	S
		1	2	3	4	5
6	7	8	9	10	11	12
13	14	15	16	17	18	19
20	21	22	23	24	25	26
27	28	29	30	31		

August

S	M	T	W	T	F	S
					1	2
3	4	5	6	7	8	9
10	11	12	13	14	15	16
17	18	19	20	21	22	23
24/31	25	26	27	28	29	30

September

S	M	T	W	T	F	S
	1	2	3	4	5	6
7	8	9	10	11	12	13
14	15	16	17	18	19	20
21	22	23	24	25	26	27
28	29	30				

October

S	M	T	W	T	F	S
			1	2	3	4
5	6	7	8	9	10	11
12	13	14	15	16	17	18
19	20	21	22	23	24	25
26	27	28	29	30	31	

November

S	M	T	W	T	F	S
						1
2	3	4	5	6	7	8
9	10	11	12	13	14	15
16	17	18	19	20	21	22
23/30	24	25	26	27	28	29

December

S	M	T	W	T	F	S
	1	2	3	4	5	6
7	8	9	10	11	12	13
14	15	16	17	18	19	20
21	22	23	24	25	26	27
28	29	30	31			

Circle these dates on the calendar.

March 7	June 2nd
September 25	5/13/09
April 15th	8/20/09
January 23rd	10/31/09

On this calendar, what day of the week is . . .

July 4th	Friday	11/16/09	______
February 10th	______	1/14/09	______
May 22nd	______	3/5/09	______

F ORDINAL NUMBERS

1st	11th	21st
2nd	12th	22nd
3rd	13th	23rd
4th	14th	24th
5th	15th	25th
6th	16th	26th
7th	17th	27th
8th	18th	28th
9th	19th	29th
10th	20th	30th

Write the correct ordinal number.

third	______	seventh	______
fifteenth	______	twenty-first	______
second	______	twelfth	______
thirtieth	______	eighteenth	______

G WRITING ASSESSMENT: Months of the Year

Look at the abbreviation. Write the correct month of the year.

MAR ______	DEC ______	APR ______
AUG ______	FEB ______	JUN ______
NOV ______	JAN ______	MAY ______
SEP ______	OCT ______	JUL ______

Go to the next page

H CLOCK TIMES

2:00	______	______	______	______

I WRITING ASSESSMENT: Fill Out the Forms

First Name: ____________ Last Name: ____________

Date of Birth: ____________ Place of Birth: ____________

Signature: ____________ Today's Date: ____________

Last Name: ____________ First Name: ____________

Date of Birth: ___ Month ___ Day ___ Year Today's Date: ___ Month ___ Day ___ Year Signature: ____________

J WRITING ASSESSMENT: Day & Date

What day is it? ....

What's today's date? ....

K WRITING ASSESSMENT: Future Plans

What are you going to do tomorrow? Tell about five or more things you are going to do. Use a separate sheet of paper.

L SPEAKING ASSESSMENT

I can ask and answer questions about dates, time, and weather:

Ask	Answer	
☐	☐	What day is it today?
☐	☐	What's today's date? What's the date today?
☐	☐	What day is it tomorrow?
☐	☐	What's tomorrow's date?
☐	☐	What time is it?
☐	☐	What's your birthdate?
☐	☐	What's the weather forecast for tomorrow?

I can ask and answer questions about common activities and time:

What time do you usually . . .

Ask	Answer	
☐	☐	get up?
☐	☐	eat breakfast?
☐	☐	go to school?
☐	☐	eat lunch?
☐	☐	eat dinner?
☐	☐	go to bed?

What time are you going to . . .

Ask	Answer	
☐	☐	get up tomorrow?
☐	☐	eat breakfast tomorrow?
☐	☐	go to school tomorrow?
☐	☐	eat lunch tomorrow?
☐	☐	eat dinner tomorrow?
☐	☐	go to bed tomorrow?

STOP

Name ______________________________

Date ______________ Class ______________

15

A MEDICAL CARE: Parts of the Body & Ailments

Choose the correct answer.

Example:

Her _____ hurts. She has _____.

Ⓐ throat . . a sore throat
Ⓑ ear . . an earache
● head . . a headache
Ⓓ tooth . . a toothache

1. Her _____ hurts. She has _____.

Ⓐ back . . a backache
Ⓑ ear . . an earache
Ⓒ stomach . . a stomachache
Ⓓ throat . . a sore throat

2. He has _____. He wants some _____.

Ⓐ a fever . . cold
Ⓑ a toothache . . candy
Ⓒ a cold . . hot dogs
Ⓓ a cold . . cold medicine

3. He has _____. He wants some _____.

Ⓐ a cough . . cough syrup
Ⓑ a stomachache . . antacid tablets
Ⓒ an earache . . ear drops
Ⓓ a headache . . aspirin

4. Betsy has a stomachache because she _____ all day yesterday.

Ⓐ eats cookies
Ⓑ ate cookies
Ⓒ rests
Ⓓ rested

5. Robert has a backache because he _____ all day.

Ⓐ talked
Ⓑ sang
Ⓒ planted flowers
Ⓓ cried

6. Peggy has a sore throat because she _____ all day.

Ⓐ shouted
Ⓑ listened to loud music
Ⓒ rode her bike
Ⓓ studied

7. Carl called the _____ because he has _____.

Ⓐ doctor's office . . a fever
Ⓑ doctor's office . . a toothache
Ⓒ dentist's office . . a fever
Ⓓ dentist's office . . a toothache

1 Ⓐ Ⓑ Ⓒ Ⓓ	3 Ⓐ Ⓑ Ⓒ Ⓓ	5 Ⓐ Ⓑ Ⓒ Ⓓ	7 Ⓐ Ⓑ Ⓒ Ⓓ
2 Ⓐ Ⓑ Ⓒ Ⓓ	4 Ⓐ Ⓑ Ⓒ Ⓓ	6 Ⓐ Ⓑ Ⓒ Ⓓ	

Go to the next page

B GRAMMAR IN CONTEXT: Calling for Medical Appointments & Emergency Assistance

Choose the correct answer to complete the conversation.

Example:

_____ Doctor Carter, please?

- Ⓐ Are you
- Ⓑ This is
- Ⓒ May you speak with
- ● May I speak with

8. _____

- Ⓐ Who's calling?
- Ⓑ Who called?
- Ⓒ Who do you call?
- Ⓓ How do you feel?

9. _____ Ted Rogers. I have a terrible backache.

- Ⓐ You are
- Ⓑ He's
- Ⓒ This is
- Ⓓ Hello

10. I'm _____ to hear that.

- Ⓐ glad
- Ⓑ fine
- Ⓒ okay
- Ⓓ sorry

11. Can I _____?

- Ⓐ seem to be the problem
- Ⓑ make an appointment
- Ⓒ feel fine
- Ⓓ what's the matter

12. Yes. Please _____ tomorrow at 2:00.

- Ⓐ hear that
- Ⓑ feel okay
- Ⓒ come in
- Ⓓ get it

13. This is an emergency! My grandfather _____!

- Ⓐ is very tired
- Ⓑ has a cold
- Ⓒ is very sick
- Ⓓ has a toothache

14. _____

- Ⓐ How does he feel today?
- Ⓑ How did he get it?
- Ⓒ Can you come in next Thursday?
- Ⓓ What's the matter?

15. I don't know. He ate dinner, and now he feels _____. And he can't talk.

- Ⓐ sorry
- Ⓑ so-so
- Ⓒ terrible
- Ⓓ not so good

Okay. An ambulance is on the way.

---

8 Ⓐ Ⓑ Ⓒ Ⓓ	10 Ⓐ Ⓑ Ⓒ Ⓓ	12 Ⓐ Ⓑ Ⓒ Ⓓ	14 Ⓐ Ⓑ Ⓒ Ⓓ
9 Ⓐ Ⓑ Ⓒ Ⓓ	11 Ⓐ Ⓑ Ⓒ Ⓓ	13 Ⓐ Ⓑ Ⓒ Ⓓ	15 Ⓐ Ⓑ Ⓒ Ⓓ

Go to the next page

Name ______________________________ Date ______________

C READING: Over-the-Counter Medications

Read the drug store directory. Choose the correct answer to complete each conversation.

DISCOUNT MEDICAL PHARMACY STORE DIRECTORY	Aisle
ASPIRIN	1
COUGH SYRUP	2
EAR DROPS	3
COLD MEDICINE	4
THROAT LOZENGES	5
ANTACID TABLETS	6

Can you help me? I need something for a sore throat.

16. Look in _____.
    - (A) Aisle 1
    - (B) Aisle 2
    - (C) Aisle 5
    - (D) Aisle 6

Excuse me. Do you have aspirin and other medicine for a headache?

17. Yes. Look in _____.
    - (A) Aisle 1
    - (B) Aisle 3
    - (C) Aisle 4
    - (D) Aisle 6

Excuse me. I'm looking for medicine for a stomachache.

18. _______________
    - (A) Ear drops are in Aisle 3.
    - (B) Antacid tablets are in Aisle 6.
    - (C) Throat lozenges are in Aisle 5.
    - (D) Cold medicine is in Aisle 4.

D LISTENING ASSESSMENT

Read and listen to the questions. Then listen to the conversation at the drug store, and answer the questions.

19. What's the matter with the person?
    - (A) She can't hear that.
    - (B) She sings on the weekend.
    - (C) She's in Aisle Two.
    - (D) She has a sore throat.

20. What's she going to buy?
    - (A) Cough syrup.
    - (B) Throat lozenges.
    - (C) Cough syrup and throat lozenges.
    - (D) Cold medicine.

16 (A) (B) (C) (D) 18 (A) (B) (C) (D) 20 (A) (B) (C) (D)

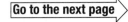

17 (A) (B) (C) (D) 19 (A) (B) (C) (D)

Go to the next page

E DRUG LABELS, DOSAGES, & FILLING/REFILLING PRESCRIPTIONS

For each conversation in the drug store, choose the correct medicine.

tsp. = teaspoon	1x / day = once a day
tab. = tablet	2x / day = twice a day
cap. = capsule	3x / day = 3 times a day

A. 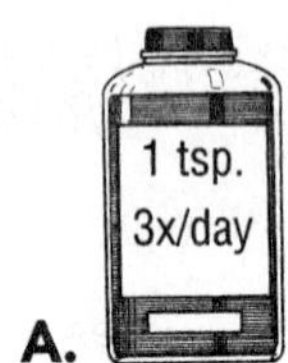

B. 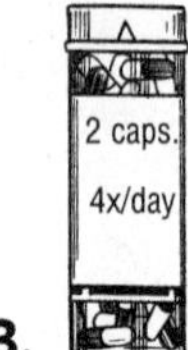

C. 

D. 

E. 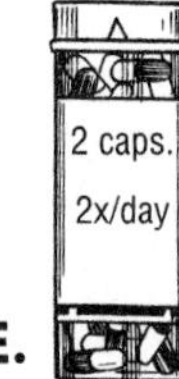

Example:
C — Take one pill twice a day. — One pill twice a day? Okay.

1. ___ Take two capsules four times a day. — I understand. Thank you.

2. ___ Do you understand the directions on the label? — Yes. I can take two capsules twice a day.

3. ___ Can you fill my prescription for cough syrup? — Yes. Please give me the prescription and take a seat. It's going to be about 20 minutes.

4. ___ Can I refill my prescription for these tablets? — Yes. You can refill this prescription one more time.

F INTERPRETING A FAHRENHEIT THERMOMETER & A DOSAGE CUP

Fill in the thermometer to show a normal body temperature of 98.6° F. (98.6 degrees Fahrenheit).

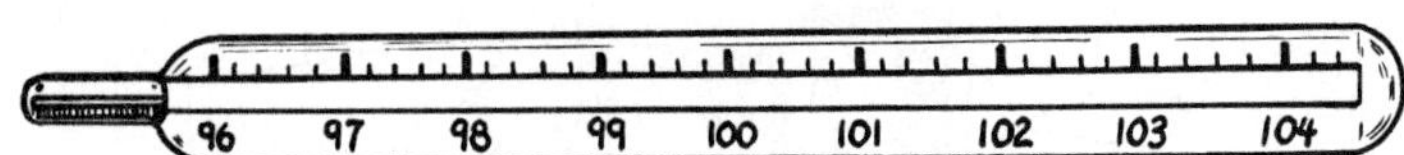

For each drug label, fill in the correct amount of medicine in the dosage cup.

G WRITING ASSESSMENT

Write about your dinner yesterday (or another day). What did you eat? Where? Who cooked the dinner? Who ate with you? Who washed the dishes? Write about it on a separate sheet of paper.

H SPEAKING ASSESSMENT

I can ask and answer these questions:

Ask	Answer	
☐	☐	How do you feel today?
☐	☐	What did you do yesterday?
☐	☐	What did you eat yesterday?
☐	☐	What did you drink yesterday?

STOP

Name ______________________________

Date ______________ Class ______________

16

A COMMON ACTIVITIES IN THE PAST

Choose the correct answer.

Example:

My friends and I _____ a movie last Saturday.

Ⓐ see
Ⓑ did see
Ⓒ saw
Ⓓ did saw

Ⓐ Ⓑ ● Ⓓ

1. He _____ a book yesterday.
   Ⓐ rode
   Ⓑ red
   Ⓒ did read
   Ⓓ read

2. I _____ a bath yesterday evening. I usually _____ a shower.
   Ⓐ took . . took
   Ⓑ took . . take
   Ⓒ take . . took
   Ⓓ take . . take

3. I usually _____ dinner for my family, but yesterday my children _____ dinner.
   Ⓐ make . . make
   Ⓑ made . . make
   Ⓒ make . . made
   Ⓓ made . . made

4. _____ lunch yesterday?
   Ⓐ Did she eat
   Ⓑ Did she ate
   Ⓒ She eat
   Ⓓ She ate

5. _____ to work today?
   Ⓐ Ms. Clark did drive
   Ⓑ Ms. Clark drove
   Ⓒ Did Ms. Clark drive
   Ⓓ Did Ms. Clark drove

6. _____ his homework last night?
   Ⓐ Did your brother
   Ⓑ Did your brother did
   Ⓒ Did your brother do
   Ⓓ Do your brother did

7. What time _____ this morning?
   Ⓐ you got up
   Ⓑ you did get up
   Ⓒ got up you
   Ⓓ did you get up

8. _____ to school yesterday?
   Ⓐ How do they go
   Ⓑ How they do go
   Ⓒ How did they go
   Ⓓ How they did go

9. _____ at the supermarket?
   Ⓐ What did they buy
   Ⓑ What they buy
   Ⓒ What did they bought
   Ⓓ What they bought

10. Did you have a big breakfast today?
    Ⓐ Yes, I do.
    Ⓑ No, I don't.
    Ⓒ Yes, they did.
    Ⓓ No, I didn't.

11. Do you and your sister go to school every day?
    Ⓐ Yes, she does.
    Ⓑ Yes, we do.
    Ⓒ Yes, she did.
    Ⓓ Yes, we did.

1 Ⓐ Ⓑ Ⓒ Ⓓ　4 Ⓐ Ⓑ Ⓒ Ⓓ　7 Ⓐ Ⓑ Ⓒ Ⓓ　10 Ⓐ Ⓑ Ⓒ Ⓓ
2 Ⓐ Ⓑ Ⓒ Ⓓ　5 Ⓐ Ⓑ Ⓒ Ⓓ　8 Ⓐ Ⓑ Ⓒ Ⓓ　11 Ⓐ Ⓑ Ⓒ Ⓓ
3 Ⓐ Ⓑ Ⓒ Ⓓ　6 Ⓐ Ⓑ Ⓒ Ⓓ　9 Ⓐ Ⓑ Ⓒ Ⓓ

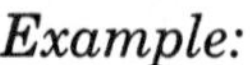

B GRAMMAR IN CONTEXT: Apologizing for Lateness at Work

Choose the correct answer to complete the conversation.

Example:

_____ I'm late.

Ⓐ You're sorry
● I'm sorry
Ⓒ He's sorry
Ⓓ She's sorry

12. _____________

Ⓐ What's going to happen?
Ⓑ What's happening?
Ⓒ What happened?
Ⓓ What happens?

13. I _____ late and I _____ the bus.

Ⓐ get up . . miss
Ⓑ did get up . . did miss
Ⓒ got up . . miss
Ⓓ got up . . missed

14. _____________

Ⓐ You understand.
Ⓑ I see.
Ⓒ You're sorry.
Ⓓ I have good excuses.

C READING: Safety Procedures

Read the safety posters. Then answer the questions on the next page.

Duck, Cover, & Hold!

What to Do At School During an Earthquake

IN A CLASSROOM:

Duck! Get down under a desk or table. (Don't go near windows, bookcases, or other tall furniture.)

Cover! Cover your head with the desk or table. Cover your eyes. (Put your face into your arm.)

Hold! Hold on to the desk or table so it stays over your head. (Furniture can move during an earthquake.)

IN THE HALL:

Drop! Sit on the floor near an inside wall. Get down on your knees. Lean over to rest on your elbows. Put your hands together behind your neck. Put your face down.

OUTSIDE:

Don't go near buildings or walls. Sit down, or use the "Drop" position.

Stop, Drop, Cover, & Roll!

What to Do If Your Clothing Is on Fire

Stop! Stop where you are. Don't run.

Drop! Drop to the ground.

Cover! Cover your face.

Roll! Roll from side to side, over and over, until the fire goes out.

12 Ⓐ Ⓑ Ⓒ Ⓓ 13 Ⓐ Ⓑ Ⓒ Ⓓ 14 Ⓐ Ⓑ Ⓒ Ⓓ

Name ______________________ Date ____________

15. Mr. Gardner's English class had an earthquake drill in their classroom today. What did the students do first?
Ⓐ They covered their eyes.
Ⓑ They went near the windows.
Ⓒ They got down under their desks.
Ⓓ They moved the furniture.

16. What didn't the students do during the earthquake drill?
Ⓐ They didn't cover their heads.
Ⓑ They didn't hold on to their desks.
Ⓒ They didn't cover their eyes.
Ⓓ They didn't roll from side to side.

17. What did students in the hall do during the earthquake drill?
Ⓐ They went to their classrooms.
Ⓑ They went outside.
Ⓒ They sat down near an inside wall.
Ⓓ They rested on the floor.

18. Your clothing is on fire. What are you going to do?
Ⓐ Duck, cover, and hold.
Ⓑ Stop, drop, cover, and roll.
Ⓒ Cover my head with a desk or table.
Ⓓ Run to a window.

D LISTENING ASSESSMENT

Read and listen to the questions. Then listen to the story, and answer the questions.

19. Which meals did she have yesterday?
Ⓐ She had breakfast and dinner.
Ⓑ She had lunch and dinner.
Ⓒ She had breakfast and lunch.
Ⓓ She had breakfast, lunch, and dinner.

20. What did she do at the mall?
Ⓐ She met her friend Bob.
Ⓑ She met her mother.
Ⓒ She ate lunch.
Ⓓ She bought a gift.

E WRITING & GRAMMAR ASSESSMENT

Example:

Did your parents wash their windows today?

No, they didn't.

They washed their car.

1. Did Sally go to the doctor this afternoon?

____

____

2. Did Mr. Lee drive a taxi today?

____

____

3. Did the students take the train to the zoo?

____

____

15 Ⓐ Ⓑ Ⓒ Ⓓ 17 Ⓐ Ⓑ Ⓒ Ⓓ 19 Ⓐ Ⓑ Ⓒ Ⓓ

16 Ⓐ Ⓑ Ⓒ Ⓓ 18 Ⓐ Ⓑ Ⓒ Ⓓ 20 Ⓐ Ⓑ Ⓒ Ⓓ

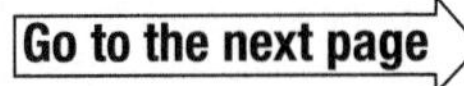

Go to the next page

F EYE CONTACT & GESTURES

For each sentence, choose the correct picture.

A

B

C

D

E

F

1. "I understand." __________
2. "I don't understand." __________
3. "I'm happy to meet you." __________
4. "I have a question." __________
5. "I'd like to introduce my friend." __________
6. "I don't know." __________

G WRITING ASSESSMENT

What did you do yesterday? Write a paragraph about all the things you did. Use a separate sheet of paper.

H SPEAKING ASSESSMENT

I can ask and answer these questions about common activities (using full sentences):

Ask	Answer	
☐	☐	What did you do yesterday?
☐	☐	Did you study English yesterday?
☐	☐	What time did you go to bed last night?
☐	☐	What time did you get up today?
☐	☐	Did you have breakfast this morning?
☐	☐	What did you have for breakfast?
☐	☐	How did you get to school today?
☐	☐	What did you do last weekend?

STOP

Name ______________________________

Date ______________ Class ______________

A BASIC FOODS & COMMON CONTAINERS

1. Do you like _____?
Yes, I do.
   - (A) cookies
   - (B) pie
   - (C) spaghetti
   - (D) cake

2. Do you like _____?
No, I don't.
   - (A) cheese
   - (B) spaghetti
   - (C) cereal
   - (D) ice cream

3. Where are the _____?
They're over there.
   - (A) cake
   - (B) bread
   - (C) cookies
   - (D) cheese

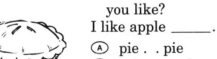

4. What kind of _____ do you like?
I like apple _____.
   - (A) pie . . pie
   - (B) cake . . cake
   - (C) bread . . bread
   - (D) cookies . . cookies

5. What did you have for dessert?
We had a pint of _____.
   - (A) cookies
   - (B) ice cream
   - (C) soda
   - (D) milk

6. What did you buy at the supermarket?
We bought a loaf of _____.
   - (A) cheese
   - (B) cereal
   - (C) bread
   - (D) cake

7. What did they drink with their lunch?
They drank a bottle of _____.
   - (A) milk
   - (B) pie
   - (C) cheese
   - (D) soda

8. What did you buy at the grocery store?
I bought a gallon of _____.
   - (A) soda
   - (B) milk
   - (C) pie
   - (D) cereal

9. What did you get at the supermarket?
I got a pound of _____.
   - (A) cheese
   - (B) bread
   - (C) ice cream
   - (D) cereal

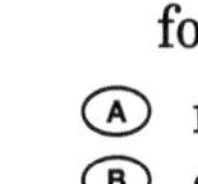

10. What do you want from the supermarket?
Please get a box of _____ for breakfast.
   - (A) milk
   - (B) cereal
   - (C) pie
   - (D) cheese

1 (A) (B) (C) (D)	3 (A) (B) (C) (D)	5 (A) (B) (C) (D)	7 (A) (B) (C) (D)	9 (A) (B) (C) (D)
2 (A) (B) (C) (D)	4 (A) (B) (C) (D)	6 (A) (B) (C) (D)	8 (A) (B) (C) (D)	10 (A) (B) (C) (D)

Go to the next page

B GRAMMAR IN CONTEXT: System of Weights Using Ounces & Pounds

Choose the correct answer to complete the conversation.

16 ounces = 1 pound (lb.)

11. How much is this _____?
    - Ⓐ bread
    - Ⓑ cake
    - Ⓒ cheese
    - Ⓓ pie

12. It's _____ per pound.
    - Ⓐ ten cents
    - Ⓑ ten dollars
    - Ⓒ one dollar
    - Ⓓ one hundred dollars

13. _____ half a pound, please?
    - Ⓐ I have
    - Ⓑ Have I
    - Ⓒ I can have
    - Ⓓ Can I have

14. _____ ounces? Okay.
    - Ⓐ 4
    - Ⓑ 8
    - Ⓒ 12
    - Ⓓ 16

15. _____ are the cookies? I want to buy two pounds.
    - Ⓐ How much
    - Ⓑ How many
    - Ⓒ Who
    - Ⓓ What

16. They're $6.00 per pound. That's going to be _____.
    - Ⓐ $3.00
    - Ⓑ $6.00
    - Ⓒ $9.00
    - Ⓓ $12.00

C READING

Read the story. Then answer the questions.

Alex Fernandez was born in El Salvador. He grew up in San Salvador, the capital city of his country. When Alex was fourteen years old, his family moved to the United States. First they lived in Dallas, Texas, and then they moved to Miami, Florida. Alex began high school in Texas. He was sad when his family moved. He liked his high school in Dallas, and he had many friends there. But Alex was also very happy in his new high school. He met many new friends there. Alex finished high school last year. Now he works in a restaurant at the Miami airport, and he studies at a computer school at night. Next year, he's going to go to college in Tampa, Florida. Alex is looking forward to next year and a very exciting future.

17. Where did Alex finish high school?
    - Ⓐ In San Salvador.
    - Ⓑ In Dallas.
    - Ⓒ In Miami.
    - Ⓓ In Tampa.

18. Which sentence is not correct?
    - Ⓐ Alex finished high school.
    - Ⓑ Alex has a job.
    - Ⓒ Alex goes to a computer school.
    - Ⓓ Alex goes to college.

11 Ⓐ Ⓑ Ⓒ Ⓓ	13 Ⓐ Ⓑ Ⓒ Ⓓ	15 Ⓐ Ⓑ Ⓒ Ⓓ	17 Ⓐ Ⓑ Ⓒ Ⓓ
12 Ⓐ Ⓑ Ⓒ Ⓓ	14 Ⓐ Ⓑ Ⓒ Ⓓ	16 Ⓐ Ⓑ Ⓒ Ⓓ	18 Ⓐ Ⓑ Ⓒ Ⓓ

Go to the next page

Name ______________________ Date ____________

D LISTENING ASSESSMENT

Read and listen to the questions. Then listen to the commercial, and answer the questions.

19. What kind of product is this commercial about?
    - (A) Shampoo.
    - (B) Window cleaner.
    - (C) Floor wax.
    - (D) Vitamins

20. How did the person get the product?
    - (A) Some friends gave the person the product.
    - (B) The person got the product at a party.
    - (C) The person got the product at a store.
    - (D) The person got the product at work.

E FOOD ADS

Look at the advertisements for food. Answer the questions.

Skim
Milk
ONE GALLON
$2.49
BUY 1
GET 1
FREE!

1. How much are two heads of lettuce? ______________
2. What's the price of three oranges? ______________
3. What's the price of six oranges? ______________
4. How much is a pound of Swiss cheese? ______________
5. How much is half a pound of Swiss cheese? ______________
6. How much are two gallons of milk? ______________

19 (A) (B) (C) (D)   20 (A) (B) (C) (D)

Go to the next page

F CLOZE READING

Read the story and circle the correct words.

I Went to Bed Early

I [go (went) did go] to bed early last night because I [was were am][1] very tired. My sister [wasn't didn't not][2] go to bed early because she [has have had][3] a lot of homework. She [did do does][4] her homework for two hours, and then she [go goes went][5] to bed.

G LEARNING SKILL: Categorizing

Write each word in the correct column.

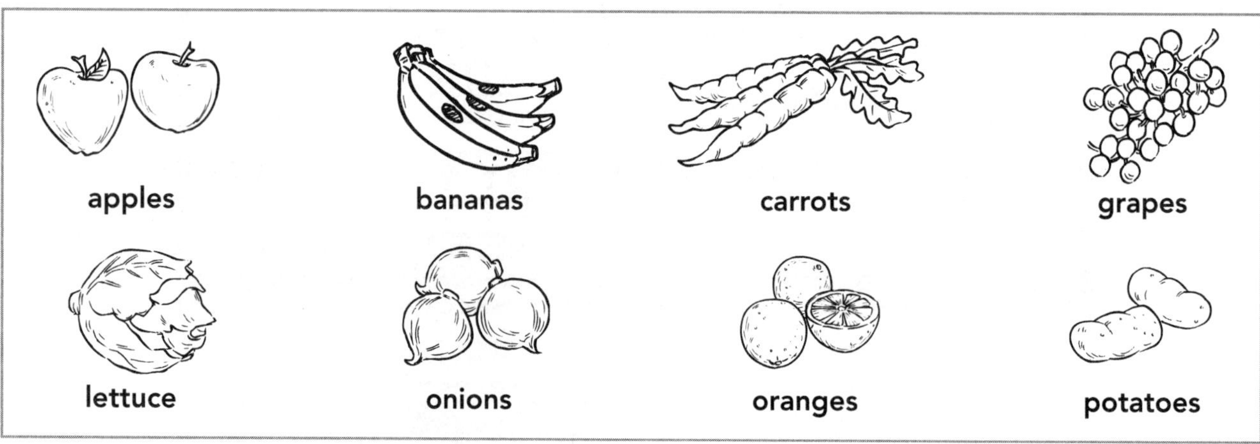

Fruits	Vegetables
apples	carrots

H WRITING ASSESSMENT

Write about your childhood. Where were you born? Where did you grow up? What did you look like? Where did you go to school? What did you do with your friends? (Use a separate sheet of paper.)

I SPEAKING ASSESSMENT

I can ask and answer these questions:

Ask	Answer	
☐	☐	What day was it yesterday?
☐	☐	What was yesterday's date?
☐	☐	Where were you yesterday?
☐	☐	Where were you born?
☐	☐	Where did you grow up?

STOP

APPENDIX

Listening Scripts

Page 3 Exercise C

Listen and circle the number you hear.

1. My address is five Main Street.
2. My address is seven Main Street.
3. My address is two Main Street.
4. My address is six Main Street.
5. My address is one Main Street.
6. My address is three Main Street.
7. My address is four Main Street.
8. My address is eight Main Street.
9. My address is ten Main Street.
10. My address is nine Main Street.

Page 4 Exercise E

Listen and write the missing numbers.

1. A. What's your phone number?
   B. My phone number is 389-7932.
2. A. What's your telephone number?
   B. My telephone number is 837-2953.
3. A. What's your apartment number?
   B. My apartment number is 6-B.
4. A. What's your address?
   B. My address is 10 Main Street.
5. A. What's your fax number?
   B. My fax number is 654-7315.
6. A. What's your license number?
   B. My license number is 2613498.

Page 5 Exercise F

Listen and write the missing letters.

1. A. What's your last name?
   B. Carter.
   A. How do you spell that?
   B. C-A-R-T-E-R.
2. A. What's your last name?
   B. Johnson.
   A. How do you spell that?
   B. J-O-H-N-S-O-N.
3. A. What's your first name?
   B. Gerald.
   A. How do you spell that?
   B. G-E-R-A-L-D.
4. A. What's your last name?
   B. Anderson.
   A. How do you spell that?
   B. A-N-D-E-R-S-O-N.
5. A. What's your first name?
   B. Phillip.
   A. How do you spell that?
   B. P-H-I-L-L-I-P.
6. A. What's your last name?
   B. Martinez.
   A. How do you spell that?
   B. M-A-R-T-I-N-E-Z.

Page 6 Exercise B

Listen and put a check under the correct picture.

1. A. Where's the book?
   B. It's on the desk.
2. A. Where's the dictionary?
   B. It's on the chair.
3. A. Where's the ruler?
   B. It's on the desk.
4. A. Where's the map?
   B. It's on the bulletin board.
5. A. Where's the globe?
   B. It's on the bookshelf.
6. A. Where's the computer?
   B. It's on the table.

Page 11 Exercise J

Listen and write the number under the correct picture.

1. Our English teacher is in the hospital.
2. Mr. and Mrs. Sanchez are in the restaurant.
3. Mary is at the dentist.
4. Billy and Jimmy are in the park.
5. Mr. and Mrs. Lee are at the social security office.
6. James is home in bed.

Page 11 Exercise K

Listen and circle the word you hear.

1. Where are you?
2. Ms. Jones is in the bank.
3. We're friends.
4. Hi. How are you?
5. Where's the newspaper?
6. He's from Korea.
7. The computer is on the table.
8. It's in the bathroom.

Page 15 Exercise C

Listen and put a check under the correct picture.

1. He's eating lunch.
2. We're drinking milk.
3. I'm playing the guitar.
4. She's playing the piano.
5. We're cooking breakfast.
6. It's in the classroom.
7. I'm reading.
8. He's watching TV.
9. She's studying mathematics.
10. They're playing baseball in the yard.

Page 20 Exercise D

Listen and write the letter or number you hear.

Ex. A. What's your first name?
   B. Mark.
   A. How do you spell that?
   B. M-A-R-K.

1. A. What's your last name?
   B. Carter.
   A. How do you spell that?
   B. C-A-R-T-E-R.
2. A. What's your telephone number?
   B. My telephone number is 354-9812.
3. A. What's your fax number?
   B. My fax number is 890-7462.
4. A. What's your first name?
   B. Julie.
   A. How do you spell that?
   B. J-U-L-I-E.
5. A. What's your telephone number?
   B. My telephone number is 672-3059.
6. A. What's your license number?
   B. My license number is 5170349.

Page 22 Exercise C

Listen and circle the word you hear.

1. We're cleaning our room.
2. He's doing his homework.
3. She's washing her hair.
4. They're fixing their car.
5. You're fixing your TV.
6. I'm feeding my cat.

Page 24 Exercise G

Listen and circle the word you hear.

1. He's studying.
2. She's doing her homework.
3. I'm feeding my cat.

Listening scripts are not provided for the achievement tests. Complete test listening scripts are included in *Side by Side Plus* Teacher's Guide 1 and Multilevel Activity & Achievement Test Book 1 (and its accompanying CD-ROM).

4. He's cleaning his yard.
5. We're fixing our car.
6. They're washing their clothes.

Page 27 Exercise C

Listen and circle the word you hear.

1. Sally's brother is very tall.
2. Their dog is very heavy.
3. The questions in my English book are very easy.
4. My friend George is single.
5. Mary's cat is very ugly!
6. This book is very cheap.

Page 32 Exercise K

Listen and circle the word you hear.

1. A. How's the weather in Rome today?
   B. It's cool.
2. A. How's the weather in Tokyo today?
   B. It's snowing.
3. A. How's the weather in Seoul today?
   B. It's sunny.
4. A. How's the weather in Shanghai today?
   B. It's hot.
5. A. How's the weather in New York today?
   B. It's raining.
6. A. How's the weather in Miami today?
   B. It's cloudy.

Page 34 Exercise O

Listen to the temperature in Fahrenheit and Celsius. Write the numbers you hear.

1. In Los Angeles, it's 86° Fahrenheit/30° Celsius.
2. In Seoul, it's 32° Fahrenheit/0° Celsius.
3. In San Juan, it's 81° Fahrenheit/27° Celsius.
4. In Hong Kong, it's 72° Fahrenheit/22° Celsius.
5. In Miami, it's 93° Fahrenheit/34° Celsius.
6. In London, it's 56° Fahrenheit/13° Celsius.
7. In Mexico City, it's 66° Fahrenheit/19° Celsius.
8. In Moscow, it's 34° Fahrenheit/1° Celsius.

Page 36 Exercise B

Listen and put a check under the correct picture.

1. In this photograph, my sister is skateboarding in the park.
2. In this photograph, my son is acting in a play.
3. In this photograph, my friends are dancing at my wedding.
4. In this photograph, my uncle is baking a cake.
5. In this photograph, my cousin is playing a game on her computer.
6. In this photograph, my husband is standing in front of our apartment building.
7. In this photograph, my grandparents are having dinner.
8. In this photograph, my aunt is planting flowers.

Page 40 Exercise E

Listen and choose the correct response.

Ex. Is he old?

1. Is it large?
2. Is she poor?
3. Is it sunny?
4. Is he quiet?

Page 43 Exercise C

Listen to the sentences about the buildings on the map. After each sentence, write the name on the correct building.

1. There's a bakery between the barber shop and the bank.
2. There's a school next to the church.
3. There's a department store across from the school and the church.
4. There's a library around the corner from the barber shop.
5. There's a hospital across from the library.
6. There's a police station next to the hospital.
7. There's a hair salon across from the barber shop.
8. There's a supermarket next to the hair salon.
9. There's a video store around the corner from the bank.
10. There's a park between the library and the video store.
11. There's a health club around the corner from the department store.
12. There's a train station across from the health club.

Page 51 Exercise D

Listen and circle the word you hear.

1. umbrellas
2. blouses
3. coats
4. computer
5. shoes
6. exercises
7. dress
8. restaurants
9. necklaces
10. earring
11. belt
12. watches
13. nieces
14. nephew
15. shirts
16. tie

Page 52 Exercise E

Listen and circle the color you hear.

1. My favorite color is blue.
2. My favorite color is green.
3. My favorite color is gray.
4. My favorite color is silver.
5. My favorite color is yellow.
6. My favorite color is orange.

Page 54 Exercise H

Listen and put a check under the correct picture.

1. I'm washing these socks.
2. He's reading this book.
3. I'm looking for these men.
4. They're using these computers.
5. We're vacuuming this rug.
6. She's playing with these dogs.
7. We're painting this garage.
8. They're listening to these radios.

Page 54 Exercise I

Listen and circle the correct word to complete the sentence.

1. This bicycle . . .
2. These exercises . . .
3. These apartment buildings . . .
4. This bracelet . . .
5. These women . . .
6. These sunglasses . . .
7. This car . . .
8. These jeans . . .
9. This refrigerator . . .

Page 61 Exercise F

Listen and circle the correct word to complete the sentence.

Ex. These dresses . . .

1. That house . . .
2. Those people . . .
3. These flowers . . .
4. This blouse . . .

Page 63 Exercise B

Listen and choose the correct response.

1. What's your name?
2. What language do you speak?
3. What do they do every day?
4. Where do you live?
5. What language do you speak?
6. What do you do every day?

Page 66 Exercise G

Listen and circle the word you hear.

1. We live in Paris.
2. Where do you live?
3. What language does he speak?
4. Every day I listen to Greek music.
5. Every day she watches English TV shows.
6. What do they eat every day?
7. Every day I sing Korean songs.
8. Every day she eats Chinese food.
9. Every day he reads Mexican newspapers.

Page 70 Exercise D

Listen and choose the correct response.

1. What kind of food do you like?
2. Do they paint houses?
3. Why does he go to that restaurant?
4. When does Mrs. Miller cook dinner?
5. Do you work in a bank?
6. Where do they live?
7. What do your children do in the park?
8. Does your friend Patty drive a taxi?
9. Why do they shop in that store?

Page 72 Exercise I

Listen and choose the correct response.

1. Do you do a different kind of sport every day?
2. Does Bob write for the school newspaper?
3. Do Mr. and Mrs. Chang live near a bus stop?
4. Does your sister baby-sit every weekend?
5. Does Timmy do a different activity every day?
6. Do your children play in the orchestra?
7. Does your son sing in the choir?
8. Do your parents go to the park every day?
9. Do you play cards with your friends?

Page 75 Exercise D

Listen and choose the correct response.

Ex. What do Patty and Peter do during the week?

1. When do you watch your favorite TV program?
2. Why do you eat Italian food?
3. Does Carlos visit his grandparents in Puerto Rico?
4. What kind of books do you like?
5. Where do your nephews live?

Page 77 Exercise C

Listen and put a check under the correct picture.

1. How often do you read them?
2. I call her every day.
3. I don't like him.
4. I wash it every weekend.
5. He calls us all the time.
6. I say "hello" to them every morning.

Page 78 Exercise G

Listen and choose the correct answer.

1. Henry's car is always very dirty.
2. My husband sometimes makes dinner.
3. My neighbors play loud music at night.
4. My grandparents rarely speak English.
5. Jane always spends a lot of time with her friends.
6. I rarely study in the library.

Page 82 Exercise N

Listen and choose the correct response.

1. Do you have curly hair?
2. Are you married?
3. Does he have brown eyes?
4. Do you have a brother?
5. Do you usually go out on weekends?
6. Is your husband heavy?
7. Do you live in the city?
8. Do you have short hair?

Page 89 Exercise H

As you listen to each story, read the sentences and check yes ***or*** no.

Jennifer and Jason

Jennifer and Jason are visiting their grandfather in California. They're sad today. Their grandfather usually takes them to the park, but he isn't taking them to the park today.

Our Boss

Our boss usually smiles at the office, but he isn't smiling today. He's upset because the people in our office aren't working very hard today. It's Friday, and everybody is thinking about the weekend.

On Vacation

When my family and I are on vacation, I always have a good time. I usually play tennis, but when it's cold, I play games on my computer and watch videos. Today is a beautiful day, and I'm swimming at the beach.

Timmy and His Brother

Timmy and his brother are watching a science fiction movie. Timmy is covering his eyes because he's scared. He doesn't like science fiction movies. Timmy's brother isn't scared. He likes science fiction movies.

Page 91 Exercise E

Listen and choose the correct response.

Ex. What are Peter and Tom doing today?

1. What do mail carriers do every day?
2. Where are you going today?
3. What do you do when you're scared?
4. Do you usually use a typewriter?
5. Where do you usually study?

Page 93 Exercise D

Listen and circle the word you hear.

1. Our teacher can speak French.
2. I can't play the piano.
3. He can paint houses.
4. My sister can play soccer.
5. They can't sing.
6. Can you drive a bus?
7. I can't read Japanese newspapers.
8. My son Tommy can play the drums.
9. Their children can't swim.
10. Can your husband cook?
11. We can't skate.
12. I can use a cash register.

Page 97 Exercise K

Listen and circle the words you hear.

1. We have to go to the supermarket.
2. My son has to play his violin every day.
3. We can use business software on our computers.
4. Boris has to speak English every day now.
5. I can't cook Italian food.
6. Apartment building superintendents have to repair locks and paint apartments.
7. That actress can't act!
8. Our children have to use a computer to do their homework.
9. Mr. Johnson can operate equipment.

Page 98 Exercise M

Listen and choose the correct answer.

1. I'm sorry. I can't go to the movies with you today. I have to go to the dentist.
2. I can't go to the party on Saturday. I have to wash my clothes.
3. I can't have lunch with you, but I can have dinner.
4. We can't go skiing this weekend. We have to paint our kitchen.
5. I'm very busy today. I have to go shopping, and I have to cook dinner for my family.
6. I can't see a play with you on Friday because I have to baby-sit. But I can see a play with you on Saturday.

Page 102 Exercise H

Listen and circle the words you hear.

1. I'm going to visit her this year.
2. I'm going to write to my uncle right away.
3. I'm going to call them this Monday.
4. When are you going to cut your hair?
5. I'm going to fix it next Tuesday.
6. We're going to see them this December.

7. They're going to visit us this winter.
8. I'm going to clean it at once.
9. We're going to spend time with them this August.
10. I'm going to wash them immediately.
11. You're going to see us next week.
12. When are you going to call the plumber?

Page 103 Exercise J

Listen to the following weather forecasts and circle the correct answers.

Today's Weather Forecast

This is Mike Martinez with today's weather forecast. This afternoon it's going to be cool and cloudy, with temperatures from 50 to 55 degrees Fahrenheit. This evening it's going to be foggy and warm, but it isn't going to rain.

This Weekend's Weather Forecast

This is Barbara Burrows with your weekend weather forecast. Tonight it's going to be clear and warm, with 60 degree temperatures. On Saturday you can swim at the beach. It's going to be sunny and very hot, with temperatures between 90 and 95 degrees Fahrenheit. But take your umbrella with you on Sunday because it's going to be cool and it's going to rain.

Monday's Weather Forecast

This is Al Alberts with Monday's weather forecast. Monday morning it's going to be cool and nice, but Monday afternoon wear your gloves and your boots because it's going to be very cold and it's going to snow! On Tuesday morning the skiing is going to be wonderful because it's going to be sunny and very warm!

Page 108 Exercise T

Listen and write the time you hear.

1. It's seven forty-five.
2. It's six fifteen.
3. It's four thirty.
4. It's nine fifteen.
5. It's midnight.
6. It's five o'clock.
7. It's a quarter to nine.
8. It's a quarter after eight.
9. It's one forty-five.
10. It's noon.
11. It's eleven thirty.
12. It's a quarter to three.

Page 113 Exercise G

Listen to the story. Fill in the correct times.

Every day at school I study English, science, mathematics, music, and Chinese. English class begins at 8:30. I go to science at 10:15 and mathematics at 11:00. We have lunch at 12:15. We go to music at 12:45, and we have Chinese at 1:30.

Page 114 Exercise B

Listen to the story. Put the number under the correct picture.

Everybody in my family is sick today.

My parents are sick.

1. My father has a stomachache.
2. My mother has a backache.

My brother and my sister are sick, too.

3. My sister Alice has an earache.
4. My brother David has a toothache.

My grandparents are also sick.

5. My grandmother has a cold.
6. My grandfather has a sore throat.
7. Even my dog is sick! He has a fever!

Yes, everybody in my family is sick today . . . everybody except me!

How do I feel today?

8. I feel fine!

Page 117 Exercise F

Listen and circle the correct answer.

Example 1: I study.
Example 2: I played cards.

1. I planted flowers.
2. I shave.
3. I cried.
4. I typed.
5. I work.
6. I shouted.
7. I clean.
8. I studied.
9. I fixed my car.
10. I paint.
11. I smile.
12. I cooked.

Page 126 Exercise I

Listen and choose the correct response.

1. When did you write to your girlfriend?
2. When does your neighbor wash his car?
3. Who did your parents visit?
4. Where does Irene do yoga?
5. When did your son go to sleep?
6. When do you clean your apartment?
7. Where did you take your grandchildren?
8. What did you make for dinner?
9. When does Carla read her e-mail?
10. When did you get up today?

Page 129 Exercise B

Listen and circle the word you hear.

1. My husband is thin.
2. She was very hungry.
3. They were tired today.
4. He was very energetic at school today.
5. My wife is at the clinic.
6. Their clothes were clean.
7. My children are very sick today.
8. My parents are home tonight.
9. He was very full this morning.
10. The Lopez family is on vacation.
11. Their neighbors are very noisy.
12. These clothes were dirty.

Page 131 Exercise E

Listen and circle the word you hear.

1. I wasn't busy yesterday.
2. We were at the movies last night.
3. They weren't home today.
4. Tom was on time for his plane.
5. It wasn't cold yesterday.
6. They weren't at the baseball game.
7. My friends were late for the party.
8. The doctor was in her office at noon.

Page 134 Exercise I

Listen and choose the correct response.

1. Where were you born?
2. Where did you grow up?
3. What was your favorite subject in school?
4. When did you move here?
5. What did you look like when you were young?
6. Did you have freckles?
7. What do you do in your spare time?
8. Did you have a favorite hero?

Page 137 Exercise F

Listen and circle the word you hear.

Ex. Is Jane rich or poor?

1. It was a nice day today.
2. My friends were thirsty at lunch.
3. Who is your favorite hero?
4. Were Mr. and Mrs. Parker at home last weekend?
5. My new couch is uncomfortable.
6. My cousins were late for their plane.
7. Before I met Howard, I was very sad.
8. Your children are very cute.

ACTIVITY WORKBOOK 1 ANSWER KEY

UNIT 1

WORKBOOK PAGE 2

A. What Are They Saying?

1. What's, name
2. address, My, is
3. your, phone number
4. your, name
5. What's, address
6. phone, My, number
7. Where are, I'm from

WORKBOOK PAGE 3

B. Name/Address/Phone Number

(Answers will vary.)

C. Listening

1. 5	6. 3
2. 7	7. 4
3. 2	8. 8
4. 6	9. 10
5. 1	10. 9

WORKBOOK PAGE 4

D. Numbers

4	2	six	eight
7	9	two	ten
1	6	seven	four
8	5	three	nine
10	3	one	five

E. Listening

1. 2	2. 5
3. 6	4. 10
5. 7, 3	6. 1, 4, 8

WORKBOOK PAGE 5

F. Listening

1. R, E	4. R, O
2. H, S, N	5. P, L
3. G, A, D	6. M, T, Z

G. What Are They Saying?

1. name
2. Hi
3. meet
4. Nice
5. you
6. My
7. is
8. Hello
9. I'm
10. to
11. you

UNIT 2

WORKBOOK PAGE 6

A. Puzzle

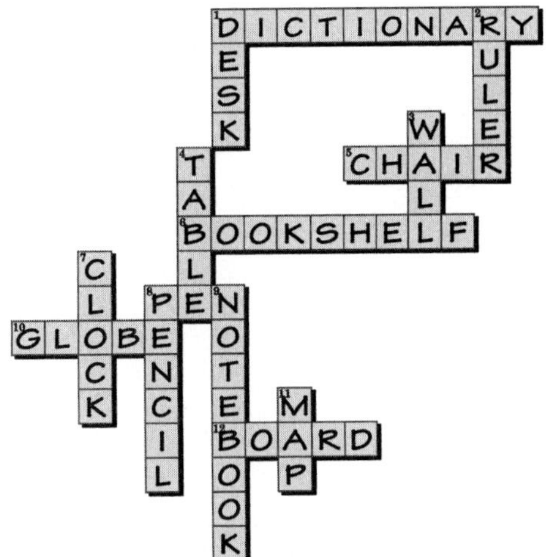

B. Listening

1.	✓	___	2.	___	✓	3.	✓	___
4.	✓	___	5.	___	✓	6.	✓	___

WORKBOOK PAGE 7

C. What Are They Saying?

1. Where, I'm, bedroom
2. are, They're, yard
3. are, We're, kitchen
4. Where, I'm, dining room
5. Where are, They're, basement
6. are, We're, attic
7. Where are, They're, living room
8. Where are, I'm, bathroom

WORKBOOK PAGE 8

D. What Are They Saying?

1. Where's, He's, garage
2. Where's, She's, living room
3. Where's, It's, classroom

E. Where Are They?

1. They
2. She
3. He
4. They
5. We
6. It
7. He
8. She
9. It

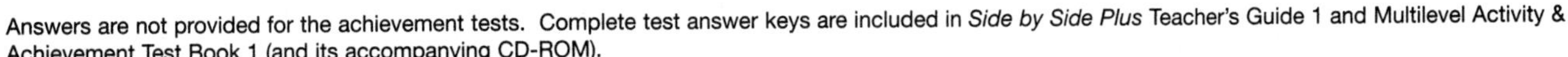
Answers are not provided for the achievement tests. Complete test answer keys are included in *Side by Side Plus* Teacher's Guide 1 and Multilevel Activity & Achievement Test Book 1 (and its accompanying CD-ROM).

F. Where Are They?

1. He's
2. They're
3. We're
4. I'm
5. It's
6. She's
7. You're
8. Where's

WORKBOOK PAGE 9

G. The Baker Family

1. in the living room
2. in the bathroom
3. in the yard
4. in the kitchen
5. in the bedroom
6. in the garage

H. Where Are They?

1. She's in the living room.
2. He's in the bathroom.
3. They're in the yard.
4. He's in the kitchen.
5. She's in the bedroom.
6. It's in the garage.

WORKBOOK PAGE 10

I. What's the Sign?

1. PARK, in the park
2. POST OFFICE, in the post office
3. RESTAURANT, in the restaurant
4. SUPERMARKET, in the supermarket
5. MOVIE THEATER, in the movie theater
6. HOSPITAL, in the hospital
7. ZOO, in the zoo
8. LIBRARY, in the library

WORKBOOK PAGE 11

J. Listening

5	1	3
2	4	6

K. Listening

1. you
2. Ms.
3. We're
4. How
5. Where's
6. He's
7. on
8. It's

L. Matching

1. c	4. g	6. d
2. e	5. b	7. f
3. a		

UNIT 3

WORKBOOK PAGE 13

A. What Are They Saying?

1. What, studying
2. doing, She's eating
3. What's, He's sleeping
4. What are, They're reading
5. What are, We're watching
6. What are, doing, I'm playing
7. What's, He's cooking

WORKBOOK PAGE 14

B. What Are They Doing?

1. eating
2. drinking
3. studying
4. reading
5. sleeping
6. teaching
7. listening
8. watching
9. cooking
10. singing
11. playing

WORKBOOK PAGE 15

C. Listening

1.	✔	___	2.	___	✔
3.	___	✔	4.	___	✔
5.	___	✔	6.	✔	___
7.	✔	___	8.	✔	___
9.	___	✔	10.	___	✔

WORKBOOK PAGE 17

E. What's the Question?

1. Where are you?
2. What's he doing?
3. Where are they?
4. What are you doing?
5. Where is he?
6. What's she doing?
7. Where is she?
8. Where are you?
9. What's he doing?
10. Where is it?
11. What are they doing?
12. Where are you?

WORKBOOK PAGE 20

CHECK-UP TEST: Units 1–3

A. *(Answers will vary.)*

B.

1. lunch
2. What's
3. singing
4. mathematics
5. meet
6. pencil

C.

1. in
2. reading
3. He's
4. watching
5. We're
6. Where's
7. doing
8. It's
9. What
10. and

D.

1. T
2. 8
3. 6
4. J
5. 7
6. 0

UNIT 4

WORKBOOK PAGE 21

A. What Are They Doing?

1. What's, cleaning his
2. doing, fixing her
3. What, my apartment
4. children, their homework
5. are, our sink

WORKBOOK PAGE 22

B. What's the Word?

1. my
2. our
3. their
4. her
5. its
6. your
7. his

C. Listening

1. our
2. his
3. her
4. their
5. your
6. my

D. Puzzle

WORKBOOK PAGE 23

E. What Are They Saying?

1. Yes, he is.
2. Yes, we are.
3. Yes, she is.
4. Yes, they are.
5. Yes, he is.
6. Yes, she is.
7. Yes, I am.
8. Yes, you are.

WORKBOOK PAGE 24

G. Listening

1. he's
2. her
3. feeding
4. yard
5. our
6. washing

WORKBOOK PAGE 25

H. What Are They Doing?

1. washing
2. cleaning
3. doing
4. reading
5. painting
6. feeding

I. What's the Word?

1. They're, their
2. Where
3. He's, his
4. Where's
5. our
6. Is
7. are
8. its

WORKBOOK PAGE 26

J. A Busy Day

1. restaurant
2. eating
3. in
4. They're
5. their
6. park
7. reading
8. listening
9. and
10. doing
11. playing
12. laundromat
13. She's
14. her
15. are
16. washing
17. his
18. fixing
19. Where's
20. library
21. What's
22. He's

UNIT 5

WORKBOOK PAGE 27

A. Matching Opposites

1. d
2. a
3. g
4. c
5. f
6. b
7. e
8. n
9. l
10. i
11. j
12. h
13. k
14. m

B. What Are They Saying?

1. tall
2. thin
3. young
4. married
5. small
6. noisy
7. expensive
8. ugly

C. Listening

1. tall
2. heavy
3. easy
4. single
5. ugly
6. cheap

WORKBOOK PAGE 28

D. What's Wrong?

1. It isn't new. It's old.
2. They aren't quiet. They're noisy.
3. It isn't large. It's small.
4. He isn't single. He's married.
5. She isn't young. She's old.
6. They aren't short. They're tall.

E. Scrambled Questions

1. Are you busy?
2. Is your dog large?
4. Are they married?
4. Am I beautiful?
5. Is English difficult?
6. Is their car new?
7. Is she tall or short?/Is she short or tall?
8. Is he noisy or quiet?/Is he quiet or noisy?

WORKBOOK PAGE 30

G. Whose Things?

1. Albert's car
2. Jenny's bicycle
3. George's guitar
4. Fred's dog
5. Kate's computer
6. Mr. Price's house
7. Jane's piano
8. Mike's TV
9. Mrs. Chang's book
10. Alice's cat

WORKBOOK PAGE 31

H. What's the Word?

1. Her
2. Their
3. His
4. Her
5. Its
6. Her
7. His
8. Their

I. Mr. and Mrs. Grant

1. Yes, he is.
2. No, he isn't.
3. No, he isn't.
4. Yes, he is.
5. Yes, she is.
6. No, she isn't.
7. Yes, she is.
8. No, it isn't.
9. Yes, it is.
10. Yes, it is.
11. No, it isn't.
12. No, they aren't.
13. Yes, they are.
14. No, it isn't.

WORKBOOK PAGE 32

J. How's the Weather?

1. It's warm.
2. It's sunny.
3. It's snowing.
4. It's raining.
5. It's cool.
6. It's hot.
7. It's cold.

K. Listening

1. cool
2. snowing
3. sunny
4. hot
5. raining
6. cloudy

WORKBOOK PAGE 33

L. What's the Number?

1. 24
2. 31
3. 72
4. 46
5. 97

M. What's the Word?

thirty-eight
eighty-three
fifty-five
ninety-nine
sixty-four

N. Number Puzzle

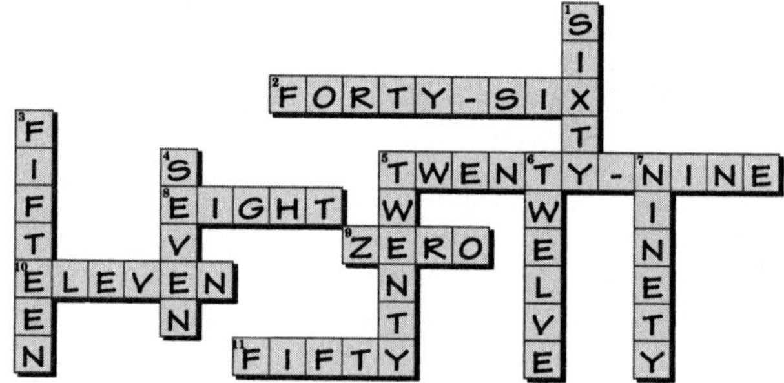

WORKBOOK PAGE 34

O. Listening

1. 86° / 30°
2. 32° / 0°
3. 81° / 27°
4. 72° / 22°
5. 93° / 34°
6. 56° / 13°
7. 66° / 19°
8. 34° / 1°

Q. Matching

1. e
2. h
3. d
4. a
5. i
6. c
7. f
8. b
9. g

UNIT 6

WORKBOOK PAGE 35

A. A Family

1.	wife	**11.**	grandfather
2.	husband	**12.**	grandmother
3.	children	**13.**	grandchildren
4.	son	**14.**	grandson
5.	daughter	**15.**	granddaughter
6.	brother	**16.**	uncle
7.	sister	**17.**	aunt
8.	father	**18.**	nephew
9.	mother	**19.**	niece
10.	grandparents	**20.**	cousin

WORKBOOK PAGE 36

B. Listening

1. ✓ ___ **2.** ___ ✓
3. ✓ ___ **4.** ___ ✓
5. ✓ ___ **6.** ✓ ___
7. ___ ✓ **8.** ✓ ___

C. The Wrong Word!

1. cheap (The others indicate size.)
2. park (The others are rooms of the house.)
3. baseball (The others are musical instruments.)
4. tall (The others describe people's appearance.)
5. dinner (The others describe the weather.)
6. rugs (The others are family members.)
7. bank (The others are classroom items.)
8. Mr. (The others are titles for women.)
9. poor (The others describe sound.)
10. sister (The others are male.)

WORKBOOK PAGE 37

D. GrammarSong

1.	smiling	**5.**	hanging	**9.**	looking
2.	living	**6.**	dancing	**10.**	hanging
3.	living	**7.**	having	**11.**	smiling
4.	looking	**8.**	crying	**12.**	Looking

WORKBOOK PAGE 38

E. An E-Mail from Los Angeles

1. It's in Los Angeles.
2. It's warm and sunny.
3. It's 78° Fahrenheit.
4. They're in the park.
5. She's reading a book.
6. He's listening to music.
7. She's Bob's sister.
8. She's riding her bicycle.
9. He's Bob's brother.
10. He's skateboarding.
11. No, they aren't.
12. They're at home.
13. She's baking.
14. He's planting flowers in the yard.
15. No, he isn't.
16. He's in New York.

WORKBOOK PAGE 40

CHECK-UP TEST: Units 4–6

A.

1. nephew
2. in
3. beach
4. its
5. on
6. reading
7. fixing
8. brushing

B.

1. Where
2. grandmother
3. niece
4. Who
5. her
6. their
7. his

C.

1. He's thin.
2. They're tall.
3. It's new.

D.

1. Are you married?
2. Are they quiet?
3. Is she young?

E.

1.	b	**3.**	b
2.	a	**4.**	b

UNIT 7

WORKBOOK PAGE 41

A. Where Is It?

1.	next to	**7.**	across from
2.	across from	**8.**	around the corner from
3.	between	**9.**	next to
4.	around the corner from	**10.**	between
5.	next to	**11.**	across from
6.	between		

WORKBOOK PAGE 42

B. What Are They Saying?

1. There's, next to
2. Is there, There's, around the corner from
3. there, There's, across from
4. Is there, There's, between
5. Is there, there, There's, Central, next to

WORKBOOK PAGE 43

C. Listening

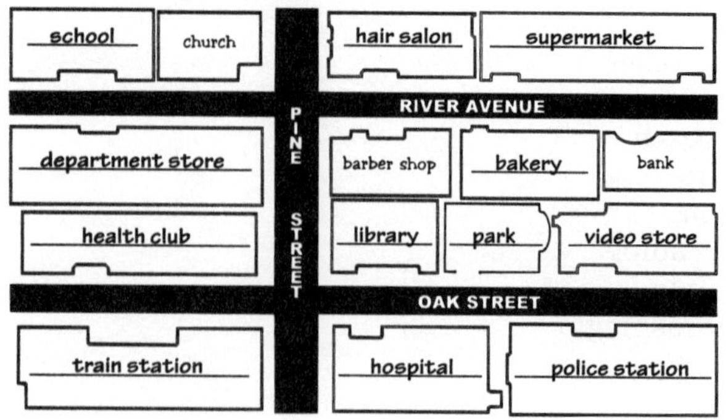

D. Yes or No?

1. No, there isn't.
2. Yes, there is.
3. No, there isn't.
4. Yes, there is.
5. Yes, there is.
6. No, there isn't.
7. No, there isn't.
8. Yes, there is.
9. No, there isn't.

WORKBOOK PAGE 45

F. What Are They Saying?

1. Is there
2. there is
3. are there
4. There's, there are
5. Is there
6. there isn't, there are
7. Are there
8. there aren't, there's
9. are there
10. There are, there's

WORKBOOK PAGE 46

G. Our Apartment Building

1. machines
2. broken
3. mice
4. escape
5. hole
6. satellite dish
7. refrigerator
8. closets
9. cats, dogs
10. stop, mailbox

WORKBOOK PAGE 47

H. Jane's Living Room

1. Yes, there is.
2. No, there isn't.
3. Yes, there are.
4. Yes, there is.
5. No, there aren't.
6. Yes, there are.
7. Yes, there are.
8. No, there isn't.
9. No, there aren't.
10. Yes, there is.
11. Yes, there is.
12. No, there isn't.
13. Yes, there are.
14. No, there isn't.

WORKBOOK PAGE 48

I. Looking For an Apartment

1. Chicago
2. sunny
3. bedroom, bathroom
4. fireplaces
5. children
6. Miami
7. beautiful
8. bedrooms
9. two
10. elevator
11. New York
12. large
13. living room
14. air conditioners
15. school
16. Dallas
17. quiet
18. dining room
19. building
20. near

UNIT 8

WORKBOOK PAGE 50

A. What's the Word?

1. tie
2. shirt
3. jacket
4. pants
5. umbrella
6. earring
7. necklace
8. blouse
9. bracelet
10. skirt
11. glasses
12. suit
13. belt
14. sock
15. shoe
16. dress
17. coat
18. purse
19. stocking
20. hat
21. watch
22. glove
23. briefcase
24. mitten
25. sweater
26. jeans
27. boot

WORKBOOK PAGE 51

B. *A* or *An*?

1. a
2. an
3. a
4. an
5. a
6. an
7. a
8. an
9. an
10. a
11. a
12. a
13. an
14. a
15. a
16. a
17. an
18. a
19. an
20. an
21. a
22. an
23. a
24. a

C. Singular/Plural

1. a hat
2. a basement
3. dresses
4. bosses
5. exercises
6. a watch
7. a glove
8. socks
9. drums
10. a room
11. earrings
12. a purse
13. nieces
14. women
15. a child
16. mice
17. a tooth
18. a person

D. Listening

1. umbrellas
2. blouses
3. coats
4. computer
5. shoes
6. exercises
7. dress
8. restaurants
9. necklaces
10. earring
11. belt
12. watches
13. nieces
14. nephew
15. shirts
16. tie

WORKBOOK PAGE 52

E. Listening

1. blue
2. green
3. gray
4. silver
5. yellow
6. orange

WORKBOOK PAGE 53

G. What Are They Looking For?

1. a pair of pants
2. a pair of gloves
3. a pair of shoes
4. a pair of jeans
5. a pair of mittens
6. a pair of boots
7. a pair of stockings
8. a pair of earrings
9. a pair of pajamas

WORKBOOK PAGE 54

H. Listening

1.	___	✓	2.	✓	___
3.	___	✓	4.	___	✓
5.	✓	___	6.	___	✓
7.	✓	___	8.	___	✓

I. Listening

1. is	4. is	7. is
2. are	5. are	8. are
3. are	6. are	9. is

WORKBOOK PAGE 55

J. This/That/These/Those

1. This hat is orange.
2. That hat is yellow.
3. These boots are brown.
4. Those boots are black.
5. This computer is expensive.
6. That computer is cheap.
7. These gloves are small.
8. Those gloves are large.
9. This tie is pretty.
10. That tie is ugly.
11. These earrings are gold.
12. Those earrings are silver.

WORKBOOK PAGE 56

K. Singular → Plural

1. Those coats are blue.
2. These bracelets are new.
3. Those watches are beautiful.
4. These are Tom's jackets.
5. These aren't your shoes.
6. Are those your earrings?
7. Those aren't your notebooks.
8. These people aren't rich.

L. Plural → Singular

1. This sweater is pretty.
2. That purse is expensive.
3. Is this your neighbor?
4. Is that your dress?
5. That's Bill's shirt.
6. This woman is my friend.
7. This isn't my glove.
8. That's her cat

M. Scrambled Sentences

1. I think that's my jacket.
2. These are my new gloves.
3. Those aren't your black boots.
4. Blue suits are very popular this year.
5. Here's a nice pair of sunglasses.
6. That's my brother's old car.

WORKBOOK PAGE 58

P. This/That/These/Those

1. This, These, this
2. That, those
3. This, This, these
4. those, that
5. This, This, these
6. those, that

WORKBOOK PAGE 59

Q. GrammarSong

1. this	10. This	19. are
2. this	11. that	20. these
3. shirt	12. This	21. those
4. That's	13. that	22. This
5. skirt	14. these	23. that
6. this	15. Are	24. These
7. hat	16. boots	25. those
8. this	17. Those	26. that
9. that	18. suits	

WORKBOOK PAGES 60–61

CHECK-UP TEST: Units 7–8

A.

1. these	5. How
2. of	6. people
3. Is there	7. there
4. earring	8. No, there isn't.

B.

1. It's around the corner from the barber shop.
2. It's across from the library.
3. It's between the clinic and the drug store.

C.

1. their (The others are demonstratives.)
2. striped (The others are colors.)
3. closet (The others are places in the community.)
4. necklace (The others are worn on the feet.)

D.

1. These gloves are large.
2. That table is broken.
3. Those shoes are black.

E.

1. These rooms are small.
2. Those aren't my pencils.
3. Are these your boots?

F.

1. is	3. are
2. are	4. is

UNIT 9

WORKBOOK PAGES 62–63

A. Interviews Around the World

1. What's
2. name
3. is
4. do
5. you
6. live
7. What
8. language
9. speak
10. do
11. you
12. eat
13. watch
14. are
15. Our
16. names
17. do
18. you
19. We
20. live
21. What
22. do
23. you
24. speak
25. do
26. do
27. we
28. sing
29. read
30. What
31. are
32. Their
33. names
34. are
35. Where
36. do
37. They
38. live
39. What
40. language
41. do
42. they
43. speak
44. do
45. do
46. they
47. eat
48. they
49. watch

B. Listening

1. a
2. b
3. a
4. a
5. b
6. b

WORKBOOK PAGES 63–64

C. People Around the World

1. Her name is Jane.
2. She lives in Montreal.
3. She plays the piano, and she listens to Canadian music.
4. What's his name?
5. Where does he live?
6. He speaks Arabic.
7. does he do
   eats, he reads Egyptian newspapers
8. Her name is Sonia.
9. Where does
   She lives in Sao Paulo.
10. does she speak
    She speaks Portuguese.
11. does she do
    She does exercises, and she plays soccer.

WORKBOOK PAGE 66

F. Eduardo's Family

1. live
2. speak
3. speaks
4. speak
5. read
6. live
7. reads
8. works
9. cook
10. work
11. clean
12. shop
13. plays
14. play
15. do
16. do

G. Listening

1. live
2. do
3. does
4. listen
5. watches
6. eat
7. sing
8. eats
9. reads

WORKBOOK PAGE 67

H. What's the Word?

1. does, lives
2. do, paint
3. does, drives
4. do, live
5. do, cook
6. does, do, sells

I. What's the Difference?

1. drives
2. work
3. plays
4. sells
5. paints
6. lives

WORKBOOK PAGE 68

K. Loud and Clear

1. Charlie, chair, kitchen, Chinese
2. Shirley, short, shoes
3. Richard, cheap, French, watch
4. washing, shirt, washing machine
5. Chen, children, bench, church
6. Sharp, English, station

UNIT 10

WORKBOOK PAGE 69

A. What's the Day?

1. Tuesday
2. Saturday
3. Wednesday
4. Sunday
5. Friday
6. Monday

B. What Are They Saying?

1. Does, he does
2. Does, she does
3. Does, he doesn't
4. What kind of
5. Does, doesn't
6. Does, he does
7. Does, she doesn't
8. When

WORKBOOK PAGE 70

C. What Are They Saying?

1. Do, I do
2. Do, they don't
3. Do, we do
4. Do, we don't
5. Do, I don't
6. Do, they do

D. Listening

1. b
2. c
3. b
4. a
5. c
6. a
7. b
8. c
9. a

WORKBOOK PAGE 71

E. Yes and No

1. doesn't cook
2. doesn't drive
3. don't play
4. don't work
5. doesn't live
6. don't exercise
7. goes
8. shop
9. wears
10. speaks
11. doesn't sing

F. What's the Word?

1. do
2. does
3. do
4. does
5. do
6. does
7. Do
8. Does
9. do
10. Do
11. does
12. does
13. do

WORKBOOK PAGE 72

H. Yes or No?

1. Yes, she does.
2. No, they don't. They play volleyball.
3. Yes, we do.
4. No, he doesn't. He sings in the choir.
5. No, I don't. I see a play.
6. Yes, they do.
7. Yes, he does.
8. No, we don't. We do yoga.

I. Listening

1. b
2. a
3. b
4. a
5. b
6. b
7. b
8. a
9. a

WORKBOOK PAGE 75

CHECK-UP TEST: Units 9–10

A.

1. plays
2. shop
3. doesn't
4. do
5. stay
6. does

B.

1. Where
2. What
3. Does
4. Why
5. When
6. What

C.

1. lives
2. does
3. cleans
4. plays
5. takes
6. rides
7. goes
8. eats

D.

1. c
2. b
3. b
4. a
5. c

UNIT 11

WORKBOOK PAGE 76

A. What Are They Saying?

1. you
2. them
3. her
4. him
5. them
6. it
7. us
8. it
9. me

WORKBOOK PAGE 77

B. What's the Word?

1. it
2. her
3. them
4. him
5. it
6. them

C. Listening

1. ___ ✔
2. ✔ ___
3. ___ ✔
4. ___ ✔
5. ✔ ___
6. ___ ✔

WORKBOOK PAGE 78

E. Write It and Say It

1. eats
2. barks
3. cleans
4. washes
5. jogs
6. reads
7. shops
8. watches
9. speaks
10. plays

F. Matching

1. c
2. e
3. a
4. g
5. b
6. f
7. d
8. h

G. Listening

1. b
2. a
3. b
4. a
5. b
6. a

WORKBOOK PAGE 80

J. What's the Word?

1. have
2. has
3. have
4. have
5. has
6. have
7. has
8. have

K. What Are They Saying?

1. Does, have, doesn't have, has
2. don't have, have
3. have, have
4. do, have, have
5. Do, have, don't have, have
6. Does, have, doesn't have, has

WORKBOOK PAGE 81

L. What's the Word?

1. long
2. curly
3. short
4. single
5. hair
6. brown
7. suburbs

M. Two Brothers

1. short
2. have
3. has
4. have
5. short
6. curly
7. tall
8. thin
9. he's
10. lives
11. has
12. in
13. plays
14. play/have
15. go
16. go
17. watches
18. reads

WORKBOOK PAGE 82

N. Listening

1. b
2. a
3. a
4. b
5. a
6. b
7. b
8. a

O. What's the Word?

1. in
2. on
3. on
4. in
5. about
6. for
7. in
8. to
9. at
10. of
11. to, on
12. to

UNIT 12

WORKBOOK PAGE 83

A. What's the Word?

1. sad
2. tired
3. hot
4. angry
5. sick
6. happy
7. hungry
8. cold
9. nervous
10. scared
11. thirsty
12. embarrassed

WORKBOOK PAGE 84

B. Tell Me Why

1. They're yawning because they're yawn when they're tired
2. She's crying because she's cries when she's sad
3. He's shivering because he's shivers when he's cold
4. I'm perspiring because I'm perspire when I'm hot
5. She's smiling because she's smiles when she's happy
6. They're eating because they're eat when they're hungry
7. We're shouting because we're shout when we're angry
8. He's covering his eyes because he's covers his eyes when he's scared

WORKBOOK PAGE 87

E. That's Strange!

1. cooks
2. study
3. walks
4. brushes
5. eats
6. dance
7. is sweeping
8. are reading
9. I'm using
10. are sleeping

WORKBOOK PAGE 88

F. What's the Question?

1. Why are you blushing?
2. Where do they play tennis?
3. When does she read her e-mail?
4. What kind of food do you like?
5. How many cats do you have?
6. What is/What's he using?
7. What kind of shows does he watch?
8. How often do you call your grandchildren?
9. What do they do every weekend?
10. Why are you smiling?
11. Where is she eating today?
12. How many sweaters are you wearing?

G. Which One Doesn't Belong?

1. we (The others are object pronouns.)
2. noisy (The others are adverbs of frequency.)
3. has (The others are forms of *do*.)
4. yoga (The others are emotions.)
5. Wednesday (The others are WH-question words.)
6. outgoing (The others are verbs.)
7. shy (The others are verbs.)
8. year (The others are times of the day.)

WORKBOOK PAGES 89–90

H. Listening

1. yes ☐ no ☑
2. yes ☐ no ☑
3. yes ☑ no ☐
4. yes ☑ no ☐
5. yes ☐ no ☑
6. yes ☑ no ☐
7. yes ☑ no ☐
8. yes ☐ no ☑
9. yes ☐ no ☑
10. yes ☐ no ☑
11. yes ☑ no ☐
12. yes ☐ no ☑

I. Loud and Clear

1. Sally, sorry, sister, sick, hospital
2. What's, scientist, speaking, experiments
3. cousin, Athens is always, busy
4. Sally's husband doesn't, clothes, closet
5. Steven is sweeping, because it's
6. Mrs. Garcia reads, newspaper, Sunday
7. students, school sometimes, zoo, bus
8. son, plays soccer, friends, Tuesday

WORKBOOK PAGE 91

CHECK-UP TEST: Units 11–12

A.

1. him
2. them
3. her
4. me
5. us

B.

1. feeding
2. goes
3. baking
4. fixes
5. washes

C.

1. is
2. do
3. Does
4. do
5. Are

D.

1. Where do they work every day?
2. When do you get together?
3. Why is he crying?
4. How many children does she have?
5. What are you drinking?

E.

1. b
2. a
3. b
4. a
5. b

UNIT 13

WORKBOOK PAGE 92

A. *Can* or *Can't*?

1. can't ski, can skate
2. can sing, can't dance
3. can paint, can't paint
4. can't speak, can speak
5. can cook, can't cook
6. can't use, can use
7. can't play, can play
8. can drive, can't drive

WORKBOOK PAGE 93

C. What's the Question?

1. Can he cook?
2. Can she ski?
3. Can they swim?
4. Can you drive a bus?
5. Can he skate?
6. Can you play baseball?

D. Listening

1. can
2. can't
3. can
4. can
5. can't
6. can
7. can't
8. can
9. can't
10. can
11. can't
12. can

WORKBOOK PAGE 94

E. Puzzle

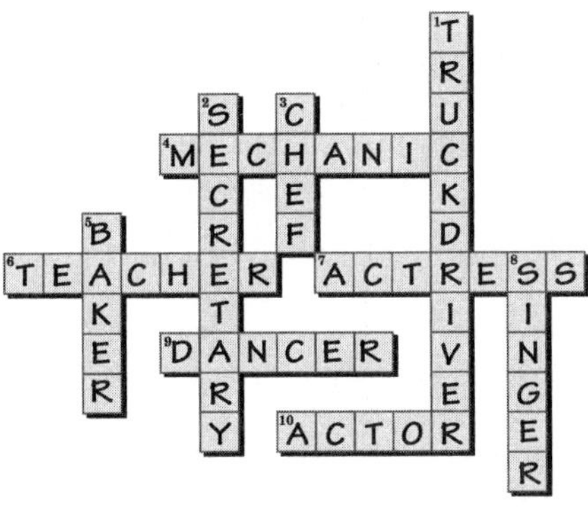

F. *Can* or *Can't*?

1. can
2. can't
3. Can, can
4. can't
5. can
6. can't
7. Can, can
8. can
9. can't, can't
10. can, can, can
11. can't, can't

WORKBOOK PAGE 96

H. What Are They Saying?

1. have to
2. has to
3. has to
4. have to, have to
5. Does, have to, does, has to
6. Do, have to, don't
7. have to
8. have to

WORKBOOK PAGE 97

I. A Busy Family

1. He has to speak to the superintendent.
2. She has to meet with Danny's teacher.
3. They have to go to the doctor.
4. He has to fix the car.
5. She has to go to the dentist.
6. She has to baby-sit.
7. They have to clean the apartment.
8. They have to plant flowers in the yard.

K. Listening

1. have to
2. has to
3. can
4. has to
5. can't
6. have to
7. can't
8. have to
9. can

WORKBOOK PAGE 98

L. They're Busy

1. can't go swimming, have to go to the dentist
2. can't go bowling, has to baby-sit
3. can't go dancing, have to work
4. can't go to a soccer game, has to study
5. can't go to a movie, have to clean the house
6. can't have dinner, have to wash my clothes

M. Listening

1. a
2. b
3. b
4. a
5. b
6. a

UNIT 14

WORKBOOK PAGE 100

A. What Are They Going to Do?

1. He's going to cook.
2. She's going to read.
3. I'm going to study English.
4. They're going to wash their car.
5. We're going to play baseball.
6. He's going to watch TV.

B. What Are They Saying?

1. What are, going to do
   I'm going to
2. What's, going to do
   He's going to
3. What's, going to do
   She's going to
4. What are, going to do
   They're going to

WORKBOOK PAGE 101

C. What Are They Going to Do?

1. going to go
2. going
3. going to go
4. is going to
5. is going to go to
6. are going
7. are going to go to
8. going to, is going to go to

WORKBOOK PAGE 102

E. Which Word Doesn't Belong?

1. Monday (The others are months.)
2. September (The others are days of the week.)
3. at once (The others are seasons.)
4. Friday (The others are months.)
5. he (The others are object pronouns.)
6. next week (The others refer to right now.)

F. What's Next?

1. August
2. Wednesday
3. April
4. winter
5. Sunday
6. December

G. Match the Sentences

1. c
2. f
3. b
4. a
5. d
6. e

H. Listening

1. this
2. right away
3. Monday
4. cut
5. Tuesday
6. December
7. winter
8. at once
9. August
10. wash
11. next
12. plumber

WORKBOOK PAGE 103

I. What's the Question?

1. are you going to do right now?
2. is she going to baby-sit?
3. are you going next April?
4. are you going to clean it?
5. are they going to do today?
6. are you going to fix the doorbell?
7. is she going to plant flowers?
8. is he going to read his e-mail?
9. are you going to bed now?

J. Listening

Today's Weather Forecast

This afternoon: cool, cloudy
This evening: foggy, warm

This Weekend's Forecast

Tonight: clear, warm
Saturday: sunny, hot
Sunday: cool, rain

Monday's Weather Forecast

Monday morning: cool, nice
Monday afternoon: cold, snow
Tuesday morning: sunny, warm

WORKBOOK PAGE 104

K. What Does Everybody Want to Do Tomorrow?

1. want to
2. wants to
3. wants to
4. want to
5. want to
6. want to
7. want to

L. Bad Weather

1. He wants to go sailing.
   It's going to rain.
2. She wants to take her son to the zoo.
   It's going to be cold.
3. They want to go jogging.
   It's going to snow.
4. He wants to go skiing.
   It's going to be warm.

WORKBOOK PAGE 105

M. Yes and No

1. They don't want to buy
2. He doesn't want to go
3. I don't want to wash
4. They don't want to play
5. He doesn't want to cook
6. We don't want to study
7. She doesn't want to dance
8. I don't want to work

N. Yes and No

1. He isn't going to go
2. I'm not going to take
3. We aren't going to go
4. She isn't going to go
5. They aren't going to clean
6. It isn't going to be
7. He isn't going to listen to
8. You aren't going to buy

WORKBOOK PAGE 106

O. What Do They Want to Be?

1. What does, want to
   She wants to be
2. Where does, want to
   She wants to work
3. What does she want to
   She wants to bake
4. What does, want to
   He wants to be
5. Where does, want to
   He wants to work
6. What does he want to
   He wants to

WORKBOOK PAGE 108

R. What Time Is It?

1. 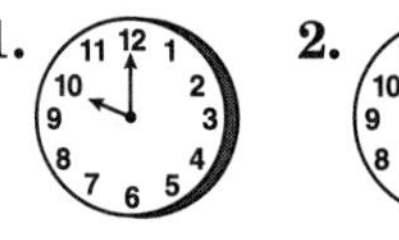
2. 
3. 
4. 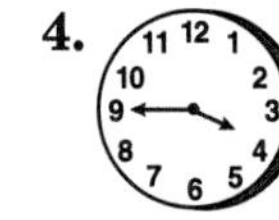
5. 
6. 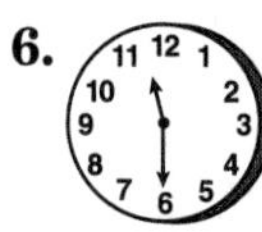
7. 
8. 

S. Which Times Are Correct?

1. b
2. b
3. a
4. a
5. b
6. b
7. a
8. b
9. b

T. Listening

1. 7:45
2. 6:15
3. 4:30
4. 9:15
5. 12:00
6. 5:00
7. 8:45
8. 8:15
9. 1:45
10. 12:00
11. 11:30
12. 2:45

WORKBOOK PAGE 109

U. Alan Chang's Day

1. He gets up at 7:15.
2. He eats breakfast at 7:45.
3. He leaves the house at 8:30.
4. He begins work at 9:00.
5. He works at a computer company.
6. He eats lunch in the cafeteria.
7. He leaves work.
8. He eats dinner at 6:00.
9. He watches videos on his new DVD player.

WORKBOOK PAGE 111

X. GrammarSong

1. week	9. February	17. to
2. year	10. April	18. to wait
3. going to	11. July	19. day
4. In	12. September	20. month
5. summer	13. December	21. right
6. fall	14. It's	22. with
7. waiting	15. after	23. to be
8. I'm going	16. past	24. you

WORKBOOK PAGES 112–113

CHECK-UP TEST: Units 13–14

A.

1. want to watch TV
   we can't
   have to study
2. wants to play tennis
   she can't
   has to go to the dentist
3. want to go dancing
   I can't
   have to work

B.

1. are	3. are	5. does
2. Do	4. do	6. Is

C.

1. I don't want to teach
2. We aren't going to bed
3. She can't bake
4. He doesn't have to go to
5. They can't speak
6. We don't have to do

D.

1. going to eat
2. she's going to go
3. she's going to have
4. she's going to take the bus

E.

1. What's she going to do tomorrow?
2. Where is he going to play tennis?
3. When are you going to go to the zoo?
4. What are they going to study next year?

F.

1. 
2. 
3. 
4. 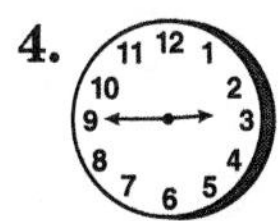
5. 

G.

English	8:30	Chinese	1:30	lunch	12:15
mathematics	11:00	science	10:15	music	12:45

UNIT 15

WORKBOOK PAGE 114

A. What's the Matter?

1. has a cold
2. has a cough
3. have an earache
4. has a stomachache
5. have a sore throat
6. has a headache
7. has a backache
8. have a fever
9. has a toothache

B. Listening

5	1	8	3
4	7	2	6

WORKBOOK PAGE 116

D. What Did You Do Yesterday?

1. cooked	2. cleaned	3. painted
4. shaved	5. typed	6. rested
7. danced	8. shouted	9. studied
10. baked	11. smiled	12. cried

WORKBOOK PAGE 117

E. What's the Word?

1. work	2. played	3. brush
4. planted	5. cook	6. studied
7. painted	8. watch	9. waited

F. Listening

1. yesterday	5. every day	9. yesterday
2. every day	6. yesterday	10. every day
3. yesterday	7. every day	11. every day
4. yesterday	8. yesterday	12. yesterday

WORKBOOK PAGE 118

G. What Did Everybody Do?

1. He cleaned	2. She typed
3. They sang	4. We skated
5. She drank	6. He ate
7. They cried	8. They barked
9. He sat	10. She rode

WORKBOOK PAGE 119

H. Puzzle

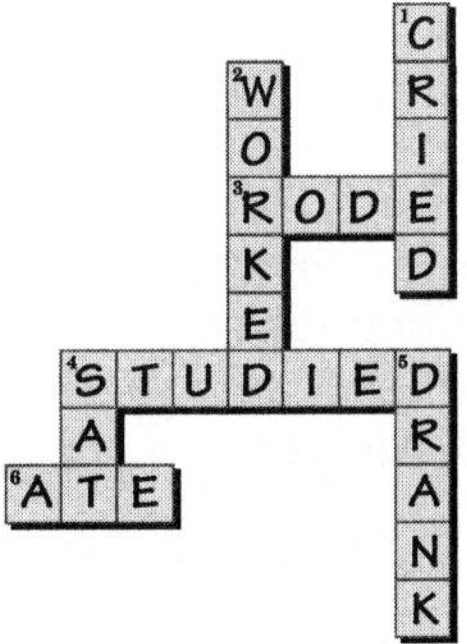

I. Peter's Day at Home

1. He cooked dinner.
2. He baked a cake.
3. He washed the car.
4. He planted flowers.
5. He painted the kitchen.
6. He fixed the sink.
7. He rested.

WORKBOOK PAGE 121

K. My Grandfather's Birthday Party

1. listened
2. danced
3. sang
4. played
5. sat
6. looked
7. laughed
8. smiled
9. cried
10. talked
11. drank
12. ate

L. Matching

1. e
2. c
3. g
4. f
5. b
6. a
7. d

UNIT 16

WORKBOOK PAGE 122

A. Correct the Sentence

1. She didn't brush her teeth.
   She brushed her hair.
2. He didn't play the violin.
   He played the piano.
3. They didn't listen to the news.
   They listened to music.
4. She didn't wait for the train.
   She waited for the bus.
5. He didn't fix his fence.
   He fixed his bicycle.
6. They didn't clean their attic.
   They cleaned their yard.
7. He didn't bake a pie.
   He baked a cake.
8. She didn't call her grandmother.
   She called her grandfather.

WORKBOOK PAGE 123

B. Alan and His Sister

1. rested
2. work
3. study
4. listened
5. watched
6. talked
7. played
8. listen
9. watch
10. play
11. studied
12. cleaned
13. cooked

C. Yes and No

1. Yes, he did.
2. No, she didn't.
3. Yes, she did.
4. No, he didn't.
5. Yes, he did.
6. Did Ellen clean
7. Did Alan talk
8. Did Alan cook
9. Did Ellen listen
10. Did Ellen watch
11. Did Alan study

WORKBOOK PAGE 124

D. What Did They Do?

1. bought
2. had
3. wrote
4. did
5. took
6. got
7. went
8. read
9. made

E. They Didn't Do What They Usually Do

1. didn't write, wrote
2. didn't have, had
3. didn't eat, ate
4. didn't get, got
5. didn't go, went
6. didn't drink, drank
7. didn't make, made
8. didn't take, took
9. didn't buy, bought
10. didn't sit, sat

WORKBOOK PAGE 126

G. What's the Answer?

1. he did
2. I didn't
3. she did
4. they didn't
5. we did
6. he didn't
7. you did
8. I didn't

H. What's the Question?

1. Did she buy
2. Did he have
3. Did you take
4. Did they go
5. Did you sit
6. Did I make

I. Listening

1. b
2. a
3. b
4. b
5. a
6. a
7. b
8. b
9. a
10. b

WORKBOOK PAGE 127

J. I'm Sorry I'm Late!

1. missed
2. had
3. forgot
4. met
5. got up
6. stole
7. had to
8. went

K. Matching

1. d
2. f
3. b
4. e
5. c
6. a
7. j
8. l
9. g
10. k
11. i
12. h

UNIT 17

WORKBOOK PAGE 129

A. A Terrible Day and a Wonderful Day!

1. were
2. were
3. was
4. was
5. were
6. was
7. was
8. were
9. was
10. were
11. was
12. were
13. were
14. was
15. were
16. was
17. was
18. were
19. were
20. was

B. Listening

1. is
2. was
3. were
4. was
5. is
6. were
7. are
8. are
9. was
10. is
11. are
12. were

WORKBOOK PAGE 130

C. Before and After

1. was, I'm healthy
2. was, he's happy
3. were, we're full
4. was, she's, comfortable
5. were, you're thin
6. was, it's shiny
7. were, they're clean
8. was, was, I'm tall
9. were, they're enormous

WORKBOOK PAGE 131

D. What's the Word?

1. Were, wasn't, was
2. Were, weren't, were
3. Was, wasn't, was
4. Were, weren't, were
5. Were, weren't, were
6. Was, wasn't, was

E. Listening

1. wasn't
2. were
3. weren't
4. was
5. wasn't
6. weren't
7. were
8. was

WORKBOOK PAGE 132

F. What's the Word?

1. did
2. didn't
3. was
4. wasn't
5. weren't
6. were
7. weren't
8. wasn't
9. Were
10. was
11. was
12. Did
13. didn't
14. didn't
15. was
16. was
17. was
18. Did
19. didn't
20. was
21. wasn't
22. didn't
23. were
24. Did
25. didn't
26. was
27. Did
28. didn't
29. Were
30. didn't
31. was
32. were
33. didn't

WORKBOOK PAGE 134

H. What Are They Saying?

1. did
2. were
3. Were
4. wasn't
5. was
6. short
7. did
8. didn't
9. curly
10. Did
11. didn't
12. freckles
13. were
14. did
15. sports
16. basketball
17. did
18. were
19. subjects
20. Did
21. hobby
22. did

I. Listening

1. b
2. b
3. a
4. b
5. a
6. b
7. a
8. b

WORKBOOK PAGES 136–137

CHECK-UP TEST: Units 15–17

A.

1. wasn't, was
2. were, was, wasn't
3. were, weren't, were

B.

1. was, I'm full
2. were, they're enormous
3. were, were, we're heavy
4. was, I'm tired

C.

1. didn't drive, drove
2. didn't arrive, arrived
3. didn't shave, shaved
4. didn't go, went
5. didn't read, read

D.

1. Did he meet
2. Did she ride
3. Did you have
4. Did they make
5. Did you see

E.

1. brushed
2. did
3. sat
4. ate
5. went
6. walked
7. bought
8. took
9. didn't take
10. didn't drive

F.

1. was
2. were
3. is
4. were
5. is
6. were
7. was
8. are

Correlation Key

Student Book Pages	Activity Workbook Pages
Chapter 1	
2	2–4 Exercises A–D
4–5	4–5 Exercises E–H
	T1–T4 (Test)
Chapter 2	
8–9	6
10–11	7
12	8–9
14	10–11
16	12
	T5–T8 (Test)
Chapter 3	
18–19	13
20–21	14–17
24	18–19
	T9–T10 (Test)
Check-Up Test	20
Chapter 4	
28	21
29–30	22–25
31	26
	T11–T12 (Test)
Chapter 5	
36–37	27
38–39	28–31
40	32–33
41	34
	T13–T14 (Test)
Chapter 6	
46–48	35–39
	T15–T18 (Test)
Check-Up Test	40
Chapter 7	
56	41
57	42
58	43–44
59–60	45
61–62	46–49
	T19–T22 (Test)
Chapter 8	
68–69	50–51
70	52
71	53
73	54–56
74	57–59
	T23–T28 (Test)
Check-Up Test	60–61
Chapter 9	
80	62–63 Exercises A, B
81	63 Exercise C–66
82	67–68
	T29–T30 (Test)
Chapter 10	
88	69
89	70–71
90–91	72–73
95	74
	T31–T34 (Test)
Check-Up Test	75
Chapter 11	
100	76–77
101	78–79
102	80
103	81–82
	T35–T36 (Test)
Chapter 12	
108–109	83–86
110–111	87–90
	T37–T38 (Test)
Check-Up Test	91
Chapter 13	
118	92–93 Exercise B
119	93 Exercise C–95
122	96–97
123	98–99
	T39–T42 (Test)
Chapter 14	
128	100
129	101
130–131	102–103 Exercise I
133	103 Exercise J–107
134–135	108–111
	T43–T46 (Test)
Check-Up Test	112–113
Chapter 15	
142	114–115
143	116–117
144–145	118–121
	T47–T50 (Test)
Chapter 16	
150	122–123
151	124–125
152	126
153	127–128
	T51–T54 (Test)
Chapter 17	
158	129
159	130
160	131
161	132–133
163	134–135
	T55–T58 (Test)
Check-Up Test	136–137

SIDE by SIDE Activity Workbook Audio Program

The *Side by Side* Activity Workbook Audio CDs contain all workbook listening activities and GrammarRaps and GrammarSongs for entertaining language practice through rhythm and music. Students can use the Audio Program to extend their language learning through self-study outside the classroom.

Audio Program Contents

Track	Page	Activity
CD 1		
1		Introduction
Chapter 1		
2	p. 3	Exercise C Listening
3	p. 4	Exercise E Listening
4	p. 5	Exercise F Listening
5	p. 5	Exercise H GrammarRap
Chapter 2		
6	p. 6	Exercise B Listening
7	p. 11	Exercise J Listening
8	p. 11	Exercise K Listening
9	p. 12	Exercise M GrammarRap
10	p. 12	Exercise N GrammarRap
Chapter 3		
11	p. 15	Exercise C Listening
12	p. 16	Exercise D GrammarRap
13	p. 18	Exercise F GrammarRap
Check-Up Test: Chapters 1–3		
14	p. 20	Exercise D Listening
Chapter 4		
15	p. 22	Exercise C Listening
16	p. 24	Exercise F GrammarRap
17	p. 24	Exercise G Listening
Chapter 5		
18	p. 27	Exercise C Listening
19	p. 29	Exercise F GrammarRap
20	p. 32	Exercise K Listening
21	p. 34	Exercise O Listening
22	p. 34	Exercise P GrammarRap
Chapter 6		
23	p. 36	Exercise B Listening
24	p. 37	Exercise D GrammarSong
25	p. 39	Exercise F GrammarRap
Check-Up Test: Chapters 4–6		
26	p. 40	Exercise E Listening
Chapter 7		
27	p. 43	Exercise C Listening
28	p. 44	Exercise E GrammarRap
29	p. 49	Exercise J GrammarRap
Chapter 8		
30	p. 51	Exercise D Listening
31	p. 52	Exercise E Listening
32	p. 54	Exercise H Listening
33	p. 54	Exercise I Listening
34	p. 57	Exercise N GrammarRap
35	p. 57	Exercise O GrammarRap
36	p. 59	Exercise Q GrammarSong
Check-Up Test: Chapters 7–8		
37	p. 61	Exercise F Listening
Chapter 9		
38	p. 63	Exercise B Listening
39	p. 65	Exercise E GrammarRap
40	p. 66	Exercise G Listening
41	p. 68	Exercise J Listen and Pronounce

Track	Page	Activity
CD 2		
1		Introduction
Chapter 10		
2	p. 70	Exercise D Listening
3	p. 72	Exercise I Listening
4	p. 73	Exercise J GrammarRap
Check-Up Test: Chapters 9–10		
5	p. 75	Exercise D Listening
Chapter 11		
6	p. 77	Exercise C Listening
7	p. 78	Exercise G Listening
8	p. 79	Exercise I GrammarRap
9	p. 82	Exercise N Listening
Chapter 12		
10	p. 85	Exercise C GrammarRap
11	p. 85	Exercise D GrammarRap
12	p. 89	Exercise H Listening
Check-Up Test: Chapters 11–12		
13	p. 91	Exercise E Listening
Chapter 13		
14	p. 93	Exercise D Listening
15	p. 95	Exercise G GrammarRap
16	p. 97	Exercise K Listening
17	p. 98	Exercise M Listening
18	p. 99	Exercise N GrammarRap
19	p. 99	Exercise O GrammarRap
Chapter 14		
20	p. 101	Exercise D GrammarRap
21	p. 102	Exercise H Listening
22	p. 103	Exercise J Listening
23	p. 107	Exercise Q GrammarRap
24	p. 108	Exercise T Listening
25	p. 110	Exercise W GrammarRap
26	p. 111	Exercise X GrammarSong
Check-Up Test: Chapters 13–14		
27	p. 113	Exercise G Listening
Chapter 15		
28	p. 114	Exercise B Listening
29	p. 115	Exercise C GrammarRap
30	p. 117	Exercise F Listening
31	p. 120	Exercise J GrammarRap
Chapter 16		
32	p. 125	Exercise F GrammarRap Rhyming Game
33	p. 126	Exercise I Listening
34	p. 128	Exercise L GrammarRap
35	p. 128	Exercise M GrammarRap
Chapter 17		
36	p. 129	Exercise B Listening
37	p. 131	Exercise E Listening
38	p. 133	Exercise G Grammar Rap
39	p. 134	Exercise I Listening
40	p. 135	Exercise J GrammarRap
Check-Up Test: Chapters 15–17		
41	p. 137	Exercise F Listening